BLUECOAT AND PIONEER

BLUECOAT AND PIONEER

The Recollections of
John Benton Hart
1864–1868

Edited by John Hart

UNIVERSITY OF OKLAHOMA PRESS : NORMAN

Chapter 1 appeared in part as "Under Moonlight in Missouri," in *Kansas History* 37, no. 3 (Autumn 2014): 180–99, and in *The Kansas City Star Magazine,* October 12, 2014, 6–12.

Chapter 2 appeared in an earlier form as "A New Account of the Battle of Platte Bridge," in *Kansas History* 38, no. 1 (Spring 2015): 50–53.

Chapter 5 appeared in part as "A Hell-Bent Ride on a Snortin' Prince of a Mule," in *True West,* August 2017, 38–43.

LIBRARY OF CONGRESS CATALOGING-IN-PUBLICATION DATA

Names: Hart, John Benton, 1842–1928, author. | Hart, John, 1948– editor and compiler.
Title: Bluecoat and pioneer : the recollections of John Benton Hart, 1864–1868 / edited by John Hart.
Description: Norman, OK : University of Oklahoma Press, [2019] | Includes bibliographical references and index.
Identifiers: LCCN 2018016986 | ISBN 978-0-8061-6175-4 (hardcover : alk. paper)
Subjects: LCSH: Hart, John Benton, 1842–1928. | United States. Army. Kansas Cavalry Regiment, 11th (1862–1865)—Biography. | Platte Bridge, Battle of, Wyo., 1865. | Red Cloud's War, 1866–1867. | Soldiers—United States—Diaries. | Bozeman Trail—History—Sources. | Frontier and pioneer life—Montana. | Fort C. F. Smith (Mont.)—History—Sources. | Missouri—History—Civil War, 1861–1865—Personal narratives. | United States—History—Civil War, 1861–1865—Personal narratives.
Classification: LCC E83.863 .H36 2019 | DDC 973.7/481092 [B]—dc23
LC record available at https://lccn.loc.gov/2018016986

The paper in this book meets the guidelines for permanence and durability of the Committee on Production Guidelines for Book Longevity of the Council on Library Resources, Inc. ∞

1 2 3 4 5 6 7 8 9 10

To Harry Hart, Lawrence Hart, and Jeanne McGahey Hart
in partial fulfillment of the hopes they had

CONTENTS

ILLUSTRATIONS

FIGURES

MAPS

ACKNOWLEDGMENTS

The three principal settings of these memoirs—Missouri, southern Wyoming, and southern Montana—require thanks to three separate sets of informants.

For the chapter concerning the Confederate invasion of Missouri, I am especially grateful to Daniel Smith and Mike Calvert, of the Civil War Round Tables of Kansas City and Western Missouri respectively, for their help in matching the John Benton Hart account to the landscape and the calendar. Thanks also to historians Mark A. Lause, Darryl Levings, and Eli Paul for their counsel and expertise.

For the Platte Bridge segment, I was greatly assisted by historians Doug Cubbison, Todd Guenther, Stephen Haack, Tom Rea, Johanna Wickman, and Richard C. Young of the Fort Caspar Museum in Casper, Wyoming. A special nod goes to Brenda Tippin, a descendant of Louis P. Guinard, nephew and assistant of Louis Guinard of Platte River Bridge.

For assistance regarding Bozeman Trail events, my thanks go especially to Kim Ostermyer and Judy Slack of the Wyoming Room, Sheridan Public Library, Sheridan, Wyoming; to Christine Fleming of the Bighorn Canyon National Recreation Area; and to historians Marc H. Abrams and John D. McDermott.

Internet or no, reference librarians remain the angels of historical research. My warm thanks to all of them, including those at the Denver Public Library; the Emporia Public Library in Emporia, Kansas; the Joint Legislative Council Library in Denver; the Marin County Free Library in San Rafael, California; the National Archives; the North Platte Public Library in North Platte, Nebraska; the U.S. Army Military Research Collection, Carlisle Barracks, Pennsylvania; and the Wyoming Historical Society, Wheatland. I must also note the assistance of the office of Yeulen Willett, Colorado state representative, District 54.

For assistance in rounding up historical photographs, I appreciate the help of Lisa Caprino of the Huntington Library; Ikumi Crocoll and Emerson Hunton of the Newberry Library, Chicago; Cindy Hagen of Little Bighorn

Battlefield National Monument, Crow Agency, Montana; Marlea D. Leljedal of the U.S. Army Heritage and Education Center in Carlisle, Pennsylvania; Ann Rogers and Marilyn Sanders of the Osage County Historical Society, Lyndon, Kansas; Jennifer Sanchez of the Norlin Library at the University of Colorado, Boulder; and Suzi Taylor of the Wyoming State Archives, Cheyenne.

Thanks also to Virgil Dean at *Kansas History* magazine and Darryl Levings at the *Kansas City Star*—and to Kevin Brock, Stephanie Evans, Gerry Krieg, and Charles Rankin for helping this book along its road at the University of Oklahoma Press.

I am grateful to my wife, Helen Schoenhals Hart, for her company at old battlefields and graveyards, and above all for diverting energy from her own work to do the prodigious job of scanning this mass of manuscripts into computer-usable form.

BLUECOAT AND PIONEER

INTRODUCTION

In 1918 John Benton Hart, then in his mid-seventies, sat down at his home in Harts Basin, near Delta, Colorado, and began to tell stories of a three-year period in his youth: his days as a member of the Eleventh Kansas Cavalry, fighting in Missouri and on the frontier, and a subsequent year spent as a civilian jack-of-all-trades doing risky work for the U.S. Army on the Bozeman Trail to Montana in the middle of the Indian resistance campaign known as Red Cloud's War (1866–68).

This late debriefing apparently was not Hart's idea. "It was always hard to persuade him to impart to me knowledge of by-gone days," his son, Harry, recalled. It was Harry, an aspiring writer, who wanted to capture this testimony of an era receding into memory. But once started, the old man seems to have thrown himself into it, recalling certain peak events with cinematic vividness. The several resulting manuscripts would amount to over 100,000 words.

Memory does battle with time, and a half-century lag between the events and their retelling is not ideal. It is also not so uncommon for such accounts. All over the West at about this time, aging frontiersmen were recording their experiences. The present body of work is unusual in that its publication occurs not 50 or 100 but 150 years after the events it describes. None of this material was published before 2014, and the bulk of it appears here for the first time in print.

In some cases John Hart's testimony supplements what is known. We have, for example, one of exactly three accounts left behind by men who rode out under doomed Lieutenant Caspar Collins at the Battle of Platte Bridge on July 26, 1865, and one of three eyewitness reports of the engagement known as the Hayfield Fight in southern Montana two years later. In a few cases Hart opens entirely new territory. Most strikingly, he provides details of an assignment carrying the mail between the beleaguered forts on the Bozeman Trail. If this is correct, it is news for historians: no mailman named Hart is otherwise recorded for this stretch.

THE LIFE OF JOHN BENTON HART

John Benton Hart's life shows the classic nineteenth-century westward drift, shifting as it did from Pennsylvania to Ohio, then on to Missouri and Kansas, to present-day Wyoming and Montana, and finally ending on Colorado's Western Slope.

Very little is known about Hart's early years, and his memoir adds exactly nothing to the facts of record. He was born in Uniontown, Pennsylvania, on July 10, 1842, along with his fraternal twin brother, Hugh, to Nathaniel Hart and his wife Belinda (née Reynolds). When Belinda died in 1853, the numerous family was living in eastern Ohio. Nathaniel then moved it to Buchanan County, Missouri, north of Kansas City, where he remarried. Two of his brothers, John's uncles, had already reached the area.

On May 30, 1854, President Franklin Pierce signed the Kansas-Nebraska Act, allowing the residents of new western territories to make the decision for or against allowing slavery. The result was a rush by northerners and southerners alike to settle Kansas and thus influence the outcome there. For Nathaniel Carl Hart and his brothers, the move was a short but risky one. One uncle had several close calls with

Privates John Benton "Johnny" Hart (right) and Hugh F. Hart.
Collection of John Hart.

proslavery neighbors. An early history reports: "In one instance, after escaping from the field where they came in on him, they left a notice at the house, if he did not leave the Territory they would hang him on sight."[1] For "Bleeding Kansas," the Civil War, which arrived a few years later, was only an intensification of an ongoing local conflict.

On September 9, 1862, at Camp Lyon near Fort Leavenworth, John Benton Hart volunteered for the Eleventh Kansas Infantry, then in the process of organization. The roll gives his residence as Grasshopper Falls (now called Valley Falls), Kansas, and describes him as brown haired, blue eyed, having a fair complexion, and just five feet, five inches tall; he apparently kept a boyish appearance well into his twenties. Everyone knew him as "Johnny," and so he shall be here.

Hart was wounded during the Battle of Prairie Grove, Arkansas (December 7, 1862).[2] His memoir says nothing about this event, though at one point it shows him exhibiting the resulting scar as proof of battlefield experience.

When Confederate major general Sterling Price threatened Kansas City in October 1864, the Eleventh Kansas, which had been converted to a casualty regiment, was key to the defense. Johnny's regiment was one of the units sent out under Major General James G. Blunt to resist Price's march from Lexington, Missouri, toward the Kansas line. He took part in the Second Battle of Lexington (October 19), and the Battles of the Little Blue (October 21), the Big Blue (October 22–23), and Westport (October 23) as well as in the subsequent pursuit of Price toward the Arkansas River, events Hart vividly describes.

That job done, Johnny and his comrades looked forward to discharge; out west, though, another kind of war was ready to draw them in. After the Sand Creek Massacre of November 29, 1864, in which a force of white Coloradans under Colonel John Chivington attacked and destroyed a peaceful Indian encampment, several tribes formed an alliance aimed at nothing less than rolling back the creeping white invasion. The Eleventh Kansas was hurried west across the wintry plains.

The memoir picks up in July 1865 on the eve of a notorious event in western history, the Battle of Platte Bridge on the Oregon Trail near modern Casper, Wyoming. Hart was one of the detachment of twenty-odd men that went out under Lieutenant Caspar Collins to relieve a beleaguered supply train, riding into a massive ambush.

Company I was mustered out at Fort Leavenworth on September 26, 1865. For a couple of years Johnny leaves no trace. When his story resumes, it is the spring of 1867, and he and brother Hugh are in North Platte, Nebraska, then the rip-roaring terminus of the rapidly extending Union Pacific Railroad, looking for work and a way west to the newly opened goldfields of Montana.[3] They signed on as "bullwhackers," or ox wranglers, with a train of freight wagons bound for Fort C. F. Smith on the Bozeman Trail. Johnny tells us much about the details and mechanics of shifting freight by a method that was on the verge of disappearing.

Arriving at Fort C. F. Smith, Johnny and Hugh left the train (refusing an offer of permanent employment with Wells Fargo) to take up the life of hangers on and contractors filling the needs of the army posts during the next phase of the Indian conflicts, Red Cloud's War. The brothers found work cutting wood, supplying meat, and cutting hay—the last of which landed them in the fierce Hayfield Fight of August 1, 1867. That fall, Johnny says, he received the dangerous job of carrying mail between Fort C. F. Smith and the next post down the line, Fort Phil Kearny, ninety miles south along the base of the Bighorn Mountains in Wyoming.

Johnny's stay at Fort C. F. Smith lasted as long as the fort did. In the summer of 1868, when the government abandoned its unsustainable outposts along the Bozeman Trail, the brothers returned to Kansas.

Johnny married Corrinna Siceloff in Leavenworth in 1871 and helped found the Elk County town of Canola (fused into modern Grenola in 1879). His first three

John Benton Hart, 1895.
Collection of John Hart.

children were born in Canola, where brother Hugh died in 1873.[4]

By 1880 Johnny had moved to remote Lake City, Colorado, where he supported his family as a miner. Complaining of the climate and altitude, he looked for a cattle ranch on the Western Slope, where a vast swath of land had recently been wrested from the Utes. In 1882 he homesteaded a valley, still called Harts Basin, in Delta County, moving the family there the following year. There ensued quiet decades as a prosperous rancher. He served one two-year term in the Colorado House of Representatives (1895–96) as a member of the briefly dominant prolabor Populist Party. John Benton Hart died at home in 1928.[5]

John Benton Hart and Corrinna Siceloff Hart, date unknown.
Collection of John Hart.

THE MANUSCRIPT

The earliest date found on the manuscript pages of Hart's memoir is 1918, the latest 1923. A number of episodes are found both in typescript and in earlier handwritten versions.

These are the components I have drawn on here:

> "Sweet Potatoes and Other Stories" is a fair copy in what is probably Harry's writing. It covers the first several days of the confrontation with General Price in Missouri in 1864.
>
> "My Bunkies," a typescript, repeats the same incidents, often more extensively, and continues the account to the end of Price's Raid.
>
> "Meeting an Indian Half Way" is a brief typescript, with some handwritten additions, recounting a minor encounter before the Battle of Platte Bridge. It is dated 1918.
>
> "Battle of Ganard's [Guinard's] Bridge" is the main narrative of the events of July 25–26, 1865.
>
> "Over the Oregon Trail," comprising some 90,000 words, is a typescript dated 1923, with many handwritten emendations. It begins with the spring of 1867 and follows the movements of Johnny and Hugh until their departure from Fort C. F. Smith in the summer of 1868. Since many of the edits concern factual matters that only the old man would have known, I have accepted them as authorial intention.[6]

An additional manuscript, "Trail Twins," in typescript or very neat longhand, is essentially a revision of "Over the Oregon Trail," with the earlier revisions incorporated. I have relied on it only as a reference where the markups of "Over the Oregon Trail" are illegible. But Harry's preface to "Trail Twins" is interesting for the warranty it offers:

> I wish to mention, the statements herein are true to the best of my knowledge. I have known an old timer, . . . now over 84 years old. It was always hard to persuade him to impart to me knowledge of by-gone days. He was a close observer, a clear describer of events and possessed a remarkable memory. When told [that] in a few years all of his class of men would go, and it would be just and right in him to relate to me just how he and his companions eked out their lives ahead of civilization, without any of the comforts of a well regulated community of civilized beings, he said, "Where certain events are not known they are not missed."

All of these texts seem to reflect a mingling of two voices: the rather plainspoken, repetitive, and often naturally eloquent voice of the elder Hart, and the more rhetorical style injected by the younger. The difference is palpable. Here is what I take to be Johnny talking:

> They were firing before any of the others were and men would jump against the wheels with side and shoulder as they spun around and kicked back from their position. It was astonishing how quick these men could load their cannon after firing. How in deadly earnest they worked and so accurate and unerring.

Here, I surmise, is Harry embroidering:

> These Indians were surging around us like an onrushing tide striking against a bluff and rebounding back in a wicked undercurrent across a rocky reef intent in its power of weight and force to snuff out all life.

There is also a good deal of dialogue, which sometimes has an inflated or wooden sound, that I suspect shows Harry's touch. It seems to be a way of imparting wads of information or stating expected noble sentiments:

> "Boys," Al Colvin said, "I wish to talk to you for a moment about the medicine pole. The time is appropriate . . . even if death does stare us in the face."

> "Oh that's all right, I always aid boys of both sides when they are in distress. It's my duty, because after all we are our brothers' keepers."

Johnny's version of events is often self-aggrandizing but also often self-deprecating. He seems to depict himself as the brilliant problem solver, able to deal with any situation. At the same time he acknowledges—and proves by many anecdotes—his mischievous side. Incessantly in trouble, he seems always able to talk his way out of serious consequences.

He also comes across as tolerant, almost sweet. At least in hindsight he has hardly a bad word to say about the Confederates he had fought. When it comes to the Native Americans, he is not free of the attitudes of whites of his era, yet he seems to have had a knack for bridging cultural divides. He describes friendships with Crows and seems to have greatly admired the Mountain Crow chief Blackfoot.

How reliable is this witness? On points where his accounts overlap other available information, they seem to match up reasonably well. Now and then, to be sure, a slippage is evident. For instance, he overstates the number of casualties at the

Platte Bridge battle yet gives the proper total for the government losses on that date: his memory has combined the toll of several engagements into one. In describing the Missouri campaign, he seems to scramble known events somewhat, as if arranging them for maximum effect. There is undoubtedly some storyteller's license but, where facts can be checked, little outright invention. This is reassuring when we come to certain episodes that cannot be verified at all.

Johnny's narrative rule may be like the one he describes prevailing at a Mountain Crow war dance: "Each warrior must show and act out with life and energy just how he executed each maneuver, and what he accomplished for his safety, and in capturing and slaying his enemy. They were allowed to exaggerate somewhat, but not so far as to be utterly false."

EDITORIAL REMARKS

This book contains approximately one-third of the available material. Only in chapter 2, "With Caspar Collins at Platte Bridge," is every word reproduced. The Missouri segment is represented by about half; less than a third of "Over the Oregon Trail" is here. I have tried to leave blocks of text intact, resorting rarely to ellipses.

The original texts are full of spelling, punctuation, and grammatical errors. To avoid letting these become a distraction, I have silently corrected spelling and much of the punctuation as errors probably attributable to the scribe. But I have left actual word choices, like "went" for "gone," alone. Except where misunderstanding threatens, I have also respected the narrator's habit (either Johnny's or Harry's) of omitting the pronouns "I" and "we."

1

UNDER MOONLIGHT IN MISSOURI

The Eleventh Kansas Cavalry was organized initially as an infantry regiment in the fall of 1862 and saw its first serious action at the Battle of Prairie Grove, Arkansas, on December 7. The following April the regiment was mounted—converted to cavalry—and placed under the command of Colonel Thomas Moonlight. This strikingly named military man was born in Scotland. In the United States by 1850, he settled in Leavenworth County, Kansas, in 1860. Moonlight would earn much praise for his Civil War service and much blame for some blunders made in fighting Indians later on.[1] Johnny, for his part, idolized his regimental commander.

Private John Benton Hart.
Collection of John Hart.

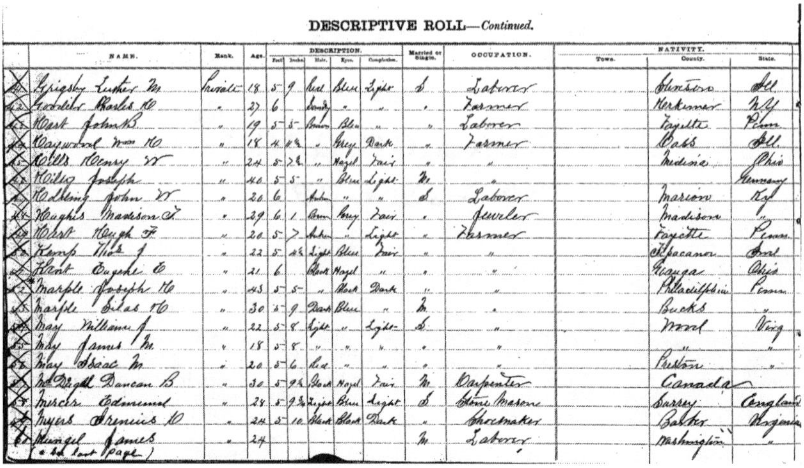

DESCRIPTIVE ROLL—*Continued.*

	NAME.	Rank.	Age.	Feet	Inches	Hair.	Eyes.	Complexion.	Married or Single.	OCCUPATION.	Town.	County.	State.
41	Grigsby Luther M.	Private	18	5	9	Red	Blue	Light	S	Laborer		Clinton	Ill
42	Goodelle Charles W	"	27	6		Sandy	"	"	"	Farmer		Herkimer	N.Y.
43	Hart John B.	"	19	5	5	Brown	Blue	"	"	Laborer		Fayette	Penn
44	Haywood Wm W	"	18	4	4½	"	Grey	Dark	"	Farmer		Cass	Ill.
45	Hills Henry W	"	24	5	7½	"	Hazel	Fair	"	"		Medina	Ohio
46	Hills Joseph	"	40	5	5	"	Blue	Light	M	"			Germany
47	Holding John W	"	20	6		Auburn	"	"	S	Laborer		Marion	Ky
48	Hughes Madison T.	"	29	6	1	Brown	Grey	Fair	"	Jeweler		Madison	"
49	Hurst Hugh F.	"	20	5	7	Auburn	"	Light	"	Farmer		Fayette	Penn
50	Kemp Thos J	"	22	5	4½	Light	Blue	Fair	"	"		Tippecanoe	Ind
51	Kent Eugene E	"	21	6		Black	Hazel	"	"	"		Geauga	Ohio
52	*Marple Joseph W	"	43	5	5	"	Black	Dark	"	"		Philadelphia	Penn
53	Marple Silas W	"	30	5	9	Dark	Blue	"	M	"		Bucks	"
54	May William J	"	22	5	8	Light	"	Light	S	"		Wood	Virg
55	May James M.	"	18	5	8	"	"	"	"	"		"	"
56	May Isaac M	"	20	5	6	Red	"	"	"	"		Preston	"
57	McDeigh Duncan B	"	30	5	9½	Black	Hazel	Fair	M	Carpenter		Canada	
58	Mercer Edmund	"	28	5	9¾	Light	Blue	Light	S	Stone Mason		Surrey	England
59	Myers Irenius W	"	24	5	10	Black	Black	Dark	"	Shoemaker		Barbour	Virginia
60	Mungel James	"	24						M	Laborer		Washington	"
	(* see last page)												

Colonel Thomas Moonlight. Born in Scotland in 1833, he set sail for America at age thirteen and served in the U.S. Army from 1853–58. Upon the outbreak of war in 1861, Moonlight raised a light battery and was commissioned captain of artillery, but on September 20, 1862, he mustered as lieutenant colonel of the Eleventh Kansas Cavalry, becoming commander in the spring of 1863.

Library of Congress, Prints and Photographs Division, LC-USZ62-44452.

Major General Sterling Price. Born in 1809, he became successively a Congressman, celebrated general in the Mexican-American War, and Governor of Missouri (1853 to 1857). Initially opposed to secession from the Union, this slave-holder switched sides in response to what he saw as heavy-handed federal intervention. Unreconciled after the war, he took his troops to Mexico, seeking service under Emperor Maximilian. He died in poverty in St. Louis in 1867.

Kansas State Historical Society.

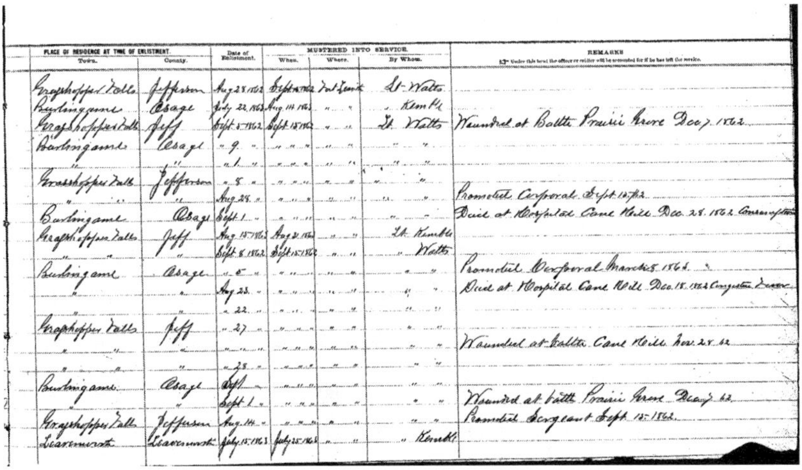

A page of the *Roster and Descriptive Roll, Eleventh Regiment, Cavalry, Kansas Civil War Volunteers* recalls a time when whole communities signed up together and a single battle could decimate a family or a village. John B. Hart enlisted on September 5, 1864; his brother Hugh F. Hart on August 15 of the following year, joining many others from the towns of Grasshopper Falls (now Valley Falls) and Burlingame, Kansas.
Kansas State Historical Society.

The Eleventh Kansas spent the middle years of the war engaging in small actions against Confederates and guerillas on either side of the Kansas-Missouri state line. Johnny's company would have been in eastern Kansas when word came of a much larger threat to the region in the autumn of 1864.[2]

Major General Sterling Price invaded Missouri in September 1864 with more than ten thousand men in a desperate attempt to divert Union forces from the East, to recruit volunteers and capture supplies, and perhaps to influence the November elections. After failing to destroy the garrison of Fort Davidson at Pilot Knob, Price aborted a planned assault on St. Louis and turned west toward Jefferson City, the state capital, which he threatened but also chose not to attack. He worked his way on toward Kansas, creating short-lived jubilation among Confederate sympathizers as he passed but not provoking the full-scale pro-Southern uprising he apparently banked on. While Major General Samuel R. Curtis dug in to defend Westport and Kansas City, Major General James Blunt moved east with two thousand men, including the Eleventh Kansas, to locate Price and then to impede his advance. Meanwhile, larger forces under Major Generals Alfred Pleasonton and Andrew J. Smith were closing in on the invaders from the rear. Blunt urged Curtis to march eastward and face the Confederates at the Little Blue River on October 21, but his superior had to

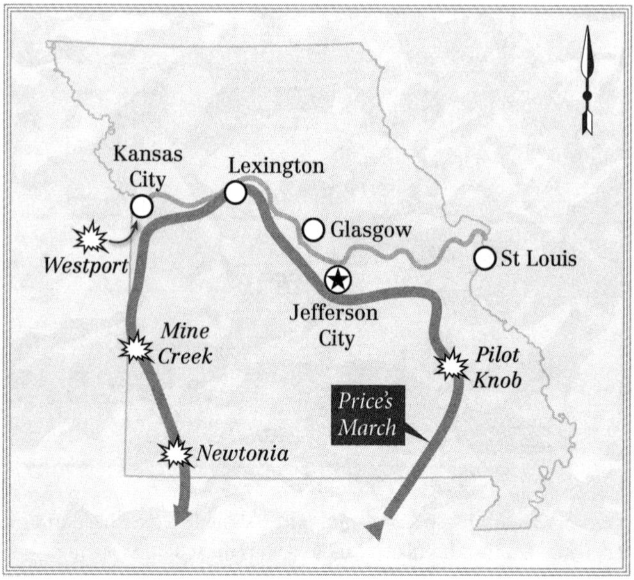

The Confederate invasion of Missouri, September–October 1864. Begun as a full-scale invasion with designs on St. Louis, Sterling Price's campaign deteriorated into a raid for men and supplies before finally descending into an exhausted flight toward safety.
Map by Gerry Krieg. Copyright © 2019 by John Hart.

decline: the Kansas State Militia, an essential part of his force, would not go that far into Missouri. Blunt, and notably Moonlight, nonetheless made an effective stand at the Little Blue before retreating grudgingly through Independence to the main Union position along the Blue (also called Big Blue) River.

On October 22 General Price located an unguarded ford on the Big Blue, penetrated and flanked the Union defenses, and drove the Federals back on Westport, then a separate town south of Kansas City. On the same day, a messenger from Curtis made it through to General Pleasonton, who at last accelerated what had been a leisurely advance. It would have shocked Johnny, who thought he was part of a closely coordinated campaign, to know that Curtis and Pleasonton had not been directly in touch for several days: the telegraph lines were down.

On October 23 the battle surged back and forth across Brush Creek south of Westport. Union troops were already gaining when Pleasonton, having forced his own way across the Big Blue, appeared out of the streamside timber. Price quickly disengaged and began his long retreat back toward the Arkansas River, punctuated by several more pitched battles with the pursuing Union forces.

Price's invasion, historians agree, did little to change the course or even to delay

Major General James Gillpatrick Blunt. Born in Maine and trained as a physician in Ohio, Blunt moved his family and practice to Kansas in 1856. A friend of "Jayhawker" James H. Lane, he served in Lane's irregular force until this was absorbed into the Union Army. Blunt's standing rose with victory in the Battle of Prairie Grove in late 1862, and fell with a heavy loss to Quantrill's Raiders the following year. He was called back from the frontier to help deal with Price's invasion, redeeming his reputation. *Library of Congress, Prints and Photographs Division, LC-DIG-cwpb-06819.*

Major General Alfred Pleasonton of Washington, D.C., was a career officer whose lackluster service in the eastern theater of the Civil War resulted in his transfer to the Trans-Mississippi in 1864. His pursuit of Price reestablished his reputation; his policy of amnesty for Confederate prisoners resulted in many going west as "galvanized Yankees." Two towns, in Kansas and California, bear his name, albeit misspelled as "Pleasanton." *Library of Congress, Prints and Photographs Division, LOT 14043-2, no. 260 [P&P].*

the conclusion of the larger war, but its scale and regional importance were huge. This campaign has surely gotten less than its share of discussion. A hundred years would pass before these events received their first thorough modern treatment, Howard Monnett's *Action before Westport* (1964); more than fifty more went by before publication of Kyle S. Sinisi's *The Last Hurrah* (2015) and Mark Lause's *The Collapse of Price's Raid* (2016). Johnny's recollections might have been useful to all.[3]

Written down half a century after the events, Hart's account cannot be read as a literal guide to the last days of Price's raid. The chronological and spatial framework he provides is sometimes questionable. At one point he speaks of a sixteen-day running fight leading up to the Battle of Westport; the calendar allows five days.

Yet Johnny captures well the enlisted man's experience of a prolonged cavalry campaign, the round-the-clock movements, and the snatched sleeps. Time is not so much stretched as it is rearranged. Company I's journey from Hickman Mills, Missouri, where the Kansans' march began on October 17, to Lexington and back and down the Kansas-Missouri line to Fayetteville, Arkansas, on November 4 encompassed every bit of sixteen days (and many nights) in the saddle. General Curtis estimated the distance traveled at 850 miles.[4]

Unlike some other contemporary witnesses, Hart did not yearn for the larger eastern battlefields but took with utmost seriousness his role as a defender of Kansas.[5] His lack of personal animosity toward the Confederates (whom he always calls "the Johnnies") extended also to Southern sympathizers he encountered. Also notable are the almost affectionate interactions he reports between officers and men. As Johnny wrote, "the officers in the Civil War would talk to their men, somewhat sociable at times. They could dine with their men in a pinch and not feel lowered by so doing."

Blunt's force reached Lexington, after an all-night march from Holden, on the morning of Tuesday, October 18, and saw its first action on Wednesday. Johnny appears to conflate the two days. He opens on a theme that will resound many times: the search for provisions.

We marched through Lexington, and went into camp a little way outside of town. As there could not be enough corn provided for our horses from the merchants in town, something had to be done. Andy [Andrew G.] Todd and myself,[6] and some others, were detailed to go under the command of a sergeant out among the farms and get what was needed. So, off we went for near a mile and a half to a big house, and on arriving there found plenty of corn of which we took one wagon load.

But just as the wagon load of corn was being driven off, Andy Todd and I sat down on the porch of the house where the people lived for a little rest. We were expected to bring up the rear in a few minutes.

While resting here the lady of the house came out on the porch where we were, and asked us if we would like some bread and milk. We replied that we would. She went back into the house, but she left an impression with us, for she seemed kind, had a neat appearance, a soft voice and wore earrings that looked like diamonds. In a little while a Negro woman came out with lightbread and milk. She cut slice after slice for us, and we had a feast, nothing in our lives tasted so good as that lightbread and milk. We thanked the lady of the house who was standing in the doorway, then made for our horses.

Just as we were mounted, the lady came running out to where we were. She threw her arms up and grabbed me by the trouser leg, and now the ear rings were gone, her ears were bleeding, her hair was down over her shoulders and face and the pretty dress she wore all torn to pieces. "Come!" she said, "they are killing my father, come in the house quick! Oh, please, come!" . . .

Back we went pell-mell into the house, through two rooms and started up a flight of stairs; here we pulled out our guns. "That's right, boys. God bless you," she said, and all the time kept hurrying us up the stairs. As soon as we were on the landing could hear arrogant demanding voices through a door. The lady opened a door and pushed us into the room.

There was a very old gentleman sitting in a high backed rickety-looking chair. His hair was white and his face nearly as white, and his hands looked lean and bony and thin. His head was pushed back against the back of the chair, his head was all bruised up and bleeding a little. There was two men from the Fifteenth Kansas, pushing the barrels of their revolvers against the old gentleman's forehead, hissing through their teeth, "Where's your money, old man? Where's your money?" I poked my gun into one fellow's neck and at the same time jerked him off his feet while Andy Todd did the same with the other one. They did not make very much resistance. Down the stairs they went with not very much ceremony, but somehow they managed to take a sack of silverware with them. We was going to make them leave that, but the lady said, "Let them have it! Let them take it! Get them out of here! That's all I want!" Out of the house they went, and we after them like a couple of bulldogs.

In the yard once more the lady thanked us, indeed, she had been doing so every minute it seemed to us. Then the mother soul in her bared itself free. She wanted to save, to pay a debt of gratitude to two boys in blue; while the blood of her race wore the gray. "Price," she said, "will be here in fifteen minutes and my husband is a colonel in his Southern Army, a man with influence and pull. You may be killed going now. You may get killed, you can't get away, it's too late. I will guarantee you boys protection, you will not be mistreated." And, as if to punctuate her plea for us like an orderly from Heaven, we could hear firing on the pickets. The lady said it was Price's men. No we said, we would have to go, and go we must. "Well," she said, "remember both of you if you are ever wounded or in trouble of any kind, please let me know and I will pay the price no matter what it is. You boys saved my father—and goodbye."

We rode away with all the haste we could after what she had told us, about Price being so near, who knows, maybe it was so. Just as we were riding out of view from the house, Andy Todd glanced back over his shoulder, saw the lady kneeling facing us as if praying for us. "That's an angel of a woman, she's good, Johnny," he said. We rode on for about a mile when we met the Negro coming back with the corn.[7] He was scared, we told him to take the corn back to the lady and tell her that we would not take anything from her.

The Fifteenth Kansas Volunteer Cavalry was commanded by Colonel Charles R. Jennison, a notorious pro-Union guerrilla, or Jayhawker. Jennison had been forced to give up command of another unit early in the war in part because it too often engaged in such pillage as Johnny describes. During Price's raid, the Fifteenth Kansas made up the core of the First Brigade, one of the two brigades Blunt took into Missouri.[8]

The narrator's idealization of the Southern lady seems extreme. But unlike some other sentimentalized passages, this one is present in the plainer first version of the events as well as in the more self-conscious second version.

The little detachment hurried through hostile Lexington with revolvers drawn and caught up with Company I. They received a light scolding from 1st Lieutenant William Y. Drew: "You fellows are always fooling around somewhere when you're needed. Fall in line and be good for a while, if it's in you."[9]

First Lieutenant William Y. Drew was one of two lieutenants in Company I. After the Battle of the Little Blue, he replaced Captain James E. Greer as company commander. Later he would provide important testimony to events at Platte Bridge station in July 1865. *Civil War Collection, U.S. Army Heritage and Education Center, Carlisle, Pa.*

Our company lined up in the middle afternoon about one half mile south of the fairground and two miles south of Lexington. We were dismounted and lined up facing south (or was it northeast?) toward Price's men across a sweet potato patch; some of the potatoes were dug and heaped up in hills; there was corn, some of it in shocks and some still uncut: an ideal place for a hungry horse and soldier. Was eying one of those sweet potato piles about twenty feet in front of me and longed for just one of them. And like a flash left the ranks headlong for one of them. Just as I picked up one nice big fat fellow an officer ordered me back. And it seemed like every one of the boys in that line had something to say about that sweet potato. "What are you going to do with that potato?" "Give me a bite!" "Going to send it home to Ma?" And last a little bit of a dried-up fellow asked, "Let me carry it for you for a while, Johnny?" I wanted to knock that dried-up lad a rap, but dared not.[10] That potato was crowded into my shirt bosom against a time when it could be baked.

Price's army advanced against the Federals, and the fighting retreat began. Johnny describes a tactic by which Blunt divided his force into two equal units. While one group made a stand against the Confederates, the second would retire to improvise a new defensive line. As its position became untenable, the forward group would fall back through the rear group and take its turn preparing a new line. Johnny describes this "saving and protecting maneuver" correctly, but according to Blunt and others, the tactic was employed only later, west of the Little Blue. The reality on the evening of October 19 was, if anything, more impressive: the Eleventh Kansas alone—about one-quarter of the available Union force—covered the Blunt's retreat.[11]

Our next stand was on a ridge where we could see all around. The Johnnies were executing a flank movement on us and it was hurrying our boys to get through our lines and on ahead to their next stand.

Presently Company I was ordered to fall back in platoons. There was a large gate that had been opened nearly on top of a little rise for the artillery to go through. Along came a man with a howitzer on double quick; while there was plenty of room for him to get through, he couldn't do it; but just had to jam the tongue of the carriage against a gate post a foot square and split it up into splinters. Colonel Moonlight, who was nearby, ordered the officer in charge, Captain [James E. Greer of] Company I, to dismount a platoon of men and get the howitzer up the hill.[12]

The Johnnies were firing on us here pretty heavy, and the delay was getting us into it worse every minute. I grabbed ahold of a wheel, while others got a hold anywhere they could to help the good work along. The old howitzer was moving right along up that hill, pretty good, when a shot from the rear came in and hit the trunion in such a manner that the lead was forced into fine little drops of spray. My arm just then was near the top of the wheel, so the underside of my arm was just peppered with red hot lead clear into the skin.

I jumped up into the air, don't know how far, whirled around and grabbed my trousers and then my arm; but when that lead was pulled out or rubbed loose it felt like cactus stickers into my flesh. I did not know how bad the wound was or how many times I had been shot. At least must have done a few record-breaking stunts in a very short time. For Colonel Moonlight laughed until his side ached am very sure; he seemed to be having the time of his life. "Did something hit you, Johnny? What in the world do you want to hop around like that for?" "Yes," I said, "something did hit me all right, my arm is full of little pieces of red-hot lead." "Does it hurt?" he said, and rode away laughing, and on, way in advance, I could still hear him laugh.

The last encounter of the day was a twilight skirmish at one of the crossings of Fire Prairie Creek, a site not now identifiable.

Our place this time was a rather hard one. We had to cut a new road through trees and brush as best we could and at that it was crooked, in the form of a big horseshoe. You see the Johnnies had burnt the bridge, just enough to let the end next to us fall down into the water, so that a part of the abutment had to be torn out and thrown into the creek, therefore the new road had to be built so as to get to water. All the troops had to go into the water then up the slanting floor of the bridge, it was the only way to cross in a short time. We expected a lively time there, if the Johnnies crowded us very hard. We were not disappointed.

Soon the men came crowding through there, but most of them had considerable of a time getting up the slanting floor of the bridge. It became wet in a little while causing horses' feet to slide back down and some of them fell and rolled down causing more trouble. It couldn't be helped, there was not enough time to do better. Most of our men managed to get through that crooked road in good time; but it was growing dark and still the road was yet crowded with the last remnant of our men.

Suddenly the Johnnies crowded into the lane . . . in the rear of our men. Immediately everything in that lane became a fighting bunch, all mixed up. It was evident they were being crowded pretty hard from the noise and the commotion they made. They passed the word forward, "They are cutting the rear all to hell." Every soldier knows what that means. He does not have to be knocked [down] to understand.

Company I was ordered to line up just where our new road commenced on the left side of the road; and two companies were lined up on the right side of the road. It was dark and I do not know what two companies were lined up over there. . . . Colonel Moonlight rode up and down in front of our company, begging us to hold our fire, and with each word bringing his hand down good and hard, as if for emphasis, on his thigh. . . . "Hold your fire until I say when! I'll say when, boys. Don't make a fool of yourselves." You have to see a man in action like that to appreciate the value of the man, to see the real life being lived in a few minutes. Across the colonel went to the other two companies begging them like he had us to hold our fire. We didn't want to hold our fire, but it is well that we did, many thanks to the colonel.[13]

After all our men in the lane had just about gained the welcome protection of our new road, which allowed the Johnnies to come up close to us, the order was given to fire. "Fire!" Colonel Moonlight yelled, at the top of his voice. It was almost as bright as day. Three companies emptied their rifles into that lane full of horses and men. Then the order came to empty our revolvers: "Shoot low in there, every man," which we did. The Johnnies stopped crowding, they were down, horses and men. Everything in a bunch. It looked pretty hard from what we could see by the flash of our guns, but it had to be done. Everybody had a chance after that to draw a long breath. Never again did they crowd us so fast and furious as that, especially after dark.

In the small hours of Thursday, October 20, the Federals camped somewhat east of the Little Blue River, shifting to the west bank after daylight. Blunt describes a day of relative ease at this spot, but Johnny recalls a far briefer break in the action.

Unknown to him, the commanders were in the middle of a tactical debate. General Blunt saw the west bank of the Little Blue as the best place for a definitive stand against Price and unsuccessfully urged General Curtis to move forward; Curtis instead instructed Blunt to pull the bulk of his force back to Independence, leaving Colonel Moonlight and four hundred men at the river to face the Confederate assault early on Friday, the twenty-first. Their unexpectedly effective delaying action developed into the Battle of the Little Blue, with significant losses to the Confederate side.[14] Johnny, however, got side-tracked into a peripheral adventure.

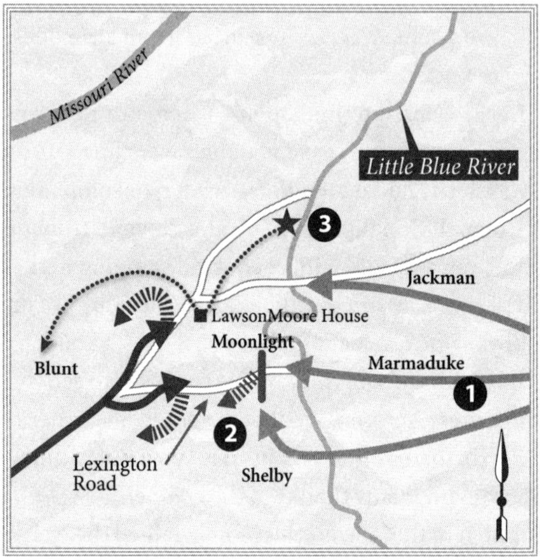

The Battle of the Little Blue, October 21, 1864. Three columns of Confederates pressed across the river from the east (1). A small force under Moonlight, later reinforced, put up stout resistance (2). Johnny's Company I, guarding a ford to the north (3), missed this action, escaping cross-country (dotted line) past the home of Lawson Moore to rejoin the main army later in the day.

Map by Gerry Krieg. Copyright © 2019 by John Hart.

All our men had safely crossed a good sized creek [the Little Blue River] on a splendid good bridge, which was immediately covered afterward with all kinds of inflammable material. Artillery was stationed on both sides of the road on our side of the creek, so as to rake the bridge. One regiment, and the Second Kansas and the Second Colorado, held the place and burnt the bridge, which forced the Johnnies to find a ford. This being anticipated, Company I under the command of Captain Greer was ordered to go down the valley and hold two fords, the first one a little more than four miles down the creek below the bridge, the second one a mile and a half still farther down. Captain Greer held the first ford and detailed Lieutenant Drew and twenty men to go and hold the second ford as long as possible.[15] Now this creek had rather steep banks which were muddy and dangerous, but out in the stream, the creek bottom was firm and good. This gave us some slight advantage. Everyone was ordered to not build any fires as that would be sure to give us away to our enemies.

After a while it began to be light and then we could build fires. And then, out from my saddle pocket, I pulled my old sweet potato and placed it in a bed of hot coals to bake. All the fellows around there crowded around my fire, asking dozens of questions and giving advice about my potato. One little fellow wanted me to save him an eye, another one wanted to hold it for me on a board while I ate it, and still another said that sweet potatoes was dangerous to have inside of one, 'cause his old aunt got blowed up by eatin' one, one time. Had to watch them, to keep them from stealing my sweet potato.

Had just about got my sweet potato good and hot, when a picket fired a shot and right on the heels of that shot came the order to fall in. Quick as I could, and that wasn't long, raked my potato out of the coals and shoved it into my saddle pocket and away we went. You see our boys had had a couple of hours of pretty good rest and it seemed a little uncanny somehow, everything for a time being so still and quiet there. Up on a little ridge we went, and there hailed some soldiers down in the timber. They said they were Yankees, soon however they proved to be Johnnies, for they came for us. Across a field we "hit it up" but were losing ground, so Lieutenant Drew ordered us to make for a house up on a hill where there could be seen a big gate and a girl standing outside by the house.

Lieutenant Drew hallooed to her to please open the gate and let us go through. Quick, she ran like a deer and opened the gate for us, and held it open until we all got through, and held that gate, mind you, under fire, while dozens of bullets were whizzing by with their intended mission of death. Every one of us boys thanked that girl . . . as we went through the opened way on a dead run; some of them said "God bless you." Then when we were through, the girl shut the gate and ran into the house.

Away we went into a cornfield like a bunch of Indians, scared half to death, for behind was five to one against us, all eager to take us prisoners. The corn in the field was high and our horses tore a swath through this forty feet wide. We got away all right, but it was a good run. Up on a little ridge a quarter of a mile away Lieutenant Drew looked back toward the house where the girl had opened the gate for us, and could see the Johnnies were going back below the house and some of them were firing into the house. Lieutenant Drew shook his fist at them, saying, "You fellows hurt a hair of that girl's head and I will come back here and blow your crowd into hell!"

It is tempting to identify this building as the Lawson Moore house, which still overlooks the Little Blue valley on East Blue Mills Road. Yet it should have been vacated under General Order No. 11 of August 1863, which ordered the rural inhabitants of four Missouri counties, including Jackson County, to leave their homes. Perhaps this building had been reoccupied at some point in the months afterward.

For a long time our little bunch of men rode after that, until finally Lieutenant Drew said, "We must be about far enough back, the artillery firing sounds away back in the rear of us now." So all hands then rode to the top of a little ridge and looked over; much to our surprise, there below in the road was cavalry, marching four abreast as far as we could see up and down the road. Lieutenant Drew asked them who they were. They replied, "We are Marmaduke's men," and laughed, and then again "Jim Lane's Tads" rolled up to us from a dozen throats. Their captain ordered "Fire!" without any preliminary maneuvers whatever, which they did and quick, too, and then a big bunch of their men came on a run for us; there was nothing to do but run for it, back over the way we came; but hold, whoa, stop, before we knew it, we were right in front of another column of cavalry marching four abreast coming toward us some three hundred yards away. This rattled all of our little band, because we had just crossed over down there a few minutes before, and surely there was not a single trooper anywhere [in] sight. It was folly to turn back, death to go ahead, so the only way out was to run with them a race for our lives.

Down to a house along a little creek we rode and jumped our horses over a fallen tree close by the side of the house, when there was a better way around the house; but didn't know it, being pressed so hard we were a little rattled, or couldn't think fast enough, don't know which. Then the people in the house commenced firing at us, which made our position still worse; so out into a cornfield we went, couldn't find no hole to crawl into; had to do something. At the edge of this cornfield was a swamp, and that swamp didn't look a bit inviting to our men, especially when everything depended on a few precious moments.

"Into it!" Lieutenant Drew shouted. "We can't be taken prisoners here!" And into it we went, and by good fortune made the other side easier than expected, as slough grass held up our horses pretty good considering the weight of our steeds. As we gained the bank and solid footing once more, here in front of us was a steep hill that had to be made on double-quick, which tried our horses and worried us.

Here Jim Lane's Tads, who had by this time gained considerable distance on us, began to shower a perfect rain of bullets over our heads. Everyone after that went for himself up that hill, getting behind big trees, something in the fashion a wild turkey will do in the wild woods to evade the man with a gun. You see, our horses were all fresh mounts and were able to hold their own; while our enemy's horses were pretty good too, but they couldn't go into the wind quite so keen as ours, and that is the only reason our outfit got out of the jaws of two columns of steel and muscle and up on the hillside in the comparatively safe refuge of the timber.

But nearly halfway up this hill, my "bunkie," Tom Roderick (the second one to be killed) got shot in the back, and fell off his horse.[16] Lieutenant Drew examined him in a hurry, and Tom was begging us not to leave him, so I started back to him. "Go on!" Lieutenant Drew ordered. "You can't help him now, his back is broke." "Well," I said, "[I] don't want to leave him here, that's pretty tough." "Yes it is, Johnny, but some more of us will get it, if we don't get out of here!"

Up on the top of the hill, just before we went scurrying away, one more look we must have, down through the trees to where our comrade lay, and something hard for our eyes there to stand we saw. The Johnnies were shooting Tom Roderick to death, finishing him then and there; but that, even, was some consolation as it put him out of his misery.

Away we went hunting our company. . . . We had to make a ride away out to one side to get around the Johnnies coming up the valley. It was evident the Johnnies must have crossed the ford where Captain Greer and the rest of our company was last seen on duty. What had become of them? That was the question. If they had to fall back, why was we not notified in time? . . . When we did finally get in [we were] an angry bunch and there had to be an explanation. The truth of the thing was that Captain Greer fell back when the first shot was fired across the creek and that he got scared at the ford ordering his men to fall back leaving us in ignorance of his move; therefore we were flanked and came very near being taken prisoners.[17]

After this incident nearly everyone in Company I called Captain Greer a coward, and would not go willingly into tight places with him in command without a kick and a grumble. The morale of the soldiers under him was gone. Eventually Captain Greer left his command and went to Kansas City, turning the company over to Lieutenant Drew who then commanded as acting captain. Captain Greer was not a soldier and could not face bullets without great mental strain. At the same time he was a good intelligent man. He did come back and wear his spurs with honor later in battles with the Indians.

Major General John S. Marmaduke, whose column the company encountered, was one of three division commanders under Price. But their claim to be "Jim Lane's Tads" was ironic. James Henry Lane was a prominent Jayhawker, a U.S. senator from Kansas, and very much in the present campaign as an aide-de-camp to General Curtis.

It was west of the Little Blue that Blunt divided his forces as earlier described, making stand after stand. The afternoon closed with a street fight in Independence, where Johnny was slightly wounded by a shot from a window.

Around midnight, Company I arrived at a site on the Blue River previously fortified by the Kansas militia. This was apparently Simmons Ford in modern Blue River Park. Recent research seems to establish a poignant fact: Moonlight's men were not supposed to be here. The colonel had actually been ordered to Hinkle's Ford, two miles upriver to the south, which was consequently left unguarded.[18]

At this point "Sweet Potatoes and Other Stories" ends, and "My Bunkies" continues the story. The following incident is dated Saturday, October 22, the eve of the Battle of Westport proper. Johnny describes an unsuccessful Confederate thrust across the river at Simmons Ford—quite unaware that Price was even then in the process of piercing the Union lines at Hinkle's Ford.

We were about three or four miles southwest of Westport at a ford (on the Blue). We were having it hot and heavy. All were angry and nervous. The Johnnies had crossed the ford and were coming and forming too sure of themselves to suit our company. We were held in a line close up where we could see a Johnny officer riding a white horse and coaxing his men to hold the line. He rode back and forth on a run. All our men tried to shoot his horse from under him, but he seemed to be charmed. This was one thing that exasperated us.

Someone hallooed "Charge!" and away we went after that officer riding the white horse. Into the Johnnies we bolted. After that officer we ran around and around, and came near capturing him a dozen times in a dozen minutes. Finally the officer discovering we wanted him, he dived into the ford where his horse fell down and the fine officer tumbled into the water rolling under a wagon. We caused a jam at that ford and stopped the Johnnies from crossing over to our side and whipped them plumb out capturing a bunch of prisoners on the side for our pains. But this charge without authorized orders from an officer was a bad move even if it was successful and did a lot of good.

Colonel Moonlight raged and swore and rested for breath, and then started in on us again. "Boys," he said, "we are fighting this campaign for a principle, for what we think is right. Don't ever charge again without orders from an officer, be honorable, be dependable. Your charge was successful, because unexpected on all sides; but if it hadn't have been, we would be in a fine position now. You have stood firm against shot and shell before. Why weaken now? I bow my head in shame before boys I trusted and considered equal to anything under the sun."

Then Colonel Moonlight rode on down the line saying something about "how foolish some people are even after they have been trained."

On the afternoon of Saturday, October 22, General Blunt heard artillery to his south and understood that Price had crossed the river on the Union right. Moonlight retreated west toward Shawnee Mission, Kansas, before joining in a vigorous counterattack.[19] Company I was engaged again Sunday morning in the Battle of Westport proper, first pushing forward and then retreating as Price recovered ground. Johnny describes these events only in summary and may have conflated the two days' actions.

Our next battle was about six miles from what was then the baby Kansas City. It was called the Battle of Westport and the end of the Price advance. Westport was the big town then. Price forced us by Westport in a mighty hard drive, flanked us and drove us off the field about used up. This was on Sunday morning and this time we lost sixteen men out of the company.[20] We had been fighting five to one.

Price moved up south of Westport and commenced to throwing shells into Westport. We were whipped this day good and plenty and we all were feeling mighty blue. Sixteen out of our company when we counted off did not make for very pleasant thoughts just then. Down, down in the blues we had sunk and blacker and blacker the awful thing crowded over our eyes. Lieutenant Drew

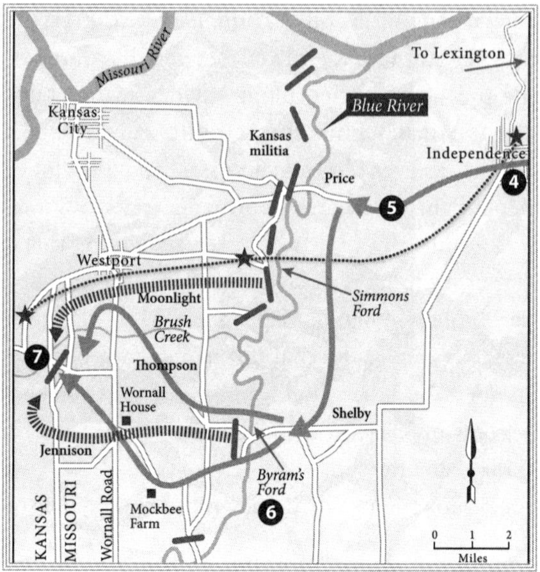

The Battle of the Big Blue, October 22, 1864. After the street fight in Independence (4), Johnny's unit snatched some sleep at Simmons Ford (star). In the morning Price feigned a direct attack on Kansas City (5), but his subordinate Brigadier General J. O. Shelby breached the Union defenses at Hinkle's Ford and Byram's Ford (6). By day's end Union forces were arranged north of Brush Creek and along the Kansas-Missouri state line (7), where the 11th Kansas Cavalry took position.

Map by Gerry Krieg. Copyright © 2019 by John Hart.

Chaos. Samuel J. Reader, Second Kansas State Militia, captured in this contemporaneous drawing the confusion of the fighting along the Big Blue on October 22, 1864, during which he became a Confederate prisoner.

Courtesy Kansas State Historical Society.

was all covered over dust and mud and his uniform half torn from his precious body. And [2nd] Lieutenant [James J.] Clancy[21] was in the same condition. It hurts soldiers to see their officers used up, especially when they were men who were always in the lead and no cowards.

Lieutenant Drew said, "Boys, there isn't so many of us now. I want those boys back."

Later on Sunday, Company I remained near Shawnee Mission, positioned to block any move by Price into Kansas. From this spot Johnny reports witnessing Pleasonton's definitive breakthrough from the east. Seeing a new Union force emerging from the woods, Confederate brigadier general Joseph O. Shelby is said to have shouted, "Charge yonder line and break it, or all is lost." Johnny, however, sees the Rebels purely on the defensive. He gives the time as "after four o'clock," though this may be on the late side.[22]

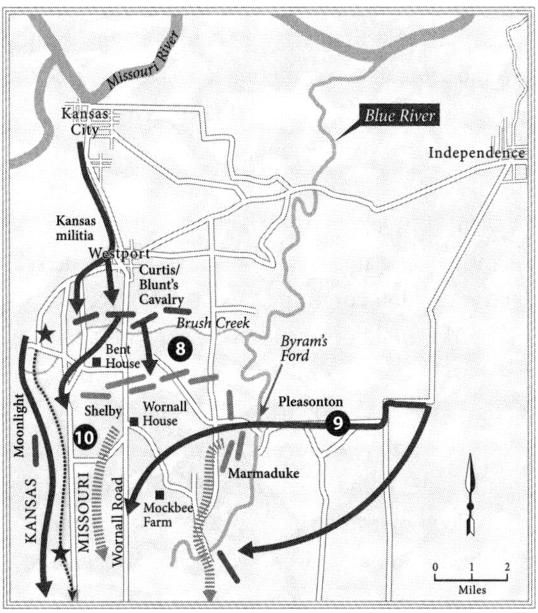

The Battle of Westport, October 23, 1864. On the climactic day of the campaign, Union forces pushed south across Brush Creek (8) while a second Northern column under Pleasonton moved in from the east (9). Moonlight's men at the Kansas line witnessed the junction of these forces, as the Confederates began their retreat from Missouri. The cornfield shelling took place near (10).

Map by Gerry Krieg. Copyright © 2019 by John Hart.

Our company and several others were on a hill where we could see away down on the Blue. The air was clear and we could see a long way. We were lined up on this hill and counting off. Something was going to happen pretty soon. We had been everywhere this Sunday and saw things changing before our eyes as in a dream. Whipped by the Johnnies in the morning and in turn they were whipped by us to a showdown and were on the retreat.

We could see at the bottom of the hill, where Johnnies were lining up and counting off, about three regiments of cavalry. About the time they were lined up and ready for action, here through the timber of the Blue came Pleasonton's cavalry, about three regiments of cavalry. They came out below us and formed as they came.

We knew there was going to be something doing pretty soon. Three thousand cavalry of Pleasonton['s] going to match their strength with an equal number of Johnnies. We shouted at the top of our voices, we stood up in our stirrups as if to make our noise carry farther. Colonel Moonlight ordered all the line officers and sergeants in front to keep us from charging. He wanted to make sure we obeyed orders. "I'll give you the charge in time, if Pleasonton's men cannot handle their end of the line. You wild-eyed, daredevil bunch, hold still! I'll say when!" Colonel Moonlight shouted.

We loved Colonel Moonlight, we worshipped him, it was heavenly to have him lecture us in his plain honest way. He had very little self-esteem, but a wonderful amount of good common sense right over his eyes balancing the front side of his head straight on ahead through calms and through storms.[23]

We knew they [Pleasonton's men] drew their sabers because of the sun's reflection on their steel. We could hear the bugle sound the charge. We could see that line of cavalry advance forward, then in a little while the bugle sounded the double quick and then the whole line of men lunged forward. They intended to do something that evening, and that line of Price cavalry would have to fight. We cheered, we were excited, we wanted to be in on that charge, and all the time that line of Johnnies stood there, they never showed the white feather, they were as good as our boys, and why not? Weren't they born under America's stars? And weren't they our brothers?

Closer and closer Pleasonton's cavalry advanced, now they were within about one hundred yards of the Johnnies, all on the double quick in earnest. And then we could see a soldier here and there along the line speed up and leave his comrades, daredevils they were, going to meet their death ahead of their time. Now our line was up close to the Johnnies and the Johnnies still stood there, don't believe they batted an eye. It was steel against steel, muscle against muscle, sand against sand, fate against fate, all in the twinkling of an eye.

We stood up in our stirrups and well nigh forgot to breathe, so intensely interested did we become watching this game of real life. Then that whole line of Johnnies fired, three thousand bullets good for three thousand Union horses, or three thousand Union lads providing they all hit the mark; but it is hard to fire true in the face of an onrush of men and horses, it is hard to keep down the quiver and tension of muscles. The eye is apt to overrate the distance and fool you on the bead and a rapid heart beating under excitement does not make for accurate shooting at the mark. And that is the answer why our boys were not stayed in the advance of their charge.

The line did reel and sway, and horses and men went down. We could see men leave their wounded horses and continue the charge on foot, unswayed, undaunted, and unwhipped. Why shouldn't we cheer? Why shouldn't we feel the wonderful thrill of a lifetime?

Now that line all mixed up, two and two waging a battle, three and three, and bunches here and there. And all the time the line widening, scattering out. It was like, excuse the comparison, six thousand dog fights on a plain waging a battle of life and death, all equally matched, all trained under fire and all brothers under our beloved American stars. Good all of them, the Yankee and the Johnny.

The outcome of that charge was in doubt for some little time, no living being could predict correct, a minute rolled by in the time of an hour. Even Colonel Moonlight, hard and seasoned as he was, forgot himself and ceased to breathe now and then, then he would catch himself and slap his leg in downright earnestness. He was a true soldier.

Round and round, up and at it, across and over and down, then all over again, continuous, everlasting and death. Then, could see breaking, running, hurrying and scurrying, the Johnnies were going, they were whipped. The Yankees did not follow them, they were too near used up and had about all they wanted before the sun went down. It was worth living a lifetime to see this charge of the Blue and the Grey.

Afterward we could see hundreds of horses down and men administering to a wounded comrade. And then an orderly came on the dead run to Colonel

Moonlight. Then the order came to march. We started out on the trot uphill and along the line of Price's retreat in between Price and the Kansas line. General Price wanted to get into Kansas, and we were determined he should not.[24]

The next episode is titled "Shelling the Johnnies out of the Bloody Lane." Bloody Lane was the name applied to Wornall's Lane (now busy Wornall Road in Kansas City) after a guerrilla force under George Todd, part of William Quantrill's effective irregular group, ambushed a party of Union soldiers there on June 17, 1863. The location is in modern Loose Park, between 51st and 55th Streets.[25]

Our company was lined up and counting off when a heavy brass battery of eight pieces from General Pleasonton drove in front of us.[26] It proved that we had at last united our forces and would wage war all together from now on, instead of two separate units as heretofore. We greeted them with all the cheers we could and went half wild, and kept it up. The officers finally restored order.

But such an outfit. Our boys looked bad and dilapidated, but these men of Pleasonton clapped anything had ever seen before. Their captain wore a cap which had nothing left to it but a rim and the cap part over the eyes. His hair was all fussed up and protruding out and above the cap rim like a garden that had gone to seed for ages. His remnant of a uniform resembled a rag wagon. On one trousers leg a large piece of carpet had been wired and tied in lieu of the missing portion long since passed from service. Both of his arms were honored by common pieces of gunnysacks patched on here and there, and he hadn't shaved for so long, his beard looked like a bramble bush. But his eyes shone keen and bright and fairly snapped with fire.[27]

The artillery men looked worse than tramps. They were all patched up with pieces of carpet and gunnysacks like their captain, and like him all unshaved. But few of them had a cap or hat, and the ones bareheaded didn't seem to miss their headgear the least bit in the world. Real soldiers they were, hardened, nonchalant and ready for anything to come before them and test their might. Their horses were large, long and poor, so that their ribs could be plainly seen. These horses looked like Kentucky pure-breds, with now and then the exception of a fat horse picked up somewhere to take the place of a horse that had died or been killed.

My position in the line was at the end of the line and was close to the captain where he was talking to General Blunt and in speaking distance of some of the men.

"Aren't you the men that is going to guard us while we pepper the Johnnies out of yonder cornfield, or wherever it is we go?" one of them asked me.

"Believe we are from the looks of things," I answered.

"Well, we left some pretty good men. If you men are as good as ours we will be all right."

"We will hold, never mind about that. We have been fighting night and day and would rather fight than eat," I answered.

"You will, will you! We'll see about that! We have been fighting night and day too. And we're in just the right temper of mind to not care for anything. Now that we are in front of General Price we intend to make him sweat blood if he advances any further." . . .

After we turned toward a large cornfield which looked as if it might be two hundred acres in extent, the land became more level. Here double-quick was sounded once more, the bugler sounding the call on the dead run. And the artillery horsemen each whipping the horse they rode and the one beside them, one quirt apiece. Most of the pieces had ten spans of horses pulling them and large horses at that. These pieces were larger and heavier than anything we had in the way of artillery under General Blunt. . . .

In front of us was a board fence. The captain and his bugler jammed their horses right into the board fence as if it was a piece of paper. The horses leaned their shoulders against the board fence and lunged, they knew what to do and the captain and his bugler braced their feet against the boards. Through they went in a couple of seconds and right behind them the artillery on the dead run. When the artillery struck the board fence it went into kindling wood in a jiffy and then they went for the rail fence. But a few seconds ahead the captain and his bugler had pushed the two top rails over, and right after them the artillery knocked that rail fence into no resemblance of a fence at all. It was a sight worth seeing, something to be proud of; true, our batteries did some wonderful work, but this battery must have been a brag battery of the East sent out to aid us, for all did splendid work and all with the bugle calls, both men and horses. . . .

After this big brass battery was clear of all fences they made an excellent run for [the] position which had been planned by some of our generals in due regard for the danger it would be placed in and the method of a quick retreat.

It was known that the cornfield was full of Johnnies and that they were protected by their artillery, so this position was not without danger, both from being charged by the Johnnies from the cornfield and their artillery fire. We could not march up the Bloody Lane to get at them, so the cornfield had to be cleared, also if we could once get into action we could everlastingly wallop everything in that field.

The captain and his artillery went like the wind. The men riding the caisson held on for dear life. A bugle call pierced the air and the first brass piece arrived at the place where it was to unlimber, the riders whipping their horses as they swerved around to a standstill and it seemed the old heavy gun rolled around on two wheels. Quickly that bunch of men ran seemingly in a picked direction, but each one was doing one thing. I remember one fellow that carried the shells, he had a carpet on one half of his seat and a wad of gunnysacks on the other and I couldn't decide which side of him deserved the most curiosity. He ran with all his might to the caisson for solid shot; he jammed his foot up against the caisson to stop himself while the soldier there handed him the solid shot, then he tore back to the brass piece hard as he could hit it up a-running in a kind of a jump and a gallop, his legs ran and his body and arms as well, but he got there and quick, too.

And the powder man, him I nearly forgot. He ran smooth and fast, like a Kentucky thoroughbred. He didn't have any patches on his seat at all, he needed them to be sure, for there was two places where his pink skin showed. You see it is very hard for artillerymen to keep the seat of their trousers from wearing out.

They were firing before any of the others were and men would jump against the wheels with side and shoulder as they spun around and kicked back from their position. It was astonishing how quick these men could load their cannon after firing. How in deadly earnest they worked and so accurate and unerring. It was splendid, and well worth while to see. The solid shot from these guns fairly made my ears pop, as we were stationed right up close, but after a while could only hear a keen sing ringing in my ears, and never afterwards could hear quite normal.

Away went the solid shot through that cornfield and could see cornstalks shoot straight up in the air when the shot hit them. The solid shot would hit the ground as intended, roll and bounce through the cornfield. There was a commotion in that cornfield as we could see rows of Johnnies mounting their horses. Our solid shot was making it so hot for them they hurriedly moved out of there. At the edge of the cornfield we could see dozens of riders leaving their horses as they had legs broken. All of them at first tried to go out of there by way of the Bloody Lane. Then the captain seeing the Johnnies going out the Bloody Lane ordered the cannon turned on the rock fence beside the Bloody Lane. And when a solid shot would hit that rock fence on an angle the rocks would fly in all directions ahead like a hundred different shots all at once flying through the air. This made it really bad business for the Johnnies in that lane that day.

Did not know the number of this company of artillery then and never have found out, but they were of the first water, the best of the land.[28]

In the aftermath, Johnny tells of intervening to help a wounded Confederate officer.

After this cornfield and Bloody Lane battle we were ordered to go up on a hill past a Johnny gun that had blown up where the Johnnies had established a temporary hospital. There were plenty of wounded soldiers belonging to Price's army there. One Southern soldier who was shot in the leg just above the knee and was an officer in spite of his years wore a splendid pair of new boots. And as I thought of aiding him another man came along and noticing his boots seized hold of his foot which was swelled inside of the boot and the wounded leg. He pulled as hard as he could to get that boot off the officer's foot, and the officer yelled in pain. I pulled a revolver on the fellow and made him go clear off the hill. He said, "You ought to be on the Southern side, that's where you belong."

I came back with my knife and cut the boots off both the wounded officer's feet. He said, "I thank you, sir. You are a gentleman. May God bless you even if you are of the North."

"Oh that's all right, I always aid boys of both sides when they are in distress. It's my duty, because after all we are our brothers' keepers."

Then I stepped around and ordered that the officer be attended to right away. The fellow looked at me for a moment. "Get at it!" I ordered. Tie a bandage, stop blood away and stayed there and saw that it was done, no one objected to my giving orders, and that surprised me. But a Southern lad is entitled to as much consideration when wounded as any other man, and this one was decent clear through and worthy.

It always made a world of difference with me in the manner another one spoke to me and how he conducted himself for his own good. There is a soft spot of comradeship running through all men, arouse that and you are accommodated.

On the morning of Monday the twenty-fifth, the pursuit of Price southward along the state line began. The first days were intense, with several night marches for the Eleventh Kansas Cavalry, taxing men and horses no less than the earlier phase of the campaign. Some incidents Johnny assigns to the retreat from Lexington almost certainly belong to the pursuit period, like this bivouac in the rain: such a drenching is recorded for the night of October 24–25, not earlier. Reverting to the "Sweet Potatoes" manuscript:

The skies became cloudy and the clouds changed to a dull dark hue, which foretold rain. It was lucky for us that night that the commissary wagons finally reached us for our rations had long since played out and we were living off the country. Just a little while we stopped and then on and on in a tiresome grind as if forever. The rain poured down all night and everybody became wet and covered more or less with mud, horses and men. Our command stopped by a cornfield near midnight for I think one hour and a half to let the horses have time to eat. Some of the boys hunched up under trees, others worn tired stopped where they were and slept as best they could out in the pouring rain. For myself rustled some poles and slabs of the fence near there and laid them side by side with one end a little higher than the other, then laid some corn fodder on that for a bed. Laid down on this sumptuous bed, curling up in a knot and pulling my long cavalry cape and coat combined over me, and then went to sleep like the rest out in the rain, but such a sleep, it was a good one and I got it in spite of the elements and the war. It refreshed me like nothing else could, not even hardtack.

Then "Fall in! Fall in!" was sounded. It sounded away off down through an earhorn and across a big canyon a mile deep, and the voice calling seemed hoarse with a weary shading mingled in with its tone. All were obedient though slow and sluggish in motion, for the machinery of our bodies was fast running down, and we couldn't get enough to eat and sufficient sleep to ever wind up a heart that was losing beats.

Keeping west of Price to block any deeper movement into Kansas, Moonlight's men missed the Battle of Mine Creek on October 25, which cost the Confederates much of their remaining strength. The long marches and skirmishes continued for several more days. During this period, Johnny made two more attempts to cook his sweet potato.

The fire for my mess was going pretty good, so out comes my sweet potato once more. It had been baked a little in the fires before and had a few bites gnawed off around the side by my humble teeth, otherwise this potato of mine nearly had its original shape. Into the coals it went once more, and I just had to sit down there on a log and stand guard over that precious sweet potato of mine. It hadn't been baking very long, just enough to nearly get it hot through, when that dreaded "Fall in! Fall in!" came clanging down the line; everything round about sprang into life and motion. I kicked my potato out of the coals, grabbed it up in my hands and brushed it off a little, then jammed it down into my saddle pocket, but the wrong one, being then careless and in such a hurry. This wrong saddle pocket the potato got into this time was the one I had been carrying cartridges in and some of them had gotten loose in some way and let the powder in the shells fall out. The saddle pocket seemed to be empty when the hot potato was crowded down into the bottom of it.

Immediately old Pones, my horse, jumped and ran away from me, as the powder in that saddle pocket hissed and sputtered flame. He mixed everybody and everything all up and made quite a commotion. Couldn't catch him, for some of the powder was wet and some dry, and every time I approached near to him off some more powder would go; then away Pones went kicking and bucking like a bronco. Lieutenant Clancy came running up demanding what was the matter, when told, he was angry.

"Johnny!" he called, "You are a hoodoo for the whole company, always you have to be doing something, and always somebody else gets the blame. When will this combination of you and the horse and the potato cease to be? Boys, get the horse! Kill it if you can't get it no other way. Put him on his horse, and trust to good luck. There is no telling what he'll do next in the midst of this inferno of hell. Don't let him cook his potato on the back of that horse." And the lieutenant went away down the line, but he was smiling.

My saddle pocket was all burnt and shriveled up, and the potato was all covered with burnt powder, so that it was necessary to throw some of it away. Couldn't eat powder. This horse and the potato mixed up everything pretty bad and made everybody mad within reach of me and the old horse. This was along close to daylight in the morning when the horse tore around. . . .

Then once more dug out my sweet potato, now worn and dusty and flavored with a very nice powder smell. Then I split it into two halves and chucked them both in the hot ashes and coals. But that was not all, an extra precaution and vigilance had to be kept up, even while I slept. So a slightly heavy stick was laid over the coals where my potato was roasting and on that stick my feet were placed to stand guard while my head slept a refreshing slumber it needed so very bad. Some part of me had to stand guard or some other man would eat my sweet potato and not I. . . .

In less than half an hour I awoke and found my sweet potato roasted fine on one side, that was good enough that near baked. So, I stuck a slice of bacon on a stick, then held it over the hot coals and soon had the grease dropping over my one-half slice of sweet potato. Then went to eating and bragging how fine my sweet potato was and smacking my lips to make the other fellows wish they had some too. I knew that bunch would make me divide if my sweet potato looked too large, but leaving one half of it in the coals saved me from trouble, but this half looked so small no one expected me to divide.

But when I brought out the other and larger half and another slice of bacon, the boys began to be a little nervous and take notice, [I] suppose they thought my potato was swelling and toasting faster than I could eat it. One fellow said, "If someone would dare me I will take that sweet potato away from Johnny. He must have a wagon load of them under the coals."

Lieutenant Clancy could stand it no longer, so he found a stick and a slice of bacon which he warmed over the coals, then sat down beside me and commenced dropping grease on the other end of my sweet potato, thus really appropriating that end. We together finished it in short order. Lieutenant Clancy thought it was very fine, think it was all he could do to eat it with all that powder flavor that was on the outside of it.

"Now, Johnny," the Lieutenant said, "that is the last of the sweet potato that has caused you some trouble and the rest of us as well. You ought to be in the guard house for not having a better supply."

Several passages evoke the continuing decay of the Confederate army. Even in retrospect Johnny is not aware of certain disputes and miscommunications that cost the Union commanders their chance to demolish Price's force completely.

Every morning we would find the graves where the Johnnies had buried their dead during the night. Usually there would be stakes or slabs marking the graves and the names of the ones that had passed on. And we would find about every two days a bunch of wounded and sick Johnnies under the care of a doctor and helpers. We always greeted them as if nothing of any consequence was between us. It was surprising how quick they would warm up to us, talk about our continuous battle that lasted day and night, and the funny things that happened along with the grind. We would laugh together, pass the tobacco around and make some fellow feel easier, and don't you ever forget that the men of the South have a way of thanking you that carries a season of hospitality that charms.

One afternoon we rode into a farm that smacked of being well kept up and from the looks of things around about the proprietor must be well to do. We were out to one side of the line of Price's retreat in search of food for our company and fodder for our horses.

We rode up to a fine brick house before going away because Lieutenant Drew wished to learn the names of the people so as to keep a record of what things we had taken belong[ing] to the right party. Lieutenant Drew made his quest known to a lady that was standing on the porch of the house who happened to be the wife of the man who owned the place, but her husband at the time was with General Price, so she said.

"Yes!" she answered. "You Yanks are welcome to our things because there is no force here that can prevent you. I suppose you men would take the house if it could be toted away handy."

"No, Madam," Lieutenant Drew answered, "we only want what is necessary to keep body and soul alive for a little while. We are up against a hard proposition."

"You men would be up against a harder proposition, if General Price had more soldiers to fight you!" The lady snapped back hard as flint.

"I realize that fact. General Price is an able general, lady. Now please do not be afraid of our outfit. We are not willingly robbing the country, we are forced to do these things because we are hungry. General Price is doing the same thing and destroying what he cannot consume to keep us from having anything. It's war and war is not kind to anybody."

"I don't care. I hate! the Yanks! I despise the pesky animals—I do!"

Then five more ladies came out on the porch. They wanted to take a good look at a Yank. They were inquisitive which is natural for the sex.

The lady of the house continued, "Why don't you have your men dressed in better clothing. I would be ashamed to go through a country looking like tramps. Do any of you know what a razor is for?"

"Dear lady, we used to have some idea what a razor is for, but that has been so long ago it seems like it has been a hundred years ago, and good clothes, we wouldn't know how to conduct ourselves in good clothes.

"Before we go away, would you ladies sing us a nice song. We are tired of this war and are all homesick. We need a little cheer even if we are 'Yanks,'" Lieutenant Drew begged. He held his hand at salute and because our lieutenant showed that much respect, we all did the same.

"We will sing you a song if you will allow us to choose our song, and will not be angry with us after we have sung the song. If you agree to that, then we will sing."

"We agree, lady. Go ahead please."

Then the lady sang a [song] . . . which the Southern lads sang occasionally to appease their appetites. Don't remember the words except the last lines, they were, "Come on ravens and crows and have a feast, for Yankee flesh shall be your meat." And when they came to flesh in their song every lady in that bunch would stomp the floor of that porch as hard as they could.

"Now what do you think of that, you men?" the lady asked.

"It is splendid, your singing shows to have had some training and your motive is well emphasized and marked. Have never heard such fine singing in all my life before. Your professor must have [been] a singing master of renown."

Then the Lieutenant thanked the lady and we rode away.

On November 4 the troops were in northern Arkansas, where the company surprised a group of exhausted Confederate soldiers.

At or near Fayetteville, Arkansas our army ceased to keep on the western side of Price as it was not necessary to continue further on that plan, we were away from the Kansas border. Here we were issued six hardtack and a handful of sugar, one ration, and it could not go very far, but that is all could be had at the time. We had to live off the country. The Johnnies would kill a beef and skin one side, cut half of the meat out, and go on if we were pushing too hard behind and then we would come along, turn the beef over, and skin the other side and cut out the other half of the meat. Here we found an ocean of abandoned wagons and mules and horses staggering around half dead. Their shoulders were worn to the bone, a hard looking bunch of stock.

In the afternoon we rode up on about twenty Johnnies sleeping beside a little creek. They were all dead for sleep which was why they did not waken when we approached. We surrounded them, covering all with revolvers, then hallowed to them to wake up. Some of them hurried to their feet, others rubbed their eyes and then discovered they were trapped. At first showed they intended to scrap, but Lieutenant Drew told them to keep quiet if they wished to live a while longer.

They were quite angry and couldn't figure out what happened. Then one of their number said in an angry mood,

"We are caught like rats in a trap. I feel disgraced."

"That is about all there is to it. You men are caught, so be good about it, if it's in you," Lieutenant Drew answered.

"If I had known you were coming, no Yank would have taken me alive. It is bad to give up your life in battle, but that is honorable compared to be caught asleep. Our lieutenant is the cause of this. He should have wakened us as agreed, and he alone is guilty. A fine man he is, worthy of nothing."

We made them come with us where they were made prisoners of war in the rear in a bull-pen.

Toward the end of the manuscript, Johnny reports a suspiciously inspirational conversation. Did it really occur about as written, or might it reflect not only the softening effect of time but also deference to his wife, Corrinna Siceloff, born in North Carolina? Son Harry remarked in a note: "If I sing 'Marching Through Georgia' must follow it up with 'Dixie.'" The anecdote might also reflect the determination during the post-Reconstruction years to downplay the issue of slavery. Certainly Johnny barely mentions that fatal matter but returns again and again to the need to preserve the strength of an undivided nation.

Our forces did not follow General Price across the Arkansas River, as by that time the Johnnies were about used up, and their coming again into Missouri was very doubtful. Then too the Arkansas rising made it extremely dangerous to cross the river, General Price just barely crossing with his troops in the nick of time. Our forces then turned back to [the] Kansas City vicinity.

Now we could march at our leisure in the daytime and sleep all the night minus the eternal rush and go and battling. They had given us a hard tussle and while they were in a bad way, we were not in a position to do much of the braggado [*sic*]. They were our honorable enemy, and a part of our blood and race; and that is the reason why they were so confounded hard to whip out of Missouri.

Our little dried-up fellow was still alive and healthy as an old-fashioned pine-knot, and more sassy and important than usual.[29] I asked him what he thought about the war in Missouri.

"Why," he answered, "it's all right. We were fighting to keep our brothers of the South with us. We need 'em, we must have 'em. We cannot afford to divide our Stars and Stripes for any kind of a trumped-up charge. We can't both be victorious over each other, but we can be a helluva nation all together.

"Ain't one of my brothers fighting in the Southern army this minute, and ain't I fighting in the North? My mother is in the South, stickin' up for the South, livin' for the South, ready to die for the South—and one of my sisters married a Northern man.

"That makes our family mixed in the land. And we're a mixed country of people. We got to take 'er all mixed, with one universal language.

"Ain't it so?"

2

AT PLATTE BRIDGE WITH CASPAR COLLINS

In the autumn of 1864, John Benton Hart and his comrades in the Eleventh Kansas Cavalry had done what they had signed up to do in 1862: protect Kansas and help preserve the Union in its time of peril. But even as they made their way back from Arkansas toward their headquarters in Paola, Kansas, events on the frontier were setting them up to fight another kind of war, one that would cost the unit more casualties than all its Civil War engagements combined.

On November 29, 1864, at Big Sandy Creek in Colorado Territory, a detachment of militia under Colonel John Chivington attacked a quiet encampment of Cheyenne and Arapaho Indians—people who, unlike some of their more combative peers, had asked for peace and had accepted a promise of federal protection. At a time when key plains tribes were awakening to the scale of the white invasion, the resulting Sand Creek Massacre was the final catalyst. It brought fractious tribal groups into alliance against the United States and unleashed a full-scale Indian war.[1]

The authorities saw what was coming and began moving forces west. On January 4, 1865, the Eleventh Kansas, badly underequipped for such a march, began its trek across the frigid plains.[2] On April 18 the regiment set up its headquarters at the strategic point on the Oregon Trail called "Platte Bridge" or "Ganard's Bridge,"

Platte Bridge Station, 1863, from a drawing made by C. Moellman, bugler with the Eleventh Ohio Cavalry. Photographs of American Military Activities, ca. 1918–81.
National Archives and Records Administration.

Platte Bridge Station, in a drawing by William Henry Jackson, 1926. Jackson, a celebrated photographer and artist, like Johnny first went west as a bullwhacker, passing through the station in 1866.
Special Collections, Harold B. Lee Library, Brigham Young University.

after its builder, Louis Guinard. From this point the men patrolled westward along the North Platte River and its western tributary, the Sweetwater, skirmishing with Indians and repairing the telegraph line, which the hostiles were constantly taking down. By late July the unit was once more at Platte Bridge. Johnny sets the scene:

All there was at Ganard's Bridge in 1865 were Ganard's double cabin close to the bridge, two squaw-men's tepas, the Telegraph Company's little fort (the Post) with a small stockade, and a small cabin close to the telegraph building.

Ganard was an old-timer, a French Canadian, an Indian trader and used to the wild frontier. He and his oldest son it was that built the bridge across the North Platte River. This bridge was twenty-six spans of thirty-six feet to the span; the timbers of which it was built were hewed out in the mountains [the Laramie Mountains] twelve miles south of where it was built across the river. This bridge must have cost Ganard at least eight thousand dollars completed. He charged $2.50 for one wagon and one team to cross the bridge, other teams in proportion.

There was another bridge about twelve miles further down the river which was built by Reshaw [John Baptiste Richard], a French Canadian too; but all freighters and emigrants were forced to pull through sand requiring two days of the hardest kind of work to make the bridge, and as there was no sand going by way of Ganard's bridge, he had all the trade in the toll bridge business at the time.[3]

Johnny's narrative comes in two pieces, "Meeting an Indian Halfway" and "The Battle of Ganard's Bridge." The former describes a preliminary brush with Indians; the latter casts new light on the Battle of Platte Bridge on July 26, 1865, the celebrated engagement in which Caspar Collins, namesake of Casper, Wyoming, was killed. Johnny's story joins a short list of eyewitness accounts of the core of this action,

George Bent (1843–1918), with his wife Magpie, or Black Bird, 1902. The son of trader William Bent and Owl Woman, the daughter of a Northern Cheyenne chief, he thought of himself as Cheyenne but moved freely between the two societies. Bent fought alongside the Indians at Platte Bridge and later worked for the government as an interpreter. His letters and memories were captured by anthropologists George Bird Grinnell and James Mooney and biographer George E. Hyde.
Special Collections and Archives, Norlin Library, University of Colorado at Boulder.

taking its place alongside the diary of Sergeant Isaac B. Pennock, the reminiscences of Private Ferdinand Erhardt, and the letters of George Bent, son of a Cheyenne mother and a white father, who fought on the Indian side.[4]

In the late spring of 1865, Cheyenne, Sioux, and Arapaho leaders, encamped in the Powder River country north of the Platte, settled on a plan of campaign. After wearing the federal garrisons down with incessant minor raids, they would mass their forces at a chosen spot and sever the Oregon Trail—permanently.[5] The first incident recorded by Johnny, in "Meeting an Indian Half Way," is not datable but seems to belong to the harassment phase of this war.

I was stationed at Ganard's Bridge on the North Platte River. The grass was poor, a sort of alkali grass, so we moved up to the foot of the mountains, went in camp on a small creek bottom, which was about twenty-five yards wide and near twenty-five feet deep. We built a fort on each bluff out of boulders. West of this creek was fine bluestem grazing ground and extended down two miles and about one half mile wide sloping up from the creek. We grazed our horses two hours in the morning and two hours in the afternoon, and on this new grass our horses were doing fine.

I was put on picket on the west side of the grazing ground about three hundred yards from the herd, where I could see all around. I was posted on a high ridge, this gave my horse a chance to eat. In about thirty minutes I thought I saw a wolf pass over a low place and in half a minute another and right along like that. I seen that they were horses, and about a foot of his back was exposed when passing through this low place. I walked to my horses, mounted, gave my hat a wave and started for the herd thoroughly scared. Away the herd ran for camp. Every horse in the herd knew what it meant as well as the herder, as we trained them by always firing a shot and waving our hats when we wanted the herd to go to camp. We wasn't a minute too soon in our run toward camp.

The Indians appeared all around about one hundred a minute. When I got half way to camp, I slowed down to walk and stopped, about one thousand yards from our fort. I seen the Indians couldn't cut me off. A lone Indian rode up to within five hundred yards of me and hallowed to me to come out! come out! I asked him to come over. He gave me a lot of abuse and I fired back the same. Finally the Indian brave dared me to come half way, calling me a coward and a squaw.

John Roderick,[6] my herding partner, was still mounted and was [in] the old boulder fort, like myself waiting for the company to saddle up and come out, and I knew he heard this challenge. I wasn't anxious to battle this Indian, as I thought he was well armed and a half breed, and I did not see any fun in it. But this Indian kept it up, daring me. I thought that if I couldn't fight one Indian to a finish, I was no good, so I yelled to him, all right I'll meet you half way. Then we both started in a walk towards each other. About four [hundred] yards ahead there was a sag just deep enough to hide me and sixty yards wide, across this sag I started in a run, anything is fair in love and war. As I climbed cautiously the opposite bank of this sag, I saw my challenger and a dozen more behind him coming under the whip. I saw the trap at a glance, whirled and put spur to my horse for camp. But where these extra Indians came from, where the place was level, is a puzzle to me today.

On coming out of this sag, I saw a squad of cavalry coming at full speed, as John Roderick told Lieutenant Drew that I had gone out to meet an Indian on the war path, half way. I held up a little, as I wanted to scrap that Indian who had tricked me. I didn't care if he was coming, thought I would slow up and dismount and get him standing on the ground. You cannot shoot off-hand from a horse that has been running with accuracy. But that dozen Indians coming further behind would be onto me before Lieutenant Drew and his boys would be up. I watched behind and ahead. Finally thought it safe to stop and fight that lone Indian, as he had shot several arrows at me, and my reinforcements would be up as soon as his would. I shot my carbine and then emptied my revolver at him. I got his horse, it laid down in about two hundred yards, but never knew whether the Indian was hit or not.

I never heard the last of going out to meet an Indian half way, all my pals took great pains to remind me about that every time we made a thrust at the Indians. John Holding was wounded.[7] We moved back to Ganard's Bridge that evening.

This minor affair exemplified a tactic the Indians employed incessantly, often with success: use a small force, in this case a single warrior, to lure soldiers out of safety and into an ambush.

On July 25, unknown to the garrison (but suspected by Guinard), several thousand Indians had converged north of the river. About one hundred of these showed themselves that day, hoping to draw out a sortie. On this occasion the bait was not taken. The chiefs sent a respected Cheyenne warrior, High Backed Wolf, to bring the advance party in. Instead, the frustrated decoys decided to take some action on their own, persuading the messenger to disregard his orders and come along.[8] Johnny's account of what ensued is subtitled "First Day: Cattle Raid."

One morning Ganard came to me stating that the Indians were coming and asking me to help him drive his cattle up close to our camp. We were camped close to Ganard's Bridge and so were in a good position to fight away the warlike Indians. Our company was camped at this bridge to aid in keeping the telegraph line open, as the Indians kept taking it down.

Four of my company saddled up and rode down the North Platte about four miles where we found Ganard's cattle and started them up towards the bridge. Ganard's squaw and her mother mounted ponies and accompanied us. We just had the cattle under good way when four Indians showed up some distance away stripped for battle and painted.

Ganard said, "There may be considerable more of these Indians showing up pretty soon." He said that we had better abandon the cattle and make for the post at the bridge. "Things do not look good, I am uneasy. My squaw she sees smoke signals—Indians gathering."

Did not like this abandon idea very well, as we had come down there for the cattle and wished to be successful rather than otherwise, so answered Ganard, "No, we will fight the Indians off, and push the cattle as fast as we can, Indian or no Indian."

The four Indians fired at us long distance; this scared the squaws so they commenced to sling the lariat onto the rumps of those cattle. So did Ganard, he was excited as much or more than the squaws.

He then told us there might be a large war party and that we had better see they did not get between us and the Post.

Eleventh Kansas boys from the camp could see us, and kept coming out to us one by one until we had eight in our party of soldiers, but the Indians had increased until there were twelve or more of them. We were keeping the Indians back three or four hundred yards behind the cattle, when we came to a damp place that was covered with water when the Platte overflowed its banks during the very highest water of the year. This place cut the river bottom across from the river to the bluff, and here sand and trash had blown in among the sage and checo shrubby growth, so that after our horses and cattle had scampered across you couldn't see a horse in some places sixty feet. But joining this there was a low bare place about one hundred yards wide, a fine place to fight Indians across.

We soldiers were firing when we could get a chance and the Indians were doing the same. After this firing had been going on a spell, we concluded to all mount and charge back across this bare place and make a cleanup of the Indians at once. But found on the other side a good bunch of Indians on the fight, far too many now for us to give battle to, so we fell back to our former position and the Indians right in our rear, crowding us a terrific pace.

A Cheyenne chief was pounding Noah Coffman on the back with an old blunt sword which made him yell for help. Pharus Hammond and myself wheeled and fired on this chief.[9] One ball slivered the chief's right wrist and another ball lodged in his neck. He fell off his pony, then jumped up and ran into a bunch of willows that grew in the middle of the damp lane. After this all the other Indians fell back to their side of the battleground. Then on closer inspection saw that the chief had fallen just at the edge of the bunch of willows and not clear out of sight as we at first supposed and lay there as if through for this world.

Pharus Hammond and I rode down and around the knobs of willow sand domes opposite where the Cheyenne chief lay, then as the surrounding bushes seemed to be free of Indians, rustled up courage and rode to the chief. Then I dismounted and seized hold of the chief's feet and pulled him out of the willows.

Then turned him over on his back. He lay still. At first thought he was dead or about so, but all at once he jumped up and attacked us like a wild animal and we had to fight for our lives. His right hand being out of commission is probably the thing that saved both our lives, his being mixed up with us in close quarters in a second, and the extra powerful Indian he was; quickness was his principal aid. We had our wits put to a severe test defending ourselves, and both of us were about out of breath, for once entirely surprised and pretty well rattled. He had seized me by the arm and would not let go at the beginning of the trouble, and even as he fell to the ground exhausted, had whirled and tossed until I felt as if my back was about broke. Then as it looked as if one or the other would have to die if he managed to stab us just right with his short saber, the chief sank down to the ground dead. We were so crazy mad at the time, did not think out the proper thing to do, so like a couple of fools that should have known better, scalped that Cheyenne chief, and the memory of it makes me feel ashamed to this day.

Several sources agree that this scalping occurred and that the victim was none other than High Backed Wolf. But who killed and mutilated him and under what circumstances? There turn out to be several other "claimants," and Johnny's account strikingly contradicts other versions.

Private William Henry Lord later claimed that he and his friend Jim Porter had "dispatched" the chief. In Lord's telling the soldiers killed the Indian, found him to be wearing a buckskin shirt "laced with the scalps of white women," and took his own scalp in revenge. The next morning they tied the trophy to a stick and waved it tauntingly at the warriors across the river.[10]

Corporal Charles Bates, in a letter written in 1924, gives a more sober account: "I removed the beaded shirt or jacket by slitting it up the front and rolling him out of it. I also took off his scalp and it was later buried in the orchard here at home." Bates is unsure of the man's tribe, and he does not mention any grisly decorations.[11] George Morton Walker, at the post and thus not an eyewitness, also named Bates while repeating the scalp-shirt story.

William Y. Drew, also at the post, tells it like this: "Two of the boys rode into the brush to find the chief, and found him lying apparently dead. One man jumped off his horse and stabbed him about the heart. He did not give the least sign of life. Then he commenced to scalp him. As soon as the knife touched his head the Indian commenced to beg, when another man shot him through the brain." Drew does not mention a scalp-ornamented shirt but adds that the soldiers had vowed revenge for the mutilation of one of an Eleventh Kansas man about ten days earlier.[12]

There are yet two more candidates for the killing. One is Mich Lajeunesse, son of Charles Lajeunesse, a trader at the post, and a Shoshone woman; Mich's sister Louisa Lajeunesse Boyd tells this story without mentioning the taking of the scalp.[13] Finally, Ferdinand Erhardt of Company K, Eleventh Kansas, assigns the action to one Henry C. Merwin, adding a sensational description of the Indian's adornments: "scalp locks with seventeen different kinds of white women's and children's hair." Erhardt places the event several days earlier and in a different location.[14]

There seems no way of determining the truth. But would Johnny have laid false claim to an incident that he, alone of all the tellers, seems to have found shameful?

Just then Sergeant Old Ike Pennock[15] came with ten more men, and ordered our mob back to the Post. Sergeant Pennock gave us a good dressing down

then and there. “Whatever you do from now on, boys,” he said, “do not ever scalp another Indian! Don’t you know a scalped Indian can never enter the Happy Hunting Ground? That everything is lost to him forever, that he has no recourse, he or his friends?”

We hurried back toward the Post, and had ridden about fifty yards, when the Indians came up to their dead and scalped chief. Then we could hear the real savage yell of a band of Indians maddened almost into blindness rage. To see and witness Indians in a rage like this can never be forgotten, and suggests the idea that man is still the most savage animal of the earth.[16]

At the Post, saw [that] Ganard and the two squaws had driven the cattle into safety, and were feeling good over it. Ganard wanted to see the scalp, said his mother-in-law would tan it, and work it into a fine specimen.

That evening I took the scalp to Ganard’s house. His mother-in-law looked the scalp over for quite a while, said it was a Cheyenne chief’s scalp, and that he was a member of the council, a big man of importance.

She then looked the scalp over a while longer. Then suddenly commenced to chew that scalp, all the while yelling and singing her inherited war song of hate. She jumped around like a colt and kept it up until she fell down on the earth floor of the cabin exhausted, but kept chewing that scalp in a barbarous manner. She was getting even, eking out the hate of her race on one scalp of the Cheyenne.

Mr. Ganard slapped himself and laughed. It was great fun for him, and his squaw kept singing their scalp song in almost regular measured time. Their song of triumph, and especially so, as both these squaws were Rees [Arikaras], who had always been at war with the Cheyenne, so gloried in the death of their enemies. To me this sort of thing was disgusting. Had enough of Indians for one day, so turned and walked away, out of tune with myself and all the wide world.

Here is another knot of mysteries. As previously discussed, Lord and Bates each claimed to have kept the scalp. Historian Todd Guenther has the shirt, not the scalp, as the object of this celebration and thinks that Lajeunesse’s sister Louisa was the celebrant. Mrs. Boyd herself is silent on the subject.[17] Also, Guinard’s nephew Louis P. Guinard would later testify in court proceedings that his uncle had disappeared on June 6, seven weeks before these events. In any case, both the elder Guinard’s relations and Lajeunesse’s sister were Shoshones, not Arikaras.[18]

At this point Johnny's thoughts turn to tensions among the men along the trail and to the celebrated figure of Caspar Collins.

One company at Ganard's Bridge were "fillers in," that is, enlisted men who were filling the places of those who had died of sickness, or in battle with the Indians. And some there were whom we called "galvanized infantry." They had been Confederate soldiers taken prisoners during the Civil War, and who had been in a prison in Chicago. They had been given the opportunity to enlist and fight Indians in Wyoming and Montana.[19]

But to a man they were our bitter enemies. There were fine fellows among them, considerate and sensible, while others were of the worst type, as is the case with all collections of men from over the country. It was understood at the time that the Southern Confederacy had given them permission to enlist to fight Indians in the North, though I have never had this point verified. There was a good full company of them first at Ganard's Bridge, but about half of them deserted.

Lieutenant Caspar Collins was their commander, a fine officer and a splendid man all around. Was informed at the time he was the youngest officer in the army.

Johnny is confused here. Caspar Collins, the son of Lieutenant Colonel William O. Collins, was not in charge of the "galvanized Yankees." In fact he arrived at the post only on the eve of the Platte Bridge battle and by sheer coincidence, pausing there on his way back to his own Eleventh Ohio Cavalry company at Sweetwater Station after a trip to Fort Laramie.[20]

This confusion, however, may mask another reality. The main tension among the troops along the Oregon Trail in Wyoming was not between volunteers and "galvanized" soldiers, it was between the Eleventh Kansas Cavalry and the Eleventh Ohio, who shared the work of protecting the trail and telegraph line. On July 12, for example, when a detachment of Ohio troops under Captain Henry Bretney arrived at Platte Bridge, he and Captain Greer of Johnny's Company I clashed bitterly about who was in charge.[21] By putting the Ohioan Collins in command of the "galvanized" soldiers, Johnny's memory may have conflated two different sets of men he had trouble with.

By the time of the July 26 battle, the command issue had been resolved: Major

Martin Anderson, Eleventh Kansas, had arrived to take charge of the wide district, with Greer as post commander under him.[22]

On the eve of the battle, the garrison at Platte Bridge included 74 officers and men of Company I, Eleventh Kansas; some 14 "galvanized infantry"; and a handful of stray men from other units. On the afternoon of the twenty-fifth, 10 men of Company K, Eleventh Kansas, arrived from the east with the mail—and Caspar Collins. In the small hours of the twenty-sixth, Captain Bretney arrived from the west with ten Ohioans. The total complement was then 119 men, though woefully undersupplied with arms, ammunition, and horses.[23]

On July 26—"a terrible day for our command" in Sergeant Pennock's words—the Indians got the action they wished for.[24] A column of twenty-some men—reported numbers differ slightly—issued from the fort, crossed the bridge, and rode straight into a carefully prepared trap. Johnny's chapter title is "Second Day."

The next morning there were about a dozen Indians riding up and down on the mesa across the river opposite our camp, coaxing and daring us out to fight them. They called us cowards and a few pet names they had learned from the white man. It seems we had orders not to fight the Indians unless they attacked us, so our men were content, remaining in camp. But Lieutenant Caspar Collins was impatient, he wanted to test his fighting ability with the Indians that day. His command was infantry [*sic*] and could not move quick enough to do much with the Indians on their fleet ponies. He came to our captain, Captain Greer, and asked for a detail of twenty men to go over the bridge and run those bragging Indians away. Ganard advised Lieutenant Collins and all other men not to go out and fight the Indians. He said by the Indian smokes this was a gathering of tribes.

Captain Greer told Lieutenant Collins he would have to get an order from Major Bowen [Anderson].[25] Then Lieutenant Caspar Collins went to see Major Bowen [Anderson], found that Major Bowen [Anderson] could not give an order of that kind under the existing orders from headquarters. But advised if Captain Greer would allow him, Collins, to call for volunteers and could get the men to volunteer he [Anderson] wouldn't say anything. Everything was agreeable after that, for Lieutenant Caspar Collins came and called for volunteers from the Eleventh Kansas. Twenty men and myself volunteered to go out with Lieutenant Collins at once.

It is here that Johnny's memories cut most strikingly across other accounts. He errs in giving Lieutenant Collins an infantry unit. He did not know, or had in the intervening years forgotten, that the sortie was mounted to bring in a military wagon train coming east from Sweetwater Station. He also stands alone in stating that the group consisted of volunteers. Confusion still surrounds the decision to place Collins in charge of Kansans unknown to him. Apparently the Eleventh Kansas officers to a man had found reasons to excuse themselves. But did Collins actually put himself forward, as Johnny says, or go dutifully and with a sense of doom, as elsewhere reported?[26] There are no witnesses to the key conversation between Anderson and Collins. Louisa Lajeunesse Boyd may reflect the general impression at the post in recalling that Collins volunteered. John D. McDermott suggests that Collins initially stepped forward on the assumption that he would be given a much more formidable party.[27] Johnny goes on to provide a poignant sidelight story.

Major Martin Anderson of Circleville, Kansas, took command of the Platte Bridge segment of the Oregon Trail on July 10, 1865. Controversy regarding his decisions on July 26 dogged him for years. He later served a term as Kansas state treasurer. *Kansas State Historical Society.*

Lieutenant Caspar Collins as he might have looked in 1865. A promising artist, Collins left behind many charming watercolors of the West, but his own face is preserved in only one childhood photo. This computer-generated age-progression image attempts to capture his probable appearance at age twenty. A painting by Ruth Joy Hopkins, sometimes said to be of Collins, actually is not a portrait of the young lieutenant. *Image courtesy of Michael W. Streed, SketchCop Solutions.*

Second Lieutenant George Morton Walker, Company C, Eleventh Kansas Cavalry, was an important witness to the events surrounding the Battle of Platte Bridge. Like John B. Hart, he was born in Pennsylvania, came to Kansas before the Civil War, and returned there afterward—to stay. A civil engineer who worked on railroad lines and stations, Walker died in 1918. *Kansas State Historical Society.*

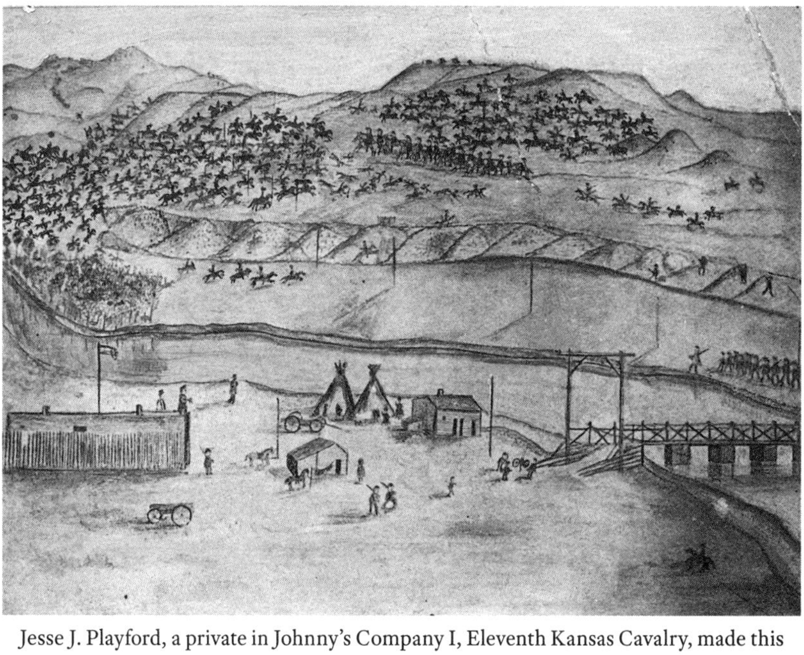

Jesse J. Playford, a private in Johnny's Company I, Eleventh Kansas Cavalry, made this watercolor of Platte Bridge Station. In the background the Collins column rides into the ambush of July 26, 1865. *Kansas State Historical Society.*

Soon we were ready, but Lieutenant Collins was determined to ride a very large grey horse that belonged to our company. He was a splendid horse but would whirl around in the ranks breaking the line. The rider could pull his bits against his neck, it made no difference. If the notion struck this horse at this time, away he would bolt where he pleased, providing he became the least excited. We warned the Lieutenant about the fault of this horse, but our efforts availed us nothing.[28]

I was in the first set of Fours. Across the bridge we marched and out on the mesa following that teasing bunch of Indians back about one half mile where we halted as wished to ascertain the whereabouts of the yelling that sounded overhead, to the sides and everywhere else. In a moment, saw we were in a trap, for two hundred warriors had rushed in behind us cutting our retreat back to the Post out of the question, and another band of Indians came out of the river bottom above the Post and so were between us and the bridge which spanned across the river.

Lieutenant Collins looked back behind us, saw both sides of the rear closing in, saw that mob of Indians coming and yelling their curdling war song. He caught his breath with a hurried whisp and exclaimed, "None of us will ever get back to the Post. We are lost! We are doomed! I am to blame for this, and I am the fool! Boys, let's fight a good fight, to the last!"[29]

Every last one of us thought the same as did the Lieutenant, and in a moment all became steeled to the summons of fate. I could see the lips of my comrades closing together tightly and the snapping of eyes suggesting a devout determination to fight out the odds to the last.

A few seconds after this the Indians closed in on us and fired, but mostly with arrows, and when an arrow missed a soldier it hit an Indian. The Indians were so numerous around us, nothing could hit the ground, arrows or bullets. And the terrific din of yelling, commotion, Indians afoot, others mounted, and last, the whirling of ponies and swirling of countless clouds of dust. These Indians were surging around us like an onrushing tide striking against a bluff and rebounding back in a wicked undercurrent across a rocky reef intent in its power of weight and force to snuff out all life. This surging mob of Indians were all stripped to the breechclout, their bodies and faces all painted in ugly grotesque shapes and colors, a hideous looking sight, and one that always rattles those not accustomed to it, be they ever so brave and steady.

It wasn't long until the Indians discovered they were killing more of their own members than of ours with arrows, so they quit and commenced to using spears.[30]

The Lieutenant's large gray mount bolted almost at the first and the last I saw of him was the big gray going over those Indian ponies as if they were so many feeble sheep.

We bunched our men and started for the bridge determined to make the attempt at all hazards. I did not notice what way or route we selected as expected to soon be among the dead, because we were outnumbered by at least twenty-five to one.

Soon discovered that to level my revolver on an Indian was about as good as to shoot him, for he would throw himself on the ground or on the side of his pony and dodge out of sight, and to get him I would have to be quick. This method gave me an opportunity to be ready for another Indian, and saved my ammunition, and at the same time believe [this] is what saved me from being scalped by the Indians that day.

These Indians seemed to drive terror among some of our men so that they lost control of themselves, and did not fight the good fight to the last, very good. I know that George McDonald yelled for me to help him, that he was lanced twice, and fell off his horse, and at that, with a loaded revolver in his scabbard. And McDonald was as brave a man as ever wore a uniform, but he lost control. And Jim Porter [met] the same fate as McDonald, good boy that he was. Both of these boys, many's the time, had stood right up to the Johnnies without flinching, and could be moved under the hottest kind of fire anywhere.[31]

Our little band was thinning out fast and the Indians were pushing us harder every second, and in a flash we were thirsty, tired and weary, fighting out a hundred years of life in a few minutes.

All at once Tip Hill yelled out, "Oh, somebody help me!"[32] On looking saw that one determined Indian had seized hold of his bridle rein and was pulling his horse out of our bunch. Tip Hill was knocking off spears with his revolver, every which way, making a heroic effort of his life as I dashed up to him. And just at this instant a Cheyenne charged in between Tip Hill and our little band and made a thrust at Tip Hill with a spear, but missed. Then seeing he had missed, whirled his spear down in front and was going to thrust Tip Hill as he rode by him. This Cheyenne was about six feet ahead of me, I must [do] something for Tip Hill then and there, so leveled my revolver on his [the Indian's] hands and shoulder so as to be sure not to make a miss and fired. Instantly that Indian threw up both hands and up went his spear about fifteen feet farther in the air; I rode under it a second before it fell down just missing my horse in the rear. That Cheyenne fell back on his pony, his mouth was open wide enough for me to crowd my doubled-up fist down his throat. Such a mouth and such a throat, an animal indeed. Tip Hill managed to get rid of the Indian holding and tugging at the bridle rein of his horse and managed once more [to] regain the thin safety of our little band of men.

All at once I gave a yell as was riding off the mesa and into the bottom some two hundred yards from the bridge, for there were the boys at the Post coming out to help us. In a few seconds after this, I knew I was safe.

Six of our little band arrived at the Post and fifteen were killed out of this twenty-one that volunteered to go out and fight Indians under Lieutenant Caspar Collins that day. Tip Hill had three arrows clinging to him, Harley Stoddard three arrows, the Captain's yellow boy two arrows and a bullet, George May three arrows, a fellow we called Strap badly wounded and I without a scratch, excepting a bruise or two.[33] Most of the boys were killed with spears. I was the only one that came out with a whole hide although was hit with a spear and a bow. I felt fine riding across Ganard's twenty-six-span bridge and couldn't see how it all happened when by rights should have been among the dead. It was a fairylike feeling that day to be alive.

On arriving in camp I, with others, was detailed to go down the river about a mile and repair the telegraph wire, as the Indians had pulled it down. Out of this party we lost five men. Others were detailed to recover at least some of our dead comrades across the river, so that all in all we lost 26 men that day.[34]

If the Indians had known the precarious state of the garrison, desperately short of ammunition, they might have carried through their plan to storm it. Instead, they turned their attention to the party Collins had been sent out to relieve: a supply train coming east under the command of Sergeant Amos J. Custard. In the resulting Battle of Red Buttes, visible from the fort, twenty-two Eleventh Kansas soldiers died.[35] Johnny says nothing about this fight; perhaps the telegraph-line expedition kept him away until the deadlier battle was over. In memory he seems to have redistributed the death toll, assigning the Red Buttes losses to the two other engagements. Only five men were killed under Collins and one more down the river near the telegraph lines. But Johnny is actually a touch conservative about the day's total government casualties: twenty-eight soldiers were lost.

Though the men feared an even worse sequel, the day's actions in fact marked the end of the tribes' attempt to sever the Oregon Trail.

The Indians scalped and terribly mutilated eighteen of our boys. We had an old German soldier in our company who was killed when out as a volunteer. He was quite gray, a man of splendid nerve and respected by all. The Indians did not scalp or mutilate his body, but they did fill his body with arrows. I pulled ninety-three arrows out of his body two days afterward when we hauled him into the Post. Lieutenant Caspar Collins was mutilated worse than any of the men, about one half of his body was carried away, his heart was cut into strings and hung on a medicine pole beside what was left of his body.

We threw shells on the mesa with an old howitzer, the shells wouldn't explode, but they would roll a long way on the mesa. The Indians would run after these shells and when they stopped rolling would stand around them and jabber and make signs.[36] Finally we shot one shell that rolled over the mesa and as usual a bunch of Indians ran after it, and after it became still for probably three minutes it exploded killing three Indians. The Indians ran away from it in all directions just like water does when you throw a rock into a pond and the waves go in every direction. After that the Indians chased no more shells, and would not go near them for some time later.

Who was the "old German soldier"? The obvious candidate is one Sebastian Nehring. The problem with this identification is that, according to other accounts, Nehring's body was spectacularly mutilated.[37] Johnny's version is plausible since Indians were known to leave bodies intact in recognition of particular bravery.

One hundred and fifty years after the events, the circumstances surrounding the death of Caspar Collins remain controversial. Was the young officer a headstrong boy or a man soberly obeying a fateful order? Generally speaking, witnesses from his own Eleventh Ohio Volunteer Cavalry tend to glorify Collins, blaming Anderson for his death; voices from the Eleventh Kansas take a more critical view of the lieutenant. Johnny was a Kansan and surely no neutral observer, though he seems rather to have admired Collins.[38]

And what about that horse? How did Collins get it and how did it behave? George Morton Walker reported that he gave the lieutenant "what was considered the best one of those used by the noncommissioned staff."[39] The story of its bolting is repeated by witnesses George Bent and Ferdinand Erhardt. Drew reported seeing the Indians dragging the fractious animal along the bluffs after the battle. George Grinnell added that the horse lived on for many years in a Cheyenne village, still giving trouble. Two observers from the post, Stephen H. Fairfield and John C. Friend, told a more flattering story: Collins, still in control of his horse, had almost reached the bridge when he turned back to help a wounded comrade.[40]

In 1867 the post at Platte Bridge was abandoned. "Burned by the Sioux," the story goes, but this operatic conclusion is apparently an invention.[41] The usable materials were actually cannibalized to build Fort Fetterman, somewhat to the east at the point where the Bozeman Trail diverged from the Oregon Trail. Many of the participants in the Platte Bridge battle, too, reappear on the Bozeman, including John Benton Hart.

3

THE WELLS FARGO MULE TRAIN

Johnny next shows up in North Platte, Nebraska, in the spring of 1867. By this time he is a civilian and in the company of his twin brother, Hugh, whom he regards as more intelligent but physically weaker and in need of protection. They are looking to make their fortune out west in the new gold-boom area around Helena, Montana. To get there, they sign on with a wagon train carrying freight to Fort C. F. Smith, an army post along the embattled Bozeman Trail.

In the summer of 1867, North Platte was taking its brief turn as the jumping-off point for the Far West. The Union Pacific Railroad, extended from Nebraska City that spring, had just brought the town into existence. Within the next few months, the line would push west to Laramie, Wyoming. Exactly when Johnny and Hugh arrived is unclear, but they may have come in on one of the very first steam trains and left with one of the very last animal-hauled wagon trains to follow the Platte River westward.[1]

Near modern Douglas, Wyoming, their route would leave the Oregon Trail and turn north on the Bozeman Trail, a new strand in the expanding web of emigrant pathways traversing Indian country and the latest flashpoint of Indian warfare.

There is a puzzle about brother Hugh. This was not the first time he had been Johnny's companion. Hugh, too, had enlisted in the Eleventh Kansas Cavalry; Hugh, too, had gone to Platte Bridge Station. Hugh's name (but not Johnny's) is found on Independence Rock on the Sweetwater River. Why does Hugh go unmentioned in all the earlier episodes of the reminiscences?

But now, together, they walked into the offices of the Wells Fargo Company in North Platte.

We went down to the Wells Fargo office and there made our wants known. A lean skinny fellow who looked as if he hadn't eaten a square meal for a year answered us. We talked for a few minutes and began to think this man would turn us down, for he said, "You fellows are only boys. It takes a man with oxen experience to handle oxen out in this wilderness of a country. Hanged if I think you all could make a decent fight with a crippled Indian, nohow."

At this moment a man came into the office.

"Any men? What luck?" he called out.

"Well, Mr. Brown, perhaps," the agent answered. "These two boys want a job bull whacking. Can you use them?"

Mr. Brown turned and looked us over, then asked.

"Boys, where are you from? Ever whack bulls?"

Both questions were poked at us as if shot from a gun.

Hugh took his time and finally answered him.

"Yes, sir, we can whack bulls, try us. We are from Kansas, and we can whack anything from a snow bird to an elephant."

"All right, boys, you're hired. Sign the contract here. Be on hand at daylight at the end of the Union Pacific Railroad yards. Find our camp out of town about two miles northwest. Put your feet under the table and eat your fill and try to be at home!"

Then Mr. Brown shot out the door of the office before we hardly knew he was gone. He was a real live man from the feet up, rather light complected, medium height.

We had a squabble with the agent over the way we wanted our contract to read; but had our way in the matter of leaving the train at Fort Smith.

Mr. Brown had put Hugh and me on our own in the matter of finding his camp, but we settled both of these matters, as we found a man and wagon going out to that very camp. The driver was kind enough to haul out our two rolls of bedding. At the camp there was plenty of tents for everybody, a big mess tent, a cook tent, sleeping quarters and plenty of everything of its kind, but nothing comfortable or convenient. There were forty-five large wagons and their trail wagons loaded at camp, also thirty wagons and trail wagons still to be loaded.[2]

On the first evening out, Johnny describes the daily routine of "corralling," or forming the wagons into a protective circle, and observes a certain lack of organization in the train.

I was aroused from my musing by the assistant foreman riding by. It then lacked but little before sundown. The assistant foreman rode on ahead of the train to locate a suitable place to corral where there had to be grass and water. Soon he stood in the middle of the road motioning to the crack bullwhacker to pull out and corral.

The train was divided in two equal halves, the right wing and the left wing. . . . The crack bullwhacker of the right wing having the lightest load of any man in the train and the best walking oxen pulled out of the road on the gee side, or right side, to the right. He drove in a half moon out, and lengthwise with the road, stopping when he came back to the road, but leaving his wagon a few feet beside the road at an angle and swinging the tongue out of the road, so as not to obstruct the road for passers-by. All the right wing followed in his track, each wagon stopping just as his near fore wheel came about two feet past the off hind wheel of the wagon before him, leaving a two feet space to go through, each man carrying his yokes and chains after unyoking so as to have them handy for yoking up in the morning, or when needed and for safe keeping.

The crack bullwhacker of the left wing pulled out on the left side, the off side, and made the other side of the oval, after which it is called a corral. This brought both lead wagons of each wing facing each other leaving a gap about twenty-five feet wide at both ends of wagon corral. This corral was a fort for the whole freight train. And this formation brought the near mess wagons, which were trailers, near each other at the rear end of [the] train. There was a right wing mess and a left wing mess. Their fires for cooking meals were built on each side of the road and outside of the corral.

After we had corralled and turned our oxen over to the night wranglers, there was a scramble to build fires over which to cook our evening meals. Some of the men did all they could, while others did nothing, being those who had not the power to force themselves and did not care. Our first evening corral did not prove a success as there was no police detail made by Mr. Brown to see that certain men did certain things. After a fashion all hands received a little food. It smacked of there being men who would have to work noon and night doing chores while others would idle around.

In the first of many special arrangements they negotiated, Hugh and John got permission from Mr. Brown to do their own cooking. As they continued to show their competence, they began to function as informal assistants to Brown. Among other things, Johnny became a night watchman to discourage pilfering and catch any miscreants. Later on, feeling that the party was not taking the threat of attack seriously, Brown had the brothers stage a false alarm, which caused a panic and disrupted the train for hours.

That evening true to agreement Mr. Brown said, "Johnny, I saw moccasin tracks this evening in a little draw beside the road, they were fresh, you'd better be wide awake tonight." "All right, I will watch carefully every minute, Mr. Brown."

There were two men at our campfire that evening; one of the men hurried down the corral to tell the news to his pals, which was the very thing we wanted. When I made my round of the train later, about all the men had something to say. Some wanted to take three to five scalps if they could get that many shots. . . .

Just at this moment three wagons of Oregon emigrants that had been turned back at Fort Laramie because they were not sufficiently supplied, or had disagreed in some manner, drove through our corral, afterwards camping on our right wing outside of the corral. They were angry with the government for turning them back. When they heard the latest Indian news they became quite scared. But soon, so far as I could make out, all were asleep in spite of the Indian scare.

After twelve o'clock at night I fired three shots with my Spencer carbine and yelled "Indians!" Mr. Brown and Hugh came out and fired several more shots with me. Then the three of us ran back to the middle of the corral yelling "Indians!" Mr. Brown yelled, "Fall in! Fall in!"

There was pandemonium in the middle of that corral instead of fall[ing] in. Bullwhackers, emigrants, women and children, all yelling at the top of their voices. No one could do anything or be heard. Two bullwhackers ran down the road like stampeded horses and as they passed the emigrants, the emigrants, mistaking them for Indians, fired at them, but missed clean. This increased the fear of bullwhackers and emigrants alike.

After this, the two bullwhackers increased their speed, running like the wind until they crossed the creek about fifty yards behind the corral, then turned up the creek. By this time having got their second wind they continued running for two miles further, when they found their feet were full of sticks and sagebrush. Then they discovered for the first time they had nothing on but their underclothes.

The night wranglers, hearing the firing, skinned out, striking the creek above the two bull wranglers, leaving the oxen to shift for themselves. In the meantime Mr. Brown detailed two men to stretch chains across both ends of the corral, but these men were so scared of the Indians Mr. Brown had to go with them. While these chains were being stretched across both ends of the corral, one man accidentally fired his rifle, which increased the excitement. It was unsafe within one quarter mile of that corral. . . .

The confusion increased as two emigrant women got into a physical fight, attacking each other and Mr. Brown. The brothers found themselves hysterical with laughter. Only toward dawn did order begin to be restored.

Mr. Brown and I went hunting for the two night wranglers and the two runaway bullwhackers. We rode up the creek yelling every few minutes. About full daylight we saw two riders going into the brush above us. Soon we came up to them and the two bullwhackers that had bolted. We told them the Indians were driven off, and for the bullwhackers to climb on behind the night wranglers' mounts, as they could not walk owing to the condition of their feet, and ride into the camp.

Here Hugh and I bubbled over and once more started to laughing again. Mr. Brown said, "If you boys don't quit laughing I'll take you over behind yonder hill and make you wish you'd never been born." So we quit it.

The two bullwhackers that bolted told the night wranglers that all had been killed at the corral, that the front of the corral was full of Indians, and that they had begun to come into the rear end as they passed out. That the Indians had fired on them, but they knocked some of the Indians right and left making an opening through them while running for the brush. . . .

When we came back to camp and yoked up, the right wing had pulled out and was going up the road, and the left wing was half strung out. I was loitering close to the tail end of the train wondering what the emigrants intended doing, when Mr. Brown rode by one of those old scrapping women.

She yelled at him, "Are you going to leave us here to fight the whole Sioux nation alone?"

"Yes," Mr. Brown answered. "I have to keep moving every day. You and your outfit can follow my train if you are afraid."

And she yelled back, "I won't go a foot! You stop that train right here and corral!"

"I tell you, lady, you and that other fighting woman can whip the whole Sioux nation."

"Yes," she said, "you will think I can, if you don't corral right away!"

I was afraid there would be another fracas with these fighting women, so yelled, "Mr. Brown! Come here a moment!"

He excused himself to the old woman, promising to come right back.

He followed me behind a wagon. I pointed up the road and said "Go ahead! And stay ahead of everything until noon. Go now!"

Near the modern Nebraska-Wyoming border, some of the men experienced the deceptiveness of western distances.

The next day we were near Chimney Rock in Nebraska. We had all the way followed the north side of the North Platte since leaving Mud Springs in Nebraska. We corralled about nine o'clock. The country around about stretched away in the distance quite level, and the distances seemed to be nearer than they really were to the eye. The air clear, the sun shining bright, a lovely day: hot in the sun, cold in the shade.

About ten of our men decided to walk to Chimney Rock, for it looked to be so close to them. They asked Hugh and I to accompany them. We refused, telling them Chimney Rock was at least seven miles away, we did not care for such a journey as that, especially after walking all morning. Had once upon a time been fooled by the distance ourselves in clear air.

That was no excuse for these men, they started walking toward the rock. After a mile some of them turned back, then more of them turned back further on, finally only two of them kept on, looking in the distance like two matches sticking up on the plain. In a few minutes these two gave up the journey, turning back and walking toward the train. They had probably walked out as far as two or three miles.

When all returned to the train, they said the eye had lied about the distance to them, since they had walked at least five miles, and Chimney Rock seemed as far away as ever.

The train left the Platte River Road (Oregon Trail), and the lifeline provided by the nearby river, to head northwest on the Bozeman Trail. For the next few days, the party traversed a region with few and feeble streams.

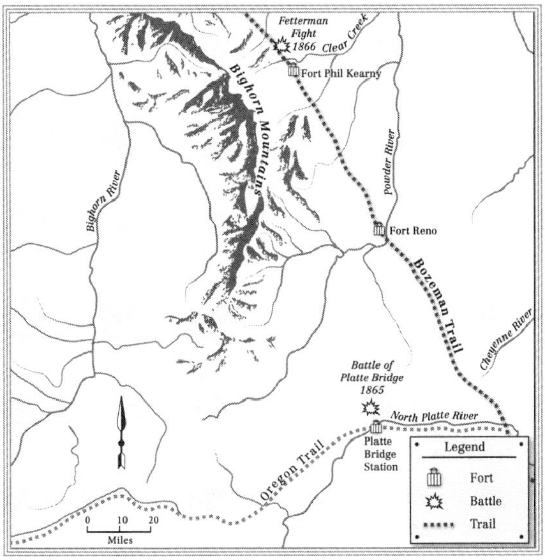

The Bozeman Trail from the North Platte River to Fort Phil Kearny, 1867.
Map by Gerry Krieg, based largely on Dee Brown, Fort Phil Kearny (Lincoln: University of Nebraska Press, 1962).

After considerable trouble, we finally arrived at the Dry Fork of the Cheyenne. There was no water in the bed of the creek, the creek had a dry smooth sandy bottom forty or fifty feet wide in places. It looked like a dry camp for the night. Everybody was disappointed, some of the men complaining and voicing their luck in swearing terms.

Mr. Brown came up. "Wait," he said, "let's see what my blessed book says about this place called the Dry Fork of the Cheyenne." After turning over a few pages and reading a bit, "Here it is! It says here, *Drive the oxen on sand in creek bottom and water will rise.*"

We followed instructions and in a few minutes heard some of the oxen were drinking and sucking in the middle of the creek bottom. A few minutes afterwards water began to rise around the oxen's feet. All of our men were in better humor directly afterwards, as that was far ahead of a dry camp.

The wagon foreman asked, "How did Mr. Brown know water would rise in the sand of this creek?"

"Oh," a little dried-up fellow from Texas answered, "Mr. Brown knows about everything there is to know, he can smell water when there is no water. If you, Mr. Wagon Boss, knew the sixteenth part of what Mr. Brown has forgotten, you would be a big man and awful wide out."

"Shut up, you rat-tailed, dried-up skeleton of a half-dead human! What do you know?"

"That may be true what you say, Mr. Boss, but when I find a place where I can be schooled, I will be able to smell water a half mile deep into the earth."

Late in the trip, Johnny improvised a solution to a problem that increasingly plagues the train—the loosening of the metal tires from the wooden rims, or "fellows."

Our wagon train finally arrived on the east side of Powder River about three miles south of Fort Reno. The ford across Powder River was directly opposite the fort, which was situated on the west side of the river. We had to corral some distance out on account of the fort reserve.

Our corral was made in good daylight before sundown. The wagon tires were in very bad condition. Driving over so much dry warm sand and dust of the road had gradually shrunk the fellows; a shower now and then did not do much to swell the wood. Driving in wedges between the tires and fellows had ceased to be of any help. Something definite had to be planned; it was impossible to go on. The tires must be set, or our train would be forced to camp at Fort Reno the rest of the summer.

The next morning Mr. Brown and I saddled up two mules and rode northward to the ford opposite Fort Reno and forded Powder River to the west side to the fort. We found a citizen [civilian] blacksmith there and tried to strike a bargain with him to re-set the wagon tires.

"How many tires have you to set, Mr. Brown?" the blacksmith asked.

"There are 150 wagons and I think all of the tires may have to be re-set and if so that would make 600 tires.[3] It will be a considerable of a job to set this many tires, but as soon as the work is completed, the money for your labor is ready, in fact I will offer you extra money if you will commence right away," Mr. Brown told him.

"Mr. Brown, it will require eight or ten days to set your tires. I have no help. Have you no blacksmith with your train?"

"No, I have not."

"Then I cannot do this work for you, I haven't the time. I positively refuse to do this work or have anything to do with your tires," the blacksmith replied.

"Well, that lands me against something pretty solid, sir."

"It cannot be helped, Mr. Brown."

"Suppose I see the quartermaster at the fort, and he talks different. What then, Mr. Blacksmith?"

"I would still refuse to undertake the work, I am half sick and no help."

Mr. Brown and I then went to see the quartermaster. He did not think the blacksmith would do the work without help.

We were thoroughly disgusted, started toward our camp. Mr. Brown concluded not to crowd the blacksmith, but to try the man once more next day. . . . Mr. Brown seemed to be falling gradually out of sight in his blues. He did not wish to have to report to Wells Fargo Company that he had failed.

We were riding slowly along, neither of us saying a word because there is nothing to talk about when you are whipped. Mr. Brown's head was slightly tilted forward, his eyes half closed. We were whipped for the present.

We were passing a moment later a rubbish pile composed of hundreds of things discarded by the fort. Among these worn out things I noticed a hundred or more heavy gunnysacks which the government uses as an outside covering to protect flour and other like goods easily damaged by long freight hauls.

I instantly realized these heavy gunnysacks would be the material to set the tires in a pinch, for I had helped do the very thing at North Platte Bridge when in the army previous to this fighting Indians. And those tires were tight and sound on the long road back to Fort Leavenworth, Kansas, where we were discharged.

"Here, Mr. Brown, it's here! I have the solution to your predicament, and mine to a certain extent. Stop!. . . . We corral here!" I called out.

"What's the matter with you, Johnny? Have you gone plumb to the dogs?" Mr. Brown turned around and looked at me, thoroughly disgusted.

Johnny explained his idea.

"We will make a double X, one for the front wheel and one for the rear wheel, that is, the likeness of a wheel, out of cottonwood logs hewn smooth. Just the right size to rest the wheels on, firm and level. In the center of this double X will be an opening large enough to let the hub pass half through into a hole dug into the ground underneath. The double X is firmly bedded to the ground. Then dig a long trench and fill with water to cool hot tires.

"We take the wheels from the wagons, being careful to number them the same number as the tires to prevent their becoming mixed. Lay all the wheels on this double X with the inside of the wheels up, this is important.

"Then we rip or cut these gunnysacks into strips about three inches wide and lay on the outside of the fellows. Tie these strips snugly with string unraveled from the gunnysacks. In the meantime, place about five tires in the fire to heat hot, evenly all around so as to force them to expand. Then wet these strips on the fellows and quickly place a hot tire over the fellows and gunnysacks pouring water on them all the time.

"Immediately run a pole through the hub and carry the wheel to a trench filled with water. Turn the wheel rapidly so as to cool the tire quickly to prevent tire from burning gunnysacks underneath. The tire will shrink enough if there is sufficient strips, not too many, or too few, to become perfectly solid.

"The tire will ring like a new one, will stand up for some time to come, also, the gunnysacks will not wear away underneath the tires as long as the tire remains tight."

"Good, Johnny! Lucky for me," Mr. Brown said. "I know that water will shrink metals when hot. If your theory doesn't work, you receive a thrashing from me. . . . Whom can we get to help us?"

"There is an old Scotchman with our train who can handle an ax well, a sort of carpenter. He can make the double X for us." . . .

Early next morning we commenced our tire setting with a vim. The dried-up Texan was to attend to the heating of the tires, for we discovered that he was somewhat of a blacksmith a little before starting to work in the morning. The Scotchman helped us in the laying of the strips around the face of the fellows. You see we had to have string wrapped around the fellows and strips about an inch and a half apart so as to hold the strips from moving out of place. The old Scotchman said, "Aye, laddie, there is a warp and a woof, we will take the warp and then we will have strings from these gunnysacks." Other men braced up the wagons underneath, so the wheels could be taken off and brought to us. This saved unloading the wagons.

We found from the first our Scotchman had good judgment. On the first wheel I thought of laying three strips on the fellows, but [I] said, if it should be too much it would split the fellows when the tire contracted.

"Aye, Johnny," our Scotchman exclaimed, "I know what you be wantin'. Just the right number of strops and no more. I was thinkin', I would be wantin' to attend to that! Hugh and me be the ones. Good it shall be and nary a miss, Johnny. And who is the father of this peculiar way of setting tires, tell me that?"

"Mr. Brown, of course," I answered. "He don't say much, but he knows something worthwhile." . . .

After we had our fellow on the first wheel in shape we poured water on the strips of gunnysacks, as a precaution against burning them, and placed a hot tire over them, which was quickly hammered into place, but not too tight. Afterward we carried it to our trench of water where it was whirled rapidly until cool.

Our Scotchman seized the wheel, carefully examined it, and tapped it with a hammer a few times. As he tapped a good ring came from the wheel, proving it was tight and able to hold its dish. Then his face became a bouquet of smiles, he became excited and acted like a young colt, he was so well pleased. "It's a success!" he hollered. "Mind you, it's a success! A grand success!"

As they approached the Bighorn Mountains, the travelers entered a well-watered country full of game. At the crossing of Crazy Woman Creek, a site of several prior ambushes by hostile Indians, Johnny made an unexpected find.

One evening a little before sundown we arrived at Crazy Woman Creek, a branch of Powder River, a stream about fifty or sixty feet wide, its water clear, averaging two to four feet deep and having a good gravel bottom.

The orders were to cross, so we did. Hugh's oxen began to drift downstream, soon coming to an island in midstream, which was about forty feet long and twenty feet wide. I let the oxen drift until I could easily get on the island without becoming much wet with the water. I jumped to the island as near as I could make it on the first effort; that put me on the off and leader side, so could nicely poke the oxen upstream, which I did.

While hurrying after the oxen I stubbed my foot against something, stopped, and pulled at a piece of leather protruding from the sand. Up it came, fastened to a sort of wicker covering or basket, the bottom of which had decayed. Discovered this to be a wicker cover over what seemed to be a demijohn. Quickly I made another effort, seizing the thong by the neck, pulling it out of the sand, and to my surprise was rewarded by finding a large demijohn filled with something. I turned the demijohn upside down in the weathered wicker cover and made for the oxen once more, but I had to wade below the oxen and make them keep on upstream until we were on the opposite side of the stream, where we corralled for the night.

After corralling, and when the first opportunity came, examined the contents of my new find, discovering to my surprise the demijohn contained excellent brandy, No. 1 fine.

At once Hugh and I realized we needed something like that for a bracer, but before this we were quite content without it. In the morning for breakfast we gave Mr. Brown a wee drink of brandy, No. 1 fine. He was surprised and quite well pleased. He looked us over rather carefully, first one then the other, puzzled; we had him fast.

"What next will you boys get hold of?" he asked. "Is it so ordered that all you upstarts have to do, is to touch a bottle out in midair somewhere and presto, what is wanted promptly comes to you?"

"No, Mr. Brown, I found this demijohn on an island in the middle of Crazy Woman Creek last evening while punching Hugh's oxen away from the island. Hugh and I sampled this brandy last evening and again this morning, so you need have no fear other than it is genuine."

"This is a nice story you are telling me, Johnny, but the worst possible feature of it is, you expect me to believe it."

"We do expect you to believe it!"

"Well how on earth? Oh, yes, probably that being the case someone last year must have had an accident on your fairy island, or set it down and forgot all about it. The parties must have been emigrants journeying toward Oregon. The weathered wicker shows it must have been in sand for at least a year, the high water in the spring covering it with sand."

"Your explanation is quite plausible, Mr. Brown, but you forgot to mention the element of luck therein contained," Hugh suggested.

"You, Johnny, must have been born lucky. The idea of finding this sort of thing in the middle of a space 60 miles square!"

Though Johnny does not mention it on this first telling, he refers later to an additional find at the creek: a packet containing a considerable amount of gold. Since Crazy Woman Creek was the site of several Indian attacks, finding lost property there was perhaps less freakish than it might appear. Warmed by the brandy, Mr. Brown was moved to repeat one of the several stories about the naming of Crazy Woman Creek.[4]

"The year before this, last summer sometime it must have been, an emigrant train camped on the bank of this very creek, now called Crazy Woman Creek. A lady belonging to the train strolled away from the train at night (it is supposed she did) and walked a few rods from camp. Instead of coming back to camp she must have gone in the opposite direction. In the meantime the embers of the campfire had died out, making no glow, and the night was almost pitch dark. It was not discovered she was missing for about an hour when she failed to return.

"The whole train crew was aroused to find her, a minute gun was fired all night. Searching parties went out into the inky dark night to find her. In every direction they went. It required their utmost efforts through the whole night and until ten o'clock the next day to find her.

"When found she was bleeding and sore, her clothes mere shreds, her mind gone, she knew nothing. She could not recognize her dear ones and never recovered. Hence, the name Crazy Woman Creek, Powder River. . . .

"Too bad, Johnny, you were not around here then, because you would immediately have found that dear lady. And her mind would have been as bright as a new silver dollar. You should have been here. I blame you for that!"

Several days later the train reached Fort Phil Kearny at the base of the Bighorn Mountains, the most notorious and beleaguered of the Bozeman Trail forts and headquarters of the newly defined Mountain District, Department of the Platte.

Mr. Brown went up to the fort the first thing to see the Wells Fargo Company agent there and remained for some time. Hugh and I later noticed Mr. Brown and the Wells Fargo agent examining the wagon tires and the train in general. After a while Mr. Brown brought the Wells Fargo agent to where Hugh and I were lounging around. He introduced the agent to us and then both of them went back to the fort.

The next morning Mr. Brown said the Wells Fargo agent would like for me to go to his office with him. Couldn't imagine what that agent could possibly want with me. Mr. Brown rode his mule and I rode the guard mule to the fort, for here, as well as the other forts, no one was allowed to pasture stock on the fort's reserve.

On arrival at the Wells Fargo office I was quite agreeably surprised at the warm greeting with which the agent made me welcome. It seemed like stepping into a man's paradise, especially after being used to so much rough talk and coarse ways much of the time every day with the train.

"Mr. Brown tells me, lad, you are quite capable," the agent said. "Mr. Brown has told me you are responsible for the setting of the tires on the wagons. It is a good job well done. I find these tires are tight on the fellows, sound and firm, even if gunnysacks were used. You saved the Company quite a blacksmith bill, and lifted Mr. Brown from an ugly predicament. Mr. Brown admits that, and gives you all the credit. You know your business. Your vigilance as train guard is of the very best. You have the ability to find out what is in a man, to repair breakdowns, to drive a shrewd bargain in managing men for the welfare of the company. Mr. Brown recommends you very highly.

"Wells Fargo Company want men like you. They scour the country continually for able men. You can care for this train during the winter and handle it as long as you wish afterwards as captain of the train. I would like for you to cancel your contract reading 'as far as Fort C. F. Smith' and sign a new one lasting for some time to come. I will not take No for an answer. Your brother can be with you all the time and be in the employ of the Company. His record also is excellent."

"Mr. Agent," I said, "thank you for considering us, but Hugh and I started for the mines. We have the gold fever. This offer breaks into our plans, and I think I will refuse your offer. At any rate I will have to talk this matter over with my brother before answering you definitely."

"Mr. Hart, you will not make much on the gold trail," he urged. "It is more apt to be fool's gold. Better figure wisely on my offer. It will be in the end by far a better trail of gold. And Mr. Brown tells me you are an adept finder of just the thing needed, even a demijohn filled with No. 1 brandy and a wallet of gold. The best third find for you will be, to cast your lot with the Wells Fargo."

"I will let you know this evening what I will do," I answered.

Then Mr. Brown and I started back to the camp. On our way going from the fort I noticed a large rock in front of Fort Phil Kearny, and soldiers on the top of that rock looking very much as if they were on duty. I asked Mr. Brown about the rock and the soldiers.[5]

"That is the lookout for the fort," he answered, "and a splendid one it is, for it enables the soldiers up there to see in all directions. There are three or four soldiers on duty on this rock the whole twenty-four hours and they are relieved each day at ten o'clock. If Indians are seen in any direction nearby, a flag is hoisted according to a code, so that the inmates of the fort can understand. It serves as a splendid alarm, not a false alarm." . . .

Hugh and I talked the matter over at camp. We could not quite come to a decision. We whittled two sticks, a long one and a short one. The long one meant I was to accept the agent's offer, the short one, that we continued our journey to the mines at Helena, Montana. Hugh held the sticks and I did the drawing. I drew the short one, so that settled the Wells Fargo business. We were to leave the train at Fort C. F. Smith, as our contract read. Immediately I rode a mule to the fort and told the agent I would not accept his offer.

On July 18 the train finally rolled into Fort C. F. Smith. With it, not yet known to Johnny, was a new commanding officer for the post, Lieutenant Colonel Luther P. Bradley, who had joined the group at Fort Phil Kearny.[6] Another cargo was more important to the brothers' future: a stock of Allin-modified Springfield breech-loading rifles, old guns retooled to be loaded through the breach rather than down the muzzle, thus allowing much more rapid firing.[7]

Our train arrived at Fort C. F. Smith in fairly good condition. Some of the oxen were about all in on the long slow trail. The wagon tires were still tight on the fellows, and sound as the day they were set at Fort Reno.

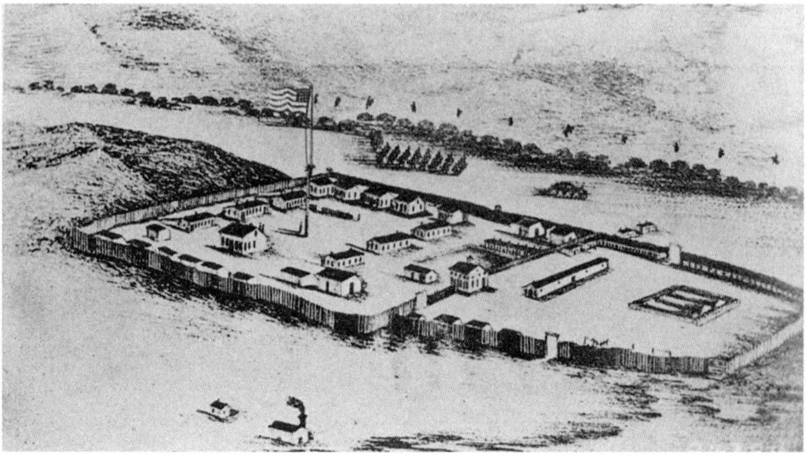

Fort Phil Kearny, Dakota Territory, 1867. Not to be confused with Fort Kearney, Nebraska, it was the headquarters of the Mountain District, a particular object of Sioux hatred, and Johnny's frequent destination as mail carrier. Reproduced from a drawing by Anton Schonbrun. *Still Photo Division, National Archives and Records Administration.*

Fort C. F. Smith, Montana Territory, 1867. This northernmost and most isolated of the Bozeman Trail forts was home to Johnny and Hugh for a year. From a sketch by Captain Isaac D'Isay, after a drawing by Anton Schonbrun. *National Archives and Records Administration.*

Everybody that could turned out to welcome us. It seemed to be something out of the usual order of things, but the train represented food and other useful things for the long winter months soon to be coming. We were two or three days unloading, weighing and attending to other necessary things before Hugh and I were released from our contract with the Wells Fargo Company. . . .

After the oxen were well rested for a few days, the train pulled into the road on back toward North Platte. Hugh and I bid Mr. Brown good-bye. . . .

As the train pulled down the road, Hugh and I stood looking for a long time. We had half a notion to follow. We missed Mr. Brown more than anything else. He was always polite, treated us square, was a good entertainer. We wanted him when he was vanishing from us. We did not realize his real value until he was gone.

Though this scene makes a nice narrative closure, it probably did not happen just this way. Wells Fargo Wagon Train No. 4 headed back southward at 3:30 A.M. on August 1, 1867, at which time the two Harts were several miles away from the fort—at a hay-cutting camp about to face a major Indian attack.[8]

4

FORT C. F. SMITH

In 1862 and 1863, gold discoveries in what is now southwestern Montana made this remote corner of the West the latest magnet for emigration from the East. In 1864 a guide named John Bozeman led a party of two thousand Americans along a newly identified route branching northwest from the Oregon Trail. We have already followed John Benton Hart along much of this "road to Montana": north through the barren headwater country of the Cheyenne River to the rich Powder River Basin, alongside the alpine Bighorn Mountains, and on to Fort C. F. Smith at the northern tip of that range.

The white invasion brought new tension to a region already far from peaceful. Most of this territory had long been the domain of the Crow tribe, but after 1840

The Bozeman Trail in the vicinities of Fort Phil Kearny and Fort C. F. Smith.

Map by Gerry Krieg, based largely on Dee Brown, Fort Phil Kearny (Lincoln: University of Nebraska Press, 1962).

it was contested by the westward-driving Lakota (Sioux).[1] By Bozeman's time the Crows had lost their grip on the Powder River but held on to the north along the Bighorn River in what is now Montana. On the premise that the enemy of my enemy is my friend, the Crows made a tentative alliance with the distant whites.

Not even the Crows liked it much when the Bozeman Trail opened, but the first wave of fortune hunters was left more or less alone.[2] Things changed when the government decided to build forts to protect travelers: Fort Reno on the Powder River, Fort Phil Kearny on Big Piney Creek at the base of the Bighorn Mountains, and Fort C. F. Smith, where the Bighorn River issues from a mighty canyon.

Though a little-noted clause in an earlier treaty allowed for such forts, the Sioux and their frequent allies, the Northern Cheyennes and the Arapahos, regarded the new intrusion as a great betrayal. Under the leadership of Sioux chief Red Cloud, they launched a coordinated and ultimately successful campaign of ambush and harassment known as Red Cloud's War. The Crows, in a difficult position, kept up relations with both sides.

On December 21, 1866, while Johnny was still in Kansas, Red Cloud's warriors had a major victory outside Fort Kearny, wiping out a detachment of soldiers lured into the field by a decoy attack on a wood-cutting party. Eighty-one whites died in this action, known as the Fetterman Fight or "Massacre," at the time the worst U.S. Army loss in Plains Indian warfare.[3]

Finding that they "could not leave for the mining district at once," the brothers began taking jobs in the environs of Fort C. F. Smith: procuring firewood, cutting hay, and later trapping and hunting to fill the meat-starved garrison's needs. They joined a civilian community of some forty-five people attached to the post and tenuously under the control of the commander there.[4]

It was a lucrative place to be, as indicated by one official report: "Your consideration of the contracts made in the Powder River Country is desired. High prices were necessarily paid because of the remoteness of the Posts, and the great risks of life and property in performing the labor that could not be done by troops. If the forms required have not always been observed, the fact that weeks instead of days, are required for the transmittal of mail matter to and from these Posts, will account for any seeming neglect."[5]

Indeed, recordkeeping at the forts, and especially at C. F. Smith, was notoriously bad.[6] This may account for an odd fact. I have not been able to turn up any document, official or unofficial, in which the presence of John or Hugh Hart at that fort is attested.

Many of the people Johnny mentions, however, were definitely on the scene, and some reportedly became his good friends. Here are some sketches of the people who appear in the excerpts printed in the following chapters, beginning with the military side:

Lieutenant Colonel Luther P. Bradley arrived in the same wagon train that brought Johnny and Hugh, having joined the group at Fort Kearny, and commanded Fort C. F. Smith until March 31, 1868.[7] What struck Johnny about him was his gold-headed cane, which the officer tapped on the floor during conversation. Johnny reports numerous contacts with him, but Bradley does not mention Johnny either in his few preserved official papers or in his diary (discussed further in chapter 7).

Lieutenant Colonel Luther P. Bradley took over command at Fort C. F. Smith just as Johnny arrived. Bradley was blamed for his slowness in sending rescue during the Hayfield Fight (August 1, 1867). Though Johnny apparently did not share this opinion, the officer's demeanor irritated the younger man to the point of defiance. *Andrew S. Burt Collection, U.S. Army Heritage and Education Center, Carlisle, Pa.*

Captain Andrew Sheridan Burt (Johnny calls him Major Burt) arrived at Fort C. F. Smith with his family at the end of November 1867. He would take over command from Bradley at the end of March 1868 and see the post through the last months of its existence.[8]

Captain Andrew Sheridan Burt commanded Fort C. F. Smith from April 1, 1867, to its abandonment. Johnny got along well with him. *Andrew S. Burt Collection, U.S. Army Heritage and Education Center, Carlisle, Pa.*

Colonel Johnathan Eugene Smith took command of Fort Phil Kearny and the entire Mountain District in July 1867. Johnny reports several contacts with him and once (as he relates in chapter 11) had to endure the company of Smith's ill-conditioned nephew on a mail trip.[9]

Second Lieutenant Alexander Wishart also appears often in these pages and in other writings about Fort C. F. Smith.

And on the civilian side, these are the men Johnny mentions repeatedly:

Jim Bridger, the aging but still active mountain man and scout, was also on the scene at Fort C. F. Smith. On the edge of retirement, Bridger had come west again as the Indian conflicts intensified in 1865; he helped establish the Bozeman forts and, after an absence, returned in the spring of 1868 to witness their abandonment. Johnny states, "I had met Mr. Bridger on the Sweetwater as a Government scout in 1865 while serving in the Eleventh Kansas Cavalry."[10]

Michel Boyer, known as Mitch, was another accomplished guide, the son of a French Canadian father and a Sioux mother. Considered second only to his mentor Bridger in trailcraft, he carried mail between the Bozeman forts on occasion. He would die at the Battle of the Little Bighorn (June 25, 1876).[11]

Michel "Mitch" Boyer, expert guide, worked along the Bozeman Trail from February to September 1867. "He is thoroughly acquainted with the country and will prove invaluable, if kept away from whiskey," Captain John Fitch Kinney at Fort C. F. Smith assessed. *National Park Service, Little Bighorn Battlefield National Monument.*

Don A. Colvin, "Al Calvin" in the manuscript, was a contractor serving the fort and the man Johnny considered his boss. A Civil War veteran, he often took the lead when things grew difficult, as at the Hayfield Fight. He was "somewhat religiously inclined," Johnny observes.[12]

Old Howard comes up frequently in the narrative as a trusted guide and advisor. There is no Howard in other accounts, but there does appear in them a Harwood, described as "an old mountaineer," and very likely the same person.[13]

Alvin Coe Leighton ("Latin" in Johnny's spelling) was one of two sutlers, or storekeepers, at the fort; more than that, he was half of the partnership of Leighton & Smith, which serviced the needs of emigrants and troops throughout this part of the West. The sutler at Fort Phil Kearny was Alvin's brother, James, whom Johnny had known while in the Eleventh Kansas.[14]

William S. McKenzie ("McKinzie" in the manuscript), usually called by his last name, was an enterprising contractor who had a hand in many Bozeman affairs. Johnny disliked McKenzie as much as he liked Al Colvin and left his employment after McKenzie acquired the interests of Colvin (in a card game, Johnny claims).[15]

Dr. Henry M. Matthews, after an earlier stint at the fort as post surgeon, returned to the region in September 1867 as a special envoy to the various Indian tribes. One of his functions was to distribute the government annuities promised to the allied Crows—a role in which he cheated the Indians and attempted to cheat Johnny, according to the memoirs.[16]

Charlie Smith, a go-between with the Crows, was Johnny's special friend and accomplice in many pranks. He does not appear in the historical record, though a John W. Smith, A. C. Leighton's partner and fellow sutler at the fort, is prominent in it. Both Smiths were talented linguists and Indian traders, but John was married to a Sioux (thought to be Oglala) woman, while Charlie was himself of mixed blood, supposedly raised in a Cheyenne village, and known to his Crow trading partners as "Shaspoosa." Moreover, John Smith may have left the fort by early 1867.[17]

John Tewksbury (Johnny recalls the name as "Stuckesberry") was the post hunter, to whom Johnny delivered quantities of meat in the fall of 1867. Johnny's relations with the much older man were touchy.[18]

Finally, Johnny frequently mentions certain Crow Indians.

Blackfoot, his key contact, was not only the leader of a Mountain Crow band but often functioned as overall chief of the tribe. Johnny dates their acquaintance to 1865. The friendship was cemented, he reports here, when Blackfoot rescued him from a close brush with the Cheyennes (see chapter 12).[19]

White Mouth and *Iron Bull*, also high-ranking Crow leaders, were additional acquaintances, and Johnny had Indian friends he called Yankee Jim and Limber Jim (though these could be alternate names for the same man).

Mountain Crow chief Iron Bull did much to support the garrison at Fort C. F. Smith, including carrying the mail for a period in the autumn of 1867. Johnny knew him, though his closest relationship was with another Crow leader, Blackfoot. *National Anthropological Archives, Smithsonian Institution, NAA INV 09850700.*

A NOTE ON SOURCES

The universe of primary sources on the Bozeman Trail is not large. It is even more restricted for the place and period Johnny experienced. We know less about Fort C. F. Smith than about Fort Phil Kearny and much less about the second, waning year of the forts than about the first.

The list begins with documents in the National Archives. The public library in Sheridan, Wyoming, has an invaluable trove of annotated copies prepared by historian Barry Hagan, whose book *"Exactly in the Right Place"* is the sole comprehensive treatment of Fort C. F. Smith.

In addition, there are five personal accounts that will be cited so often that they merit mention here:

Lieutenant Colonel Luther P. Bradley kept a diary from May 30, 1867, to May 22, 1868.[20]

Fincelius C. "Finn" Burnett was a teamster working for Colvin. He provided a short first-person account of the Hayfield Fight to historian Grace Raymond Hebard, and his recollections of this and other events underlie the biography by Robert David, *Finn Burnett, Frontiersman* (1937).[21]

Fincellius C. "Finn" Burnett, like Johnny a civilian worker along the Bozeman Trail, was a valuable if unreliable eyewitness to a number of frontier events. *Photo from Robert B. David, ed., Finn Burnett, Frontiersman (Glendale, Calif.: Arthur H. Clark, 1937), by permission of the University of Oklahoma Press.*

Private James D. Lockwood wrote of the Bozeman Trail, in the third person, in his 1893 book, *Life and Adventures of a Drummer Boy, or Seven Years a Soldier.*[22]

First Lieutenant George M. Templeton, of the Eighteenth U.S. Infantry, was at Fort C. F. Smith for twenty-two months, from its founding in August 1866 until mid-June 1868. His diary is, in Barry Hagan's words, "the sole surviving, continuous personal record of the full two years of the army's occupation of the forts along the Bozeman Trail."[23]

First Lieutenant George M. Templeton was the longest-serving officer at Fort C. F. Smith. His diary and letters underlie many accounts of what went on at the remote post. *George M. Templeton Papers, Newberry Library, 4099, 10_309.*

Second Lieutenant Alexander Wishart, noted above as a friend of Johnny's, joined Lieutenant Colonel Bradley's party on its way north to Fort C. F. Smith on July 19, 1867, and was on hand for the final days of the fort a year later. His diary, though mostly a laconic record of travels and meals shared with other officers, is a much-cited background source.[24]

5

THE HAYFIELD FIGHT

When Wells Fargo Wagon Train No. 4 departed southward in the small hours of August 1, 1867, it diminished the forces at Fort C. F. Smith. This was the moment the Sioux and Cheyennes had been waiting for.

That spring, gathered in council on Rosebud Creek northeast of the fort, they had debated how to repeat and improve on their victory at the Fetterman Fight the previous December. Unable to agree on which fort to attack, they divided their forces, sending one large group of warriors to C. F. Smith and the other to Phil Kearny. Two battles resulted: the Hayfield Fight outside Smith on August 1, and the

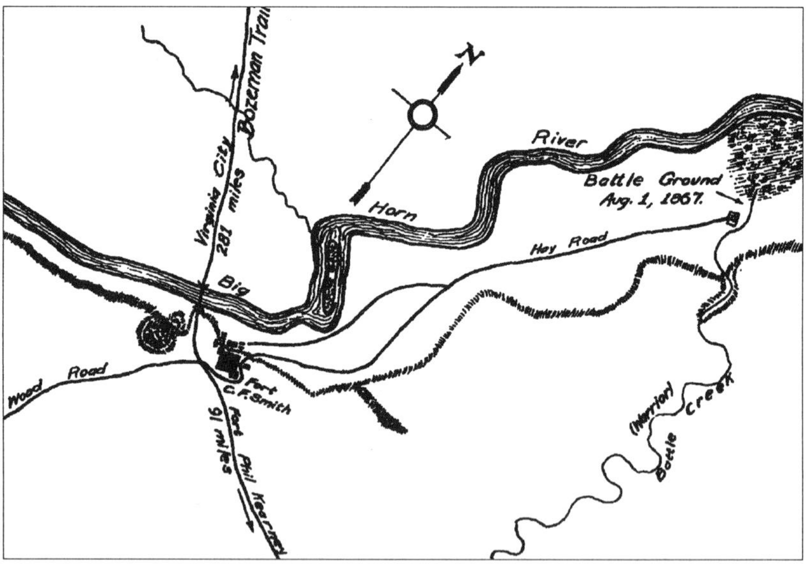

Fort C. F. Smith's environs, including the approximate location of the Hayfield battle site. Drawing from Grace Hebard and E. A. Brininstool, *The Bozeman Trail* (Cleveland: Arthur H. Clark, 1922).
By permission of the University of Oklahoma Press.

Wagon Box Fight outside Kearny a day later. This division of strength, along with the whites' newly delivered and superior firearms, may have determined the outcome of each engagement.[1]

The next day Al Colvin asked us if we would harvest hay for him a couple of weeks. When another day rolled around we were helping harvest hay of the bluestem variety for [William S.] McKenzie and Al Colvin. These men had a hay contract for Fort C. F. Smith. The hayfield was situated three miles below the fort, down the Bighorn River in a large flat valley and low river bottom on the east side of the river. There was twelve to sixteen men working in the hayfield all the time. This hay was hauled to the fort pretty green and was heavy; the loads were as large as we could conveniently haul. I did not at the time think this hay would keep, but it did and well.

To work down in the hayfield so far away from the fort was dangerous and all the men knew it. So there was always a lookout kept by our two cooks from the camp and corral. A shot fired and a flag hoisted at camp meant to come to the corral immediately. It meant Indians coming or near.

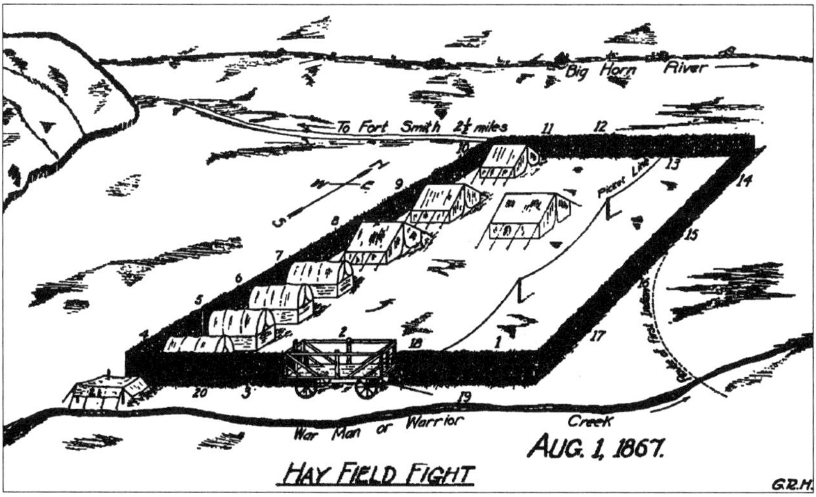

This schematic of the Hayfield Fight, based on Finn Burnett's memories many years later, fails to mention the Hart brothers. Judging by what Johnny witnessed, the pair must have been at the near end of the corral, facing Warrior Creek. Drawing from Grace Hebard and E. A. Brininstool, *The Bozeman Trail* (Cleveland: Arthur H. Clark, 1922).
By permission of the University of Oklahoma Press.

One day we were making splendid headway with the hay. Every man had a revolver hanging from his hip and a rifle on every wagon to prevent a surprise by Indians. There was a shot fired across the creek. Al Colvin went to find out what it meant as the flag at our camp had not been hoisted. He returned in a little while and said there was a lieutenant and three soldiers hunting ducks. We did not like this shooting but were powerless to prevent it. It interfered with our vigilance listening for shots fired at our corral camp.

[We] worked on for about half an hour when a shot was heard from the direction of the mowers in the lower end of the field. The mower men and teams came running up to our corral shouting, "The hills are full of Indians!"

This time the flag was up at the camp and a shot was fired. Then all hands bolted for the corral taking the wagons and teams with them.

Our corral was a large one. It was made of cottonwood trees of all sizes laid every way, one on top of another in zigzag fashion. On the outside trees had been snaked down from a ridge, then upended on the corral until it made a kind of stockade ten or twelve feet through in some places and in some places fully that high.

The treetops where they lopped over were cut off and thrown back into the corral, thus making quite a formidable place in which to fight Indians. This corral was built about fifty yards from a small creek which flowed toward the corral, then turned in a sharp angle toward the Bighorn River.

All mule teams and a few horses were turned into the corral, the wagons were pushed up so as to close the gate and chained together. The rest of the wagons not used in closing the gate to our corral were placed around the corral as best we could with what time we had to spare. Everybody, including the lieutenant and the soldiers who came in last, had just barely time to be safely in the corral.

It looked to us as if the hills in all directions were full of Indians. We loaded up our revolvers and worked digging into the earth to make corners to stop bullets. McKenzie ordered every man in the corral except the lieutenant to dig under the edge of the corral farther in, making a secondary place of refuge, in case we were stormed and greatly outnumbered. . . .

FIRST CHARGE

All men in that corral were western men except the soldiers from the fort and Hugh and me, who were half West and half East as McKenzie termed us. But we had already seen some pretty dangerous adventures. This one had already the earmarks of beating them all.

A way off we could see Indians in bunches of ten and twelve on all sides. Gradually they increased in size and kept coming nearer and nearer to us. After a while we could hear their war songs.

"That means business, boys," McKenzie exclaimed. "Don't a one of you shoot before sure of hitting an Indian or pony. Keep cool and don't become rattled."

Then after a while we heard the Indian war cry, which meant a real charge. Soon they came all yelling, but this first charge didn't amount to much, as there were only some forty odd of them. They circled round and round our corral, gradually edging in closer, riding their ponies until they came within gunshot. On being shot with our latest improved rifles [they] retired farther back into the hayfield, out of range. We learned these Indians were Sioux in this charge. In this round we accounted for seven ponies. An Indian dislikes to lose his ponies. That is his principal wealth.

Hugh and I were going outside of the corral for chunks of wood to build our corners up better, as we were stationed at the gate and more exposed than the rest of the boys.

"There is a good Indian marksman shooting across the little creek and he came near to getting me," Hugh said, as he came into the corral after one of his excursions after chunks of wood. I had the same experience and so did Al Colvin. All of us then began to be very busy trying to locate this lone Indian who was such a good shot. If we couldn't locate him he would be sure to get some of us, that was certain. We fired everywhere that [we] thought an Indian could be concealed.

The lieutenant [Sigismund Sternberg] was standing with his head and shoulders exposed close to the wagon closing the gate of the corral. He was trying to locate this very Indian we were all after. He was sure to be shot if he remained there very long. . . . I begged him to get down, telling him that Indian across the creek in nearby timber would blow his head off. We admired this lieutenant and did not want him to get hurt.

The lieutenant turned around and looked at me with perfect contempt, did not say a word. It was as if by a haughty look, he could wither me into nothing. McKenzie was our captain, and I think he should have counseled with the lieutenant.[2]

In a little while, as all expected, a dull thump was heard and our fine officer was knocked back nearly three feet, the whole side of his head blown off and some of his brains scattered on the ground beside his head where he fell. So much for a man that would not be advised. At the same time we could hear the Indian that shot him giving his cry of death.

Immediately a soldier bent over him [Sternberg], rifling for his personal things, such as watch, purse, and other articles. I called Al Colvin's attention to what the soldier [Thomas Navin] was doing.[3]

"Let him alone," he answered, "if we ever get out of here alive, will turn him over to the authorities at the fort."

Al Colvin had barely wedged back into his hole, when another dull thump was heard. We looked and sure as fate the rifling soldier had received his knockout. He was lying across the lieutenant's body, shot in the chest. I ran over and pulled the dead soldier off the lieutenant's body.

"What did you do that for?" Al Colvin asked.

"The soldier," I answered, "is a scavenger. I do not want him to bleed on the lieutenant. The lieutenant is a brave man, is entitled to respect even if dead."

SECOND CHARGE

Now there seemed to be about 500 Sioux and Cheyenne scattered here and there in large bunches close up, just barely out of range of our guns. Their war songs started up again, and to the *yep yep,* ending in a kind of a dog bark down in the throat, and then the charge, and as before all yelling like crazed demons. Swift they came on their ponies, heap big warriors, Sioux and Cheyenne. They had no clothing over their bodies except a breechclout, their limbs, arms, and head being decorated in different colors. The Sioux especially were hideous looking animals, painted in their war paint, and this sight easily rattles men who have never seen the thing before.

Before our little band of sixteen men and one soldier had time to think, the whole band rushed up close.[4] Round and round our corral they kept coming and going, round and round and yelling worse than before. They pressed hardest on the east side which was the weakest side. We could not stand up without being shot, still had to shoot through holes between the corral and among the tree tops. Quite often we got an Indian but more often a pony.

Then we discovered Indians were trying to scale our brush corral. They were numerous like bees trying to climb the front of a bee hive. We had to use our revolvers and commenced to shoot through the treetops. It was slow climbing among so many limbs and loose branches hanging down. We were getting them fast, we had to, because it would not do to allow them in the corral with us. The brush corral being built so rough and wide and high was the thing that saved us. . . .

After about fifteen minutes the charge was driven off and everything became quiet once again. The air was filled with dust caused by so many Indian ponies. It was like being in a howling wind, then enter a cave where all is dead still: the ceasing of motion and noise, extremes.

Then the lone Indian who had bothered us before commenced his fine shooting. He intended to kill more of us. Being such a good shot something had to be done as his bullets came whizzing into our corral, always close. After close observing with a field glass and watching when he fired, [we] located his hiding place. It was a wonder we had not discovered him before, as he was so close to us and did not have such a secure place as we thought. When he fired at a hat cunningly placed in a hole, all our boys would fire in the direction where smoke flared from his gun. We heard a yell of pain and his bullets stopped coming. [I] think very likely he went to his Happy Hunting Ground; at any rate he troubled us no more.

Then we had time to take a look at the two Indians shot among the brush of our corral. They were close to five and six feet up on the brush. Most everyone took a look at them making all sorts of remarks. They were right over Jack Hemphill and Larry Dolan's fighting place in the corral. Frank Manse climbed up and found the top Sioux was still alive and the one below through for good. Then a man by the name of Howard (we did not know his front name, everybody called him Old Howard) climbed up and arranged the Sioux in a sitting position in sight of his friends, the Sioux, and fixed him so he could rest easier. He would not live bit a few minutes. . . .

Some of our men wanted to finish the Sioux then and there, but Old Howard objected, saying, "let him alone! He is no coward, is entitled to respect."

Louis Richard, a half breed, asked the Sioux if he wanted to send any word to his people.

"No, you half-white dog!" the Sioux answered.

Then they gave the Sioux a drink of water.

"Now," Old Howard said, "you have hurried his death, he will die in a minute."

There were several of our men on the corral by this time looking at the Sioux when a shot was fired from the brush above the corral about two hundred feet and just missed Larry Dolan, our Irish funny man. After that we all scrambled off that corral without being told. Several wanted to finish the Sioux before going down into the corral.

"Let him die!" McKenzie ordered. "He is dying fast enough now. All keep off the corral from now on!"

But Larry Dolan or Hemphill, I don't know which one, gave him a hard knock on the head which finished him, as his head dropped forward, his body becoming still.

"Bad as I am, could not stoop to do a thing like that," said McKenzie, then bursting forth in a torrent of swear words. Al Colvin was horrified, especially as at times he was somewhat religiously inclined.

THE LOG ROUND

Our tent which was close to the creek and not far from the corral had been burned by the Indians in the second charge. There was an abundance of tin cups with finger handles to them. The Indians would take their medicine poles and reach over from the creek bed which was about four feet deep, hook a cup, then pulled it over to them into the creek where they crouched in the running water. Then a great yell would ring out punctuated with grunts and other noises denoting their glee and satisfaction.

At this point the manuscript puts a speech about medicine poles into the mouth of Al Colvin.

"A medicine pole is painted in different colors. The paint is made by the Indians themselves, is painted around the pole in rows as a usual thing. The medicine pole is from four to eight feet long according to the fancy of the warrior, and is light and small in diameter.

"A medicine man blesses the medicine pole. After that it is supposed to shield the owner from all danger. Each Indian has marks on his medicine pole which denote his name and ownership. Cheyenne are more for these medicine poles than other tribes, and the ones having medicine poles are supposed to be braver than those not having them. They must show their medicine poles before killing, which denotes fairness and is the highest type of bravery among these Indians. There are certain Indians who do not have the medicine pole, because they wish to kill in cold blood."

Could see dozens of these poles outside our corral.

Everything was burnt in our tent except the metal articles and a keg of syrup which had dried until it became thick and heavy. This keg we kept back of the tent outside and close to the creek bank, about two feet. The Indians could easily have pulled the keg of syrup into the creek, but they never did. It was strange they never thought of that.

Every once in a while an Indian would put his hand over the edge of the keg and lift out a handful of this dried syrup which was nearly candy. Afterwards we could hear his happy shouts over his venture, and in getting the sugar syrup.

"Now watch me!" Al Colvin slowly drawled, "I am going to draw a fine bead over the top of that keg about where the next Indian will likely put his hand over into the keg."

Al Colvin was the best shot among us, so we expected results. He sighted and sighted and grunted and moved around and then became still, saying softly, "The bead is fine and keen as a razor's edge."

In about a minute up went an Indian's hand and boom from Al Colvin's carbine went a bullet, a keeping time, which was quickly followed by a rage of pain. It seemed as though that Indian's hand had disappeared in the air. We never saw it go back. From that time on the Indians never bothered the keg of syrup.

The Sioux and Cheyenne never liked to take chances with a man that could shoot too close to the mark. Such a man was of the West according to their way of explaining it. It did not matter where he came from, "the West" [was] beyond their horizon somewhere, where "Heap brave men live." So the Indian preferred to have the best of the deal from the start, he did not like equal terms. But the Indian was no coward, he would take chances and come again.

Again we went to digging into the earth. It did seem like the last of us if they made many more charges as fierce and determined as the last one. When they began to climb up on our corral to get at us we had to make every shot count with a high number. We wanted to live on pretty bad just then. . . .

All of our boys were good shots and that was what counted. We were playing havoc with their ponies. An Indian would lose his squaw before his pony.

Our casualties so far were one lieutenant, one soldier, two wounded mules that would have to be shot, three more shot in the legs and several having arrows sticking in them. A few of our men were bruised up a little through dodging and hurrying around carelessly.[5]

After a while we noticed a few logs between our corral and the creek. These logs appeared to be rolling toward us at first but were coming slow. It was a little odd and uncanny this thing of life in a lifeless log. Gradually these logs crept up in their rolling way pretty close to our corral, and then there began to be shots fired at us from behind these logs by pretty good marksmen for an Indian. Stop them we must before they came too close. Our bullets would not go through them. They acted as a moving fort against our stationary one.

"Just watch me," Jack Hemphill said. "I am going to shoot right under that log and tear all that Indian's digestive tract out, if he has any."

Jack drew a fine bead holding under the log so as to make the bullet bounce up under the log as it hit the earth or go through the under portion of the log. He squirmed around quite a bit, holding his breath, fussing, and then fired. Up jumped to an Indian like a bird, all spraddled out clear above the log and yelling at the top of his voice. After that all the logs moved off toward the little creek and disappeared, much to our joy.

THIRD CHARGE

Soon after this log round, as we called it, with the Indians, there seemed to be another charge in store for us looming up in the hayfield across the little creek. The creek bothered them for it was so close to our corral. We could hear them singing their war songs to get up courage. The thing that bothered us was, perhaps this charge would be the last one. And then all of us were beginning to be pretty thirsty and hungry. We were like the Indians who did not think to pull the syrup keg into the creek when it was within two feet of the bank of the creek. So while we could have had plenty of water to drink and something to eat beforehand as we went into the corral, we did not think of that; now the Indians had destroyed it all.

Soon down on us they came, all yelling like wild creatures of some new kind of inferno, hubbub of the worst kind. Their yelling [I] suppose was to keep up their courage while on the charge and to give them more strength to fight us, but their yell is far different from the white man's yell.

This charge was almost as bad as any before and came near being fatal for us, as the ones behind kept crowding the ones in front closer in. They were jumping off their ponies and running all around our corral looking for a man to kill. Our shots were telling with deadly effect. Even so, it did look like the last of us, this crowding and jamming, especially if all should dismount and storm our temporary fort at once.

We steadily kept shooting their ponies . . . and shooting all Indians that attempted to scale our corral. If one side should be pressed pretty hard, those on the other side would rise up quickly and fire over the backs of the mules and horses and we would do the same when they were being pressed hard on their side.

It was getting pretty warm for us, disastrous for them, as their wounded and death list rapidly increased. Our stock in corral was rapidly being shot to pieces. Some of our wagons were being moved away a couple of rods, and they had commenced to move up some of the trees and stumps of the fence. To stop this we fired whole volleys in one place, which brought the desired result. If we had not chained the wagons together at the gate of the corral, all would have been up with us.

It was a regular pandemonium, a kind of miniature hell without any sulfur. By this time we were beginning to suffer in earnest for water and something to eat. We were all covered with dust, for the Indians in their scurrying of ponies and warriors continually raised clouds of dust. Doing things on the spur of the moment and having bullets and arrows tearing close to us by the dozens drew heavily on our endurance and steadiness.

However, just when we did not expect it, the Indians withdrew, greatly to our surprise. They gave it up once more and went out of gunshot. We lay all huddling up in our fighting places partly down in the ground and drew long breaths in peace for a minute.

LITTLE DOCK

During this silence or semi-silence that followed, a little soldier who was with us [Private Charles Bradley], asked McKenzie for a mule to ride to the fort.[6]

We would get killed anyhow, the little soldier said, and he would just as well die to get help from the fort as to stay here and die doing nothing.

"No!" McKenzie answered, "No mule of mine shall leave this corral, not even a mule's ear. It will not do, soldier boy, for the Sioux will surely get you within a hundred yards of this corral. It is rank suicide to attempt anything like that!"

The soldier never gave up his request for a mule to ride to the fort. Finally [he] asked Al Colvin for a mule named Little Dock, the best running mule in the corral. Al Colvin was provoked, but after a few minutes gave in, the little soldier pleaded so hard.

"All right!" Al Colvin shouted. "Take the mule, Little Dock! He's all mine anyhow, and go plumb to China if you want to!"

Then we heard Al Colvin remark to himself, "I hate to lose Little Dock. He has been with me through so many hardships and is faithful and true. He can outrun a buffalo, something few Indian ponies and white men's horses can do."

We caught Little Dock and put a blind bridle on him, for couldn't find anything better just then. Then hoisted the little soldier on his back telling him his saddle would have to be the mule's back, and wishing him a thousand Godspeeds.

We shoved wagons away from the front of the coral, then out the soldier and Little Dock went. Little Dock went walking on the front part of his hooves as if trying to walk in the air and somewhat stiff-legged but springy in his movements like a deer. Once outside of the corral the soldier turned the mule loose and prepared himself in such a manner as to hold on at all hazards. They looked mighty alone running out there into certain death.

As expected, the Indians opened up their lines on seeing the soldier coming, in the shape of a V, then closed in on him from behind. The mule, seeing so many Indians around and already scared, bolted for the swamp toward the Bighorn River. After that we held our breath, for all we could see was a cloud of dust and Indians going for the soldier in all directions. We risked our lives climbing on the corral among the logs and tree tops to watch the soldier go. We had to do it or die.

Now the Indians did not figure on Little Dock being so confounded lucky and so fast and sure of foot, or they would have killed both soldier and the mule right away.

They did not want to kill the soldier, wanted to take him alive so as to force him to die at their leisure.[7]

We were down in the corral cheering one another and preparing for another charge, when the lookout on the logs hollered, "There is something strange down there at the end of the swamp. All the Indians are going on the run toward the fort and around the end of the swamp."

We climbed upon the trees and logs of our corral to take a look. Away and there in the lead ran Little Dock and the soldier. Through McKenzie's glass could see Little Dock's front legs reaching out in front of him and they did not seem to come back, they seemed always there, so quick did he gather them. He had too much of a lead for the Indians to ever catch him. He was safe, there was no "impossible" with that soldier.

Not one of us expected the soldier to have luck like that. We cheered for the soldier, we cheered for Little Dock, we cheered for ourselves going half wild, for our hearts were beginning to warm up from under the clouds of gloom.

"How on earth did the soldier cross that swamp?" McKenzie shouted. "No man or mule in their right senses would ever dare attempt such a crazy thing. He has gained the wood road. The Sioux are too wise to cross that swamp so are going around."

The Indians knew the soldiers would soon be down there with their wagons on wheels to shoot at them. The Indians were disappointed and were coming back to us. They were going to give us one more round before the soldiers came to our aid.

CHEYENNE FOOT CHARGE

We could see this time the Indian pony was not going to figure in the charge at all. It was going to be a foot charge, the very thing we dreaded from the beginning that day, because the Sioux and Cheyenne could rush up and destroy us easily having not less than forty braves to every one of us. We were worried this time in genuine earnestness.

Charlie Smith climbed up on the corral and by the aid of a field glass [observed and] hollered down to us, "This charge is going to be Cheyenne. They are all Cheyenne. I know, because they raised me after killing my father and mother. I think an old squaw man is to lead them, and if so, it means life or death for us. A Cheyenne that has lost his standing will go if he does go until death claims him."

Their war cry once more started across the little creek. Soon here they came, all Cheyenne, one behind another in single file, even taking as long steps as they could, running like the wind and making their dog bark ending with a yelp which is loud and carries. The old squaw man was leading them. He was going to win back his glory.

They ran along across the creek close to us for about fifty yards. It would have been an easy matter for us to shoot about ten of them if all of us shot together.

"Hold your fire," McKenzie shouted, "until they jump the creek, and don't a one of you shoot until Al Colvin shoots!"

The first one to jump the creek was the squaw man, a large fellow. Just as he landed safely on our side of the creek a shot rang out and the squaw man fell to the ground toward our corral. These Cheyenne were coming fast, so it was natural to suppose more would cross the creek, but they did not. They jumped into the little creek and disappeared in a second, all at once, nearly as one Indian. All we could see was the splash of water here and there. We did not see them any more.

Soon on all sides the Cheyenne and Sioux were scurrying out and away over the distant hills. Then one of us ran to the little creek for a hat full of water. Anything that would hold water. We must have water. Then all things began to change back to their old look and we began to feel like living once more.

We rustled a pan that had not suffered too much from the tent fire to carry water in, but these things were scarce as the Indians had carried away everything they could. Al Colvin commenced to wash the dust and sweat from his face and then we began to think if all of us had a coating like he had we must be a terrible looking bunch of men.

BACK TO FORT C. F. SMITH

In a little while as expected here came the soldiers from Fort C. F. Smith. They halted about fifty yards across the creek. An orderly came over to where we were and said, "The Colonel orders you men to go to the Fort at once!"

"Yes, sir," McKenzie answered. "But we want to take our wagons and teams with us."

The orderly went away, but soon came right back on the run, once more delivering his message.

"The Colonel orders you men to come at once or be left behind!"

This made McKenzie angry, he lost his head.

"You tell the Colonel," McKenzie shouted, "we will not come without the wagons and teams. We whipped the whole Sioux nation today and can do it again."

In the meantime the ambulance had been driven up to our corral and the lieutenant and soldier placed within. We could not gather our mules and wagons together quickly and had some trouble with the wounded mules.

Al Colvin had four mule teams in this corral, McKenzie twelve four-mule teams, several horses and four yoke of oxen. The oxen were left outside of the corral as the Indian seldom bothers oxen.

As we went to the fort Al Colvin and I rode down to where Little Dock crossed the swamp. We could see his hoof marks away out in the black mud of that swamp about twenty feet. That mule must have been going hell bent when he hit that swamp.

"Well," Al Colvin said, "that mule made a splendid start at first, but the rest of the way across that swamp is unanswered. I am going to take good care of that mule from now on."

The next day, saw the little soldier. He was pretty well scratched over his back where the warriors' fingernails had scraped along, leaving their trail. They had torn most of his clothing from his body and one ear was nearly torn from his head. He couldn't do anything for two weeks afterward.

"Little Dock," he said, "is a prince of a mule, none better. He ran where he pleased. He jumped about a hundred feet out in that swamp the first jump, and about one hundred yards in the next four jumps, then we was out of it. Little Dock went tearing through the brush on the ridge between the swamp and the Bighorn River. He snorted and then smelt the wood road, then away to the fort we went. Little Dock can do more snorting than all the other mules put together. And I didn't get killed, as all you men said I would, and was the means of having the soldiers come to your aid. We are something extra, Little Dock and I."

That same morning ran across Crow Indian Jim, who said he knew the Sioux and Cheyenne were going to attack us, but had kept still because [he] did not want to be at war with them and it was none of his business. Also that we had killed and wounded over fifty Sioux and Cheyenne and had wounded and killed seventy-five ponies and that we came from the tribe of men out of the West, who shoot too well, no miss. That the Sioux and Cheyenne would never make war on our band of men again.

Johnny is just the third eyewitness to tell of the Hayfield Fight. James Lockwood included a very flowery third-person narrative in his *Life and Adventures of a Drummer Boy* (1893). Teamster Finn Burnett gave the story to Grace Hebard (1922) and later, via his granddaughter Verna, to his biographer Robert David (1937).

All agree in broad outlines. All tell of the death of Lieutenant Sternberg and the soldier (Tom Navin). Lockwood includes the ride to summon rescue—but on a horse, not a mule—while Burnett does not. Johnny provides different details, and somewhat more extensive ones, breaking the battle down into distinct phases. The accounts also differ in their lists of the men present. Neither Lockwood nor Burnett mention Larry Dolan, William McKenzie, or either Hart brother. Some of the actions ascribed to McKenzie by Johnny are credited to Colvin by the others.

Burnett gives much more space to context and aftermath. He bore a grudge all his life toward Lieutenant Colonel Bradley, charging that the commander of Fort C. F. Smith knew about the hay party's predicament and shut the gates defensively instead of sending aid. Johnny, by contrast, takes it for granted that Little Dock's heroic rider brought the first word of the fighting to the garrison.[8]

Given the inevitable divergence of eyewitness accounts, even when much fresher than these, it seems fair to say that these versions generally reinforce one other.

A soldier at the fort who witnessed Charles Bradley arrive on Little Dock, still closely pursued by Indians, wrote in his diary, "No notice was ever taken of this man's heroic deed."[9] Johnny's account helps correct this historical omission.

6

INTO THE MOUNTAINS

Fort C. F. Smith was located near the point where the powerful Bighorn River flows out of a mountain wall, dividing the Bighorn Mountains, on the southwest, from the lower Pryor Mountains, part of the same tectonic block, on the northeast. Between them the river has carved one of the West's great canyons, inundated today by a reservoir. Though the heart of the canyon was impassable, gentler terrain upstream could be reached by crossing the Pryor Mountains at a low point called Pryor (or Pryor's) Gap, from which a route called Buoyer's (or Boyer's) Cut-Off led on southward to regain the river. Resources available upstream drew supply parties from the fort. (See map on page 78.)

Hugh and I began once more to figure where we could find other employment. But on the third day Al Colvin asked Hugh and me to go on another wood hauling job. We were glad to go.

We crossed the Bighorn River at Fort C. F. Smith, then followed the river for several miles going upstream. After a while turned off into a park and later entered a canyon. There never had been a road built into this canyon, so we had a hard time of it, some of the time traveling on one side of the creek and then on the other side, and then traveling up the bed of the stream. We had to do considerable work in places in order to go through. There were hundreds of beaver dams along the creek, but no beaver. The beaver had destroyed trees, grass, all vegetation for some distance back, there was nothing left for them to live on, both sides of the creek desolate.

We were going to Pryor Gap, thence by way of Boyer's Cut-Off to the Bighorn River, where we were to make camp permanently for a time. This journey upset us all, it was so trying. Who wants to travel across country without a wagon road with heavy wagons?

After arriving above the canyon of the Bighorn River, we saw there had been a fire sometime in the past which had burned over about three hundred acres of cottonwood timber. This charred blackened mass our men were supposed to handle. We chopped these trees down, then made them into lengths of twelve and sixteen feet, then they were snaked and hauled by wagons to the river where they were thrown into the swift running water of the Bighorn River.

Al Colvin and McKenzie believed these logs would float down through the canyon to Fort C. F. Smith where they would be hauled ashore by a boom and afterwards used at the fort as firewood.

This work was not very clean as the burned outside portion of all trees soon had all men looking as if they had been drawn through a stovepipe, but Al Colvin supplied us with extra jumpers free of charge. . . .

We cut and dumped logs into the Bighorn for three weeks, but none of them ever floated through the Bighorn Canyon, so a messenger from Fort C. F. Smith told Al Colvin and McKenzie. We then packed up our outfit and started back to the fort. At this time McKenzie and a half breed went down the Bighorn Canyon in a small strong boat to find out what had become of so many logs.

While going back to Fort C. F. Smith we met a half dozen Crow Indians. We guessed a young Crow who was about to become a warrior was trying to organize a band of his own. His followers were quite young. I think they had stolen away from their tribe. Al Colvin fed them as they had no provisions. They rode back with us to the fort. Because Al Colvin fed them they called him "The man that wasn't afraid of his eatin'."

One afternoon a fool hen ran a few yards away from the road, stopped standing nearly still, an easy shot.[1] Quickly a young Crow brave ran to a rock where he leveled his obsolete rifle, taking a long time in drawing his bead on this fool hen, then fired and missed. Then we hollered, making all the fun of him we could. We said the Crow was heap no good, eye behind ear, the reason he missed. Larry Dolan told the Crow the reason he missed was because the fool hen had no gizzard. And that last remark made all the Indian lads cross and sullen.

The next day Sam House thought he would take a shot at a jackrabbit that had run a short distance from the road and then stopped and sat on his haunches, all the while watching us. It was a good shot and a tempting one. Sam House drew a bead and fired. He, too, missed entirely, which placed him in the same position on a miss as the Crow brave the day before. The young Crows were wise enough to play even, so they commenced on Sam House.

"Heap no good white man! Heap squaw man! Rabbit eyes no hit!"

McKenzie arrived at Fort C. F. Smith in his small strong boat before we did. The logs had drifted on sandbars. He hired two Michigan river logging men to go up in the canyon and push the logs off the sandbars. They were furnished with provisions, necessary tools and powder to blast jams free. These men soon proved they knew what to do, for the logs were coming down from one jam to another.

Here again we can look to Finn Burnett for a parallel yet contrasting account. Johnny has McKenzie and "a half-breed" making the canyon run. Burnett says the team consisted of Al Colvin, one Al Stevenson, and himself, and he provides much dramatic detail, adding that old man Harwood, who had been left alone upstream, followed some days later on an improvised raft.[2] Lieutenant Colonel Bradley's diary supports Johnny's version: "McKenzie came in this evening, having boated down the Big Horn, about 60 miles, running the rapids in the big canyon, a trip probably never performed by any white man before. He reports the timber lodged some 30 miles above cannot run it down on account of low water."[3] Bradley did not know of Jim Bridger's prior claim to have run the canyon—in 1825—which historians tend to credit.[4]

Johnny's next money-making plan took him back to higher ground.

Hugh went to work at the fort for the government, and I to poisoning wolves as they were quoted at two dollars and fifty cents in St. Louis. Thought would make big money. I bought a dozen bottles of strychnine and a supply of provisions. Had it delivered along with other things needed in the canyon about ten miles south of Fort C. F. Smith. There I climbed out of the canyon going south where I selected a place at the head of a short canyon.

This would put Johnny on the right, east, bank of the Bighorn River, here running southwest to northeast.

Built a shelter against a large rock eight feet high by setting a forked tree trunk in the ground eight feet from the rock. Then placed a stout pole in the fork of the tree trunk and over on top of the rock to serve the purpose of a ridgepole, then leaned poles close up all around from the ground to this ridgepole, leaving a space against the rock to build a fire and for smoke to pass out. It made quite a comfortable place after the cracks between the leaning poles were closed.

After this was finished, I went down in the canyon and packed up my provisions, blankets, and other things to my new home. I built a fire and prepared a meal, then I made a few more improvements to suit me. After that I was ready to see what I could do.

I was on a plateau about two thousand feet east of the Bighorn Canyon. This plateau ran back east to the foot of the [main mass of the Bighorn] mountains and about twelve miles, and south about eight miles to another canyon like the one I crossed to the north of it as I came in. This plateau was comparatively level. There were about three thousand elk, one thousand buffalo and large wolves everywhere. The game had never been disturbed here, to any great extent, as it was difficult for an Indian or white man to cross these canyons, so I felt quite safe there.

The one thing that bothered me was the snow, one and a half feet deep, which forced me to make a pack mule out of myself. I thought I'd start out and try my luck first thing, first taking care to have three bottles of strychnine in my pocket. I started out early in the morning of the next day filled with hope deep in my being.

Had not tramped very far when I saw a bunch of mountain sheep ahead of me. By taking a little pains I managed to stalk up to within forty yards of them. Selected a young buck and fired, shooting him in the head. I dressed him and hung him in a scrubby tree. This gave me plenty of the best kind of meat.

Then I walked up the plateau about one half mile to a point around a small clump of aspen where I could see a band of elk. I crawled up close as possibly could under the circumstances but the best I could do was in the neighborhood of one hundred yards. I concluded I could land one at that distance, so I fired at a doe. She fell, but gained her feet and ran into a bunch of small aspen, the rest of the bunch running away.

Went to the aspens carefully with my gun ready and found she was dead. I pulled and rolled her out on the clear ground covered with snow, then cut and slashed her, emptying my three bottles of strychnine in the flesh wounds while the carcass was still warm. I went back to camp quite satisfied with my day's start in the poisoning wolves business.

On the second morning again prepared breakfast early, as I wanted to see how the strychnine had worked on the wolves. Before I got to the poisoned elk

I could see a poisoned wolf about used up. He tried to run away and fell, then I knew I had him. When came to within forty yards of the elk I could see wolves lying dead in all directions, two of them almost on the elk's carcass. I stood there and counted twenty-six, a pretty good start.

Then I commenced skinning them, finding the legs on most of them frozen and some entire bodies frozen like a cake of ice, but that was an advantage in skinning. I think that morning I poisoned the giant of the wolves on that plateau. His legs being frozen, I stood him on his feet, then stood astride of him, but could not stand flat footed, only with one heel and toe. From the top of his head to the point of his muzzle was a little over twelve inches. A real giant wolf, able to kill any wild animal four times his size.

It was one o'clock before I finished skinning my first day's haul. Then I looked around a bit and saw a number of crows jumping backwards; they too had indulged in a meal of poisoned elk. Then there were dozens of magpies, they would fly to the willows growing near a spring close by, where they would fasten their feet firmly to willows and hang there upside down dead, their grip never relaxing.

I roped the pelts together, later finding it was all I could do to carry them to my home against the rock, so I divided them and made two trips. On my way home I discovered a wolf about 50 yards away that had not quite finished his meal on my elk meat, so was not killed quickly. From the looks of his wabbling in the snow he must have endured several spasms before giving up life. From the looks of things another wolf had eaten what the first wolf had expelled from his stomach; he died having only one spasm.

When I arrived at my shanty I found I had a visitor. Mr. Camp Robber (Canada jay) was making himself quite at home. He was getting into everything, and packed away all sorts of things to the bushes and trees outside. Never was there such a busy bird in all the world. He scuttled a few feet when I came into the wickiup, turned his head to one side, eying me closely all the while, as if to say, "I have been in these woods and parks and canyons long before you came, and by nature privileged to help myself to anything of yours I wish."

This saucy camp robber did not have any fear of me; it did not seem to be in his makeup. We became quite friendly, but I had to watch him closely, he was so mischievous and a natural born thief.

One evening while frying a choice steak of buffalo hump, my friend the camp robber seized the steak and scampered away outside. This incident annoyed me, but I let it pass and fried another steak. It does not require but very little grease to fry buffalo meat, as there are little streaks of fat scattered among the meat.

After a while the camp robber came back. He poked his head in the doorway slyly, acting as [if] he would like to say, "Mister, I have to eat and manners do not count here between you and me."

This bird was some company as he helped to while away the lonesome hours. His antics sometimes were quite comical, especially when there was something tied to a string that he happened to want to carry away badly. He couldn't understand why a thing couldn't be moved if he could lift it. He would scold and make more fuss than a baby two years old. I named him Ramshackle (fitted him well).

After this went to stretching pelts trapper style . . . using sticks from a bunch of alders I had previously supplied myself with. It was slow work for me, I only had seven stretched before dark. As they were stretched I hung them up against the walls of my shack to break the wind. I thought if I kept up this gait I would have to hire a man to help me stretch pelts.

On another day Johnny reports feeling threatened by the wolves, which might seem poetic justice. He titles this passage "Six big wolves."

By this time the elk and buffalo had worked east on the high end of the plateau about eight miles away. I went up this end of the plateau, and there I saw a bunch of about fifty elk in a draw, and by going around I could go close to them, the way the wind was blowing.

I had made one half of my distance winding up this draw when I heard a fine keen yelp about fifteen feet from me. Looked around and there stood six big wolves. All of them showed their teeth and hair turned the wrong way. I could shoot one of them or possibly two, but the rest of them would have me by the throat before anything else could be done, if they were attacking. And if I shot it would scare the elk. Things looked bad, and the wolf part of it was not to my liking, too dangerous, my life hung on a thread and that thread was liable to break any fraction of a second. . . .

Soon I decided to risk all. I commenced to talk ugly to them and at the same time advanced toward them, for I knew a wolf will back up a few feet even if he intends to attack afterwards. The wolves sidled off to one side in that narrow gulch, much to my surprise, but they went only a little way. After that I kept these wolves away far enough so could kill them all if they should attack. Then I started on up the gulch, this time looking sharp at every turn. And at every turn I could see the wolves coming behind at each turn I had passed.

On I went stalking the elk and the wolves were stalking me, not a very pleasant thing to have on my mind, for as sure as they came close enough while my back was turned I would be torn to pieces in less than a minute.

I finally slipped up to within fifty yards of a big bull elk, the boss of the herd. He was the largest elk I ever saw. He was pawing the snow down to the grass and on each side of him two does ate the grass as he uncovered it for them. In his humble way he was quite a provider. I stood there for several seconds watching the performance, then noticed all the other elk were pawing the snow down to the grass.

This giant elk, I noticed, had weathered many a battle for mastery of the herd. The two front prongs of one horn were broken off and about one half of the other was broken in two and gone entirely. He had had to battle giants like himself to be the survival of the fittest, and had won.

The wind changed for a moment, the six wolves were getting closer to me, and I would have to shoot quick before the elk scented me, or at the wolves. I could not shoot the giant elk who was working so hard for his wives in pawing the snow down to grass. It was not in me to make him die, so fired at a doe. She dropped and slid down to the bottom of the gulch. I skinned her then placed three bottles of strychnine in her body. Cut a thong down each foreleg of the hide and tied them together, then slung the hide over my shoulder and started for camp.

The hide being green became heavy after a while, so I commenced to drag it in the snow behind me. When I got to within 150 yards of my wikiup, heard the fine keen yelp of a band of wolves about 100 yards behind me. Instantly I slipped the thong loose from my shoulder and let the wolves have the elk hide, then made the utmost effort to gain my wickiup. Had about all the wolf annoyance [I] wished that day. I had not been to either of my baits that day. The next day I got nine [wolf] pelts, which when stretched covered my wickiup in good shape. It sometimes has a habit of getting pretty cold in Montana.

This and other wolf tales in the narrative show Johnny at his least credible or, perhaps, least informed. While the wolves of the plateau, unused to men with guns, may well have been bolder then than their modern counterparts, his continual fear of attack seems to stretch any possible truth. Zoology teaches that the "six big wolves" were hoping to scavenge part of his kill, not to make him their prey. Sometimes the author-as-editor seems to wish to deflate the drama found in the typescript. One interlineation reads: "As soon as they scented me, they ran away. They don't like the scent of man. Don't believe any wolf will attack a man if he stands firm." At another point he observes: "Always when anything runs there is something running after it. So, I ran, and the wolves ran after me."

He also shows the preference of his day, which we are still painfully unlearning, for prey over predator, mingled with some sharp observations on nature, as in this little lecture on "How wolves kill elk."

There was a band of elk and about twenty or more wolves around them. The elk were busy pawing the snow down to the grass and not paying much attention to the wolves. I saw that if an elk strayed from the herd twenty feet, the wolves would cut him out, or at least attempt to. I knew if wolves can catch an elk on level ground away from large rocks and the herd, and are up close, that elk is done for. Wolves follow a band of elk and live on them. When one strays out from the herd too far, several wolves will jump and get a firm grip with their powerful jaws and hold on, while others cut the tendons above the elk's forked hoof if they can.

The wolves holding on to the elk's hams make it hard for the elk to keep his feet; eventually the elk falls down, and when he falls, never gets up again. The wolves eat the elk alive from the rear, as the elk's front feet are too dangerous for them. The elk cannot get up on his feet, so gives up, and at first bawls that hard old bawl, and in a moment begins to bawl pitifully. The wolves will have his hind quarters eaten away and part of the entrails before the elk dies. This is horrible, but I have seen it done, and have heard the elk bleat, bleat, bleat, weaker and weaker until the end. All life on this earth lives on other life in some form or another, but some of this life-giving is far more wicked than other methods, according to what animals are seeking their meal, and the method.

This pelt-gathering expedition along with a subsequent one joined by brother Hugh and two helpers yielded a total of 150 wolf pelts. But the meat Johnny and his group brought in to the fort almost as an afterthought was of far greater value to the denizens.

At the fort that evening [we] sold all the meat we had at twenty-five cents a pound. The government beef herd had all been butchered long ago, the officers, soldiers, and citizens wanted fresh meat, thus producing a demand that smacked of being good and come to stay.

The sutler's store would only give seventy-five cents for wolf pelts, whereas expected to receive at least a dollar and a half for each pelt. This was a disappointment. Wolf hides require considerable work to handle them, but the fresh meat paid. As it was, our five days together with my other days alone on the plateau made in money one hundred and twenty dollars and fifty cents.

7

THE MYSTERIOUS MAIL CARRIER

Transporting the mail between Forts Kearny and C. F. Smith was a perennial problem during this period. In the spring of 1867, it was entrusted to several men in turn. Thereafter—most accounts agree—the mail was carried by Crow Indians. In the fall of 1867, a review of conditions at Fort C. F. Smith observed: "The system of carrying the mails between this post and Fort Phil Kearney [*sic*] I think cannot be bettered at present. Three Crow Indians at a salary altogether of $100 per mo. or an average of $44 1/3 each carry it on horseback. The mail rarely exceeds what one pack animal can carry. These Indians perform this duty with promptness and fidelity and they being on friendly terms with the hostile Sioux it is by far the safest as well as cheapest and most expeditious method."[1] The chief mail carrier is supposed to have been none other than Mountain Crow chief Iron Bull.

This arrangement appears to have come to an end, however, that fall. Early in 1868 Templeton wrote in his diary: "Our mails are received quite regularly now by the aid of Crow Indian couriers, but some foolish, irresponsible party at Fort Philip Kearny having told the boys [Iron Bull and his assistant] to hurry through, they not knowing but those were the authorized instructions, did so, thereby killing one of the public horses they were riding. This caused Bradley to discharge them and employ an old mountaineer, Mr. Harwood by name, to carry the mails."[2]

Harwood, we have already speculated, might be Johnny's advisor "Old Howard." But how do we get from "old mountaineer" to young John Benton Hart? First, though, comes Johnny's account of his getting, and first performing, the mail run.

While at the fort this time heard considerable complaint about the men carrying the mail to and from forts Phil Kearny and C. F. Smith. Made inquiries, found their names to be Old Tex (Ben Barkeley)[3] and Mich Boyer and that they drew $5.00 a day each straight time. They had formed the habit of indulging too freely in corn whiskey about three days after each trip with the mail. And on their last trip, bringing too much whiskey with them, about ten miles out they became so used up they could not go through to the fort for two days after the usual time allowed them. Therefore General [*sic*] Bradley discharged them for not being prompt, carrying whiskey, and drinking too much while on duty.[4] But all men said they could go through in spite of the Indians, that they were fearless and brave and good men away from whiskey.

Thought I might land this mail carrying job, so went up to see General Bradley. Was admitted into his office. Introduced myself and made my wants known.

There was a light tapping on the floor with what appeared to be a gold headed cane, then a short silence, then followed by:

"You are too young! Cannot trust valuable mail with you!"

Then I told him I was 22 years old.

"No! You are not!"

"It is true, I am that old."

"What have you been doing here? Tell me that!" the general snapped out, all the while tapping the floor with his gold headed cane and looking me square in the eyes like a tiger.

In that few seconds General Bradley made me angry, but held my head. He was not half so fierce as a band of wolves yelping around my heels.

Then I told him about the Hayfield Fight with the Sioux and Cheyenne, poisoning wolves, packing in meat to the fort, and sending him the snow white wolf pelt.[5]

"You were in that hayfield set-to, aha, and you sent me that white wolf pelt, many thanks for it." Then General Bradley bristled up fierce again.

"Now, I'm talking! Whom can you find that would recommend you?"

Then came a light tapping of his cane on the floor which gradually increased in velocity and loudness. "I think Al Colvin or McKenzie may recommend me, but I am not sure of that. Mr. Leighton of the sutler's store would."

"Young man, would not consider a recommendation from the sutler's store at all. Where have you been before coming here? What has been your occupation?"

"Have served three years in the Eleventh Kansas Cavalry, Sir."

"Don't believe it!"

"It is the truth, General."

"Don't believe it! Name some of your officers!"

"Colonel Moonlight, Captain Greer, Lieutenant Clancy, and—"

"Hold on! Not so fast! Have you any scars?"

"Yes, sir, two of them, General."

"Show them!"

I then showed him a scar across the heel in calf of [my] right leg.

"That's a scar, all right. Now, the other scar!"

I removed my clothes below my hips and showed him another scar high on the thigh.

"That's a second scar, sure as blazes, young man. It represents action. There are a good many men who have served a lifetime in the army who would be proud to own those scars, sir."

"I am proud of them but not proud of the pain they caused me afterwards."

"Where did you get them, sir?"

"One was given to me at Independence, Missouri, and the other one at Prairie Grove, Arkansas."

"Very well, sir. Now, do you drink whiskey?"

"No, General, never have acquired the habit so far, can get along without it."

Then came a little pause and as before a light tapping on the floor with his cane. Indeed the tapping was almost continuous, only sometimes it was light, then again like a thundering climax.

"Believe when you first came you said the price to carry the mail would be ten dollars a day, the same price the two men have been paid heretofore. You would furnish your horses and stand your own expense at that price, sir."

"No, sir. Would expect you to furnish two good horses, the buckskin and the black, furnish rations every ten days and keep my equipment up."

"That's too much. Come in and see me in the morning at 10:00 sharp, You may go now!"

I had to stand like a steer in his august presence, because he never asked me to be seated. If there is anything in this world that pays in a trade it is being diplomatic with the man before you. For that reason I resolved to drive a hard bargain with General Bradley. His tapping on the floor with his cane nearly drove me wild. I felt as if I had escaped from a tornado after leaving his office. He seemed to be all Hardy Tactics.

In the morning of another day Meacham[6] and some others tried to discourage me about carrying the mail. They thought I was not equal to the work, but I answered, if General Bradley thought I was equal to the business he would give me the job, and he was the one that counted after all.

That morning at the appointed time I went back to General Bradley's office. We agreed on everything but the horses. General Bradley said: "You have horses, why not use them?"

"That is true, General," I answered, "I have horses, but they are small and slow and cannot stand the trips. Positively must have the best horses to be had, the ones that can run three miles, and three more miles on top of that, and then have enough endurance left in them to travel all night."

Then General Bradley called in an orderly, requesting him to bring in a lieutenant and a sergeant. In less than a minute they came in.

"Lieutenant," General Bradley said, "this man wants to carry the mail. I think he is too young, but he says he has served in the Eleventh Kansas Cavalry and has scars, Civil War scars, honorable scars!"

The lieutenant doubted that I had scars.

"I can hardly believe it, General. He looks too young."

Then General Bradley ordered me to show my scars to the lieutenant, which I did, which convinced the lieutenant. Both of these officers were careful to make sure they were scars. If there is anything an officer dislikes it [is] for anyone to deceive them, and at the same time, they have respect for a man who will stand in the line and hold the line.

The lieutenant said, "Honorable scars from the Civil War are pretty good. It's enough of a recommendation for him to carry the U.S. Mail, even among these Indians."

General Bradley turned to the sergeant. "This young man says he wants the buckskin and the black. Are they in good condition?"

"Yes sir, in first class condition."

"Very well, see that no one uses them but Mr. Hart."

"I expect you to go out with the mail," the general ordered, "tomorrow evening. You are not to bring any whiskey for yourself or anyone else to this fort. If you do, you will be discharged. You may go now."

I thanked General Bradley, then backed out of his office. Was afraid he might take a notion to hit me with his cane, because he seemed to be so angry over the buckskin and the black. . . .

The news spread that I was to carry the mail; several wanted to be the second man; I refused them, saying there was not going to be any second man. Called on General Bradley, and told him I was ready to go with the mail. He said to wait another day. The next day exercised the buckskin and the black, finding them satisfactory in every way. Could shoot off the black nicely, the buckskin was a little nervous when shooting off his back.

That day had a talk with Old Tex and Boyer about the route they used. They said the distance between the forts was called 90 miles, but in reality the route by winding trail away from the road was a good 100 miles. They were bitter against General Bradley, but spoke very nice about General [*sic*] Smith who lived at Fort Phil Kearny and was in command of the three forts, Reno, Kearny, and Smith. One trip would do for me, according to the old mail carriers, and I'd be mighty lucky to make that. "But if you do arrive at Fort Phil Kearny," they said, "and General Smith offers you a drink, don't drink much at first, then you will receive a drink from him every trip afterwards."

The buckskin was a real mustang, wide thin legs, high withers, long sloping rump, was about eight inches longer than the average horse, four black hooves and the telltale tuft of whiskers between the nostrils and upper lip. He weighed one thousand and ninety pounds. The black also was a mustang, but not quite as well marked; he was an excellent horse. Folks say that the Spaniards shipped this breed of horses to North America from Arabia, they are not natives of America. Fewer vertebrae in [the] back than other breeds. There were many horses that could catch the buckskin running a quarter mile, but few a half mile. In a pinch he could run eight or ten miles.

The Indians say, "If a horse has four white feet and a white nose, feed him to the crows."

I don't think a hundred Sioux could catch me, if I had a little start, with their grass-fed ponies. The black led up fine, his head beside my knee. I sat on the lead strap to test him; very seldom did he pull the lead strap taut. Decided they were a splendid pair for the business. The scout that trained them did a complete job of it, but the poor fellow left the trail one day, taking to the road, and was ambushed by the Indians. He did ride into the fort but died a few days afterwards.[7]

Right then I began to warm up to General Bradley. He loved those two horses. No wonder he objected to letting a man have them whom he considered too young and a stranger. There is something to a man who loves noble horses.

I went to the blacksmith at the Fort and asked him if he would shoe the buckskin and the black so as to leave a barefoot track. He said he would if I would stay with him and give him instructions. The shoes were made so as to be smooth, sloping all around back to the frog of the hoof where they gradually became thinner and were without marks of any kind. The nails were driven in through holes which were hammered smooth so as not to show nail marks.

Then a small shallow dent about the size of a dime was made in the right front shoe of each horse, the Crow foot sign, but not on the other shoes.

That evening General Bradley's dapper little orderly strode up to me and said, "General Bradley orders you to appear before him at once."

I wondered if another round with him would materialize, thought I might probably yet lose the buckskin and the black. I resolved to balk if these horses were taken from me as I went toward his office. When at his office to my surprise he said,

"Young man, why are you here at Fort C. F. Smith? Have you run away from something somewhere to hide from some mean thing you have commited? Quite a number of citizens here have an accounting like that."

"No, General, I am innocent and clean, and can go anywhere I please. The worst thing [I] am guilty of so far is the eating of a magpie cobbler on an empty stomach."

"What!" General Bradley yelled. "How dare you talk to me like that! I'll have you in the guardhouse, sir. Get out of here! Go out with the mail this evening!"

General Bradley's question was rather "hard to port" and likewise mine was opposite, but I noticed a slight pretense of a smile in his face that seldom smiled. I had made it a rule to always wedge in a ridiculous answer to all who plied me too "hard to port."

FIRST TRIP CARRYING THE MAIL

Hurried down to the cabin for my Winchester and revolver which were outside of the fort where I was staying with Charlie Smith. As I passed Tewksbury's cabin he hallowed out to me.

"Johnny! You are too much of a kid to be carrying the mail. You will lose yourself, the mail will be scattered and the Sioux will scalp you. . . ."

"Thank you, Mr. Tewksbury. I think you are under-rating me a bit."

Then strode on to the cabin. How Tewksbury always knew what was going on was more than I could fathom. He knew too much about other people's business. He always sprang his news at an importune time vexing his victim unmercifully. At the same time he would accommodate anyone in a pinch and was too liberal for his own good.

I went back to the fort and prepared to go out just at dark with mail. I was issued rations for myself and horses. Then in about a half hour I started on my maiden trip. The horses, saddles, blankets, everything, suited me well.

But just as I started General Bradley's orderly came out and stopped me. In a moment General Bradley to my surprise came to where I was. The General looked over my outfit, then said, "You need a good rifle scabbard and sling." He turned to his orderly, ordering him to bring me a new rifle and equipment. When they came, the General adjusted them to suit him and to my surprise found it was just right. Then he petted the buckskin and the black and wished me a trip free from Indian trouble.

I thanked General Bradley then rode out into the night alone. And one thought uppermost in my mind for a while kept knocking for solution. Behind General Bradley's unsmiling face and apparently cold and distant disposition lived a soul worthy of just consideration. And riding out there alone in the night I resolved to win his respect and hold it.

Rode about fifteen miles from the fort feeling quite proud of my landing this job at ten dollars a day and rations. Was aroused from my happy thoughts by coming to a place where two canyons came together at the foot of the mountains. I knew this place from what had heard was dangerous because one could be easily ambushed. Here the two creeks were sandy and the water ran under the sand, but about sixty yards below me was surface water. There were cottonwoods to the water's edge and numerous beaver dams. The trail led through this place about thirty-five yards.

This was a dangerous place to cross as one could be ambushed from either side or charged. As there were some tough characters at the fort who said I would not make the first trip, thought perhaps there might be other than Indians in this place this night, so I went away below and then rode up slowly, coming to a fairly good place where I could make my way through below the regular trail. I was glad to be rid of this place for the rest of the night. From here on I did not know the trails further than had been described to me. There was a reasonably straight trail on a bench at the foot of the mountains that led over half way to Fort Phil Kearny. This trail I found without much trouble and followed it all night.

The buckskin and the black were splendid, never nagging, neighing or whinnying and holding the trail faithfully. Then after a long time something on ahead loomed up; I could tell by the buckskin's actions about what it was. My suspicions were correct, as I came nearer, I made it out to be a bear which had been following the trail. Mr. Bear hung to the trail as long as he dared then left the trail to the left of me. The horses did not like the scent of bear.

After this I traveled at a good trot, now and then loping for a change, until the break of day, but never forced the horses along too fast as I wanted them to always have their wind. Then I left the trail and rode one hundred yards through the grass where the wind had blown all the snow away; then I turned back across the trail to the right. I dismounted and brushed out the tracks of the buckskin and the black. I did this to bother anyone following my trail.

Then I went up to the mountainside about three miles at an angle where I came to [a] four or five acre park. Here I dismounted, fed the buckskin and the black corn on the opposite side of the saddle blanket, and hobbled them in good grass for the day, where the wind had blown the snow away. I took the mail and a blanket and went up in the timber out of sight. I ate my lunch cold, as I could have no fire. I saw to it, I had a peep hole toward the horses, for if Indians were trailing me, when they came within sight of the horses, they would make a rush for them; the first one touching a horse, it would be his according to Indian law.

This I would see or hear. I would shoot two or three Indians to get my horses back, but not a whole bunch. If a large bunch came, I would take the mail on my back and finish the trip on foot. This was my plan, but I never had to do it. At noon I fed the horses corn and then went back to my hiding place. A little important sort of a bird took exception to me and chirped until he became tired, this was some company.

In the evening I fed the horses, watered and un-hobbled them to free their feet from the pull of the binding hobbles, as I had to have them nimble. My arm bothered me some, as I had slept on it doubled up all day, this so the arm would go to sleep afterwards waking me up and preventing too sound sleep.

Then I saddled up and went pretty close to where I had left the trail that morning. There I took a good look all around. I mounted and once more resumed my journey toward Fort Phil Kearny. Both nights were clear and a good moon, which was a lucky thing for me, as I had to not lose my bearings and keep in mind the description of prominent landmarks General Bradley had given me. General Bradley was right in every particular, he knew; I was gradually learning.

I rode all night once more, on and on and the faithful horses seemed tireless. About twenty miles west of Fort Phil Kearny the country was chopped up and rough in the foothills of the Bighorn Mountains, but there were game trails, so I managed to travel along quite well. Before daylight I noticed tree stumps and wagon roads. Down to Fort Phil Kearny I went on a keen gallop just as day was breaking.

They were surprised at the new mail carrier. All seemed glad to see me, but not half as pleased as I was to arrive safely. A corporal took me to General Smith's headquarters, where an orderly received the mail sack and sent my horses to the stables. Then the orderly said for me to come with him. He led me into a clean warm room, said for me to lie down on a mat and take a nap until General Smith arises for the day.

Laid down on that lounge and went fast asleep in no time. Later I was awakened and taken into an adjoining room before General Smith, who shook hands with me and asked dozens of questions. He ordered brandy, invited me to take a drink. I poured out a small opener. General Smith poured out for himself a nearly full glass, then said as he noticed my small opener, "That is a small opener, Mr. Hart."

"General, I never drink much, and this one is a big one for me."

General Smith was quite grey, had a nice smile and sociable ways, but I could see he had an eye that showed cunning and shrewdness; he was a leader of men.

"General Bradley must be hard off to send a boy out with the mail alone in winter," he said. "Aren't there men up there General Bradley could find?"

"General Smith, the men up there are too smart to take chances. I am older than I look."

"All right, I will accept your explanation provided it is verified later on," the General answered.

An orderly then took me to the mechanics' mess and showed me a room I could occupy while at Fort Phil Kearny. I had breakfast then went and took a look at the buckskin and the black. They were groomed in good shape, even their hooves were cleaned out, that pleased me.

"Pretty good horses you have," the hostler said, "and the shoeing is a new one on me." I went back to my room, leaving orders for the man to wake me up in time for supper. I was tired and worn out, that first trip was a trying one. I slept all day. I was wakened for supper, which I enjoyed.

After supper an orderly came down and said General Smith wished to see me. I went up immediately. General Smith treated me kindly; so did the officers; all sociable, all human, all plying me with questions. They wanted to know all about how I came by the mail carrying. There was no backing down, I had to come through and be nice in the coming. . . .

Once again Johnny was required to tell of his battle experiences and show his scars. The officers also looked at his horses' deceptively shod hooves. Colonel Smith made him a present of a fine pair of field glasses. Thereafter, Johnny describes the sutler's store, the place where soldiers with a little extra money could buy luxuries, drink, and gamble.

I had nothing to do so I walked around and visited among the people of old Fort Phil Kearny. The Post sutler store at Fort Phil Kearny had a large stock of nearly everything. He had a saloon 20 by 40 feet and about 20 card tables and homemade chairs and stools to seat one half of a company. A bar at the side. Several tables were running, the players playing for drinks, cigars, nuts and candy. The bartenders' business was to see that no one became boozy.

At the end of this saloon was another saloon for officers, well carpeted and neatly furnished. An enlisted man or laborer was not allowed in there. I knew Mr. [Jim] Leighton as soon as I saw him for he was the sutler of the Eleventh Kansas Cavalry during the Civil War. Mr. Leighton spoke very highly of me to all the officers. "Gentlemen," he said, "Mr. Hart will give good satisfaction carrying the mail, or in anything else calling for fearlessness, trust him." And that remark helped to set me up with the best of people in old Fort Phil Kearny, which proved a valuable asset afterwards.

Fort Phil Kearny was quite a large fort, nicely graveled, had a tidy appearance. Officers' quarters two stories high. Stockade all around it with two-story bastions on opposite corners placed so as to rake both sides with cannon. Barracks for over 2,000 soldiers, a little city. This fort was situated at the head of Big Piney Creek at the foot of the Bighorn Mountains. It had a home-like air, everyone doing nearly as he pleased to a certain extent. No one must become drunk. General Smith had good order there.

Rested three days, then started back to Fort C. F. Smith, arriving there on the morning of the second night. I could make this trip in two nights easily if I had no trouble. Had two quarts of whiskey for Major [*sic*] Burt and Captain [*sic*] Wishart. Now, this was against General Bradley's orders, carrying of whiskey, but Major Burt and Captain Wishart promised to stand between me and General Bradley.[8]

I talked with a major at Fort Phil Kearny about this whiskey business, and he said, "General Bradley will never say anything as long as you carry a small amount at a time for the officers. General Bradley has had a dreadful time lately with men indulging too freely at his fort, so is more prejudiced than usual against this whiskey nightmare. Accommodate those officers once in a while sparingly, for they have been used to nips all their lives. I see you want to obey orders, which is the best thing to for you."

Major Burt and Captain Wishart came down to the cabin outside the fort about nine o'clock. I gave them one bottle of the whiskey. They pulled the cork and smelled the contents and then there was a most pleasing grin on their faces. The captain's orderly was along. He it was that measured out the nips and kept them straight. This sergeant had been with the Captain from his infancy, and now taught and cared for the captain's children faithfully.

The Orderly would pour out the nips in tin cups for the three of them, being careful to have each cup exactly holding the same amount, this was to prevent quarreling between them and have all rosy.

While resting in my bed I could not sleep, they made so much noise; so I fell to watching them. They talked for a while and then about every so often the old orderly would spin the funniest of stories. Then after a while the orderly filled their cups to a certain height once more, all the same, even to a drop. When it came to nips the orderly was boss.

Then the nips were gone. They were a disappointed bunch of men.

"Why in the name of old Mike," Major Burt asked, "didn't you bring up two bottles, Johnny?"

"I did, Major, but this second one I will turn over to the orderly sergeant. He must put it in his pocket and take it to the fort and there later on give you men your nips, because if General Bradley finds this out he will discharge me."

"That is a wise idea, Johnny, the Sergeant will take care of us at the fort. And never have a fear, Johnny, we will take care of you and the General," Major Burt answered.

Out toward the fort they walked straight as a string and quite happy. Paid ten dollars for the whiskey in Fort Phil Kearny sutler store. I received twenty-five dollars for it at Fort C. F. Smith in the cabin.

In the evening I went up to the fort. While there, General Bradley's orderly strode up to me and said, "General Bradley orders you to appear before him at once."

This dapper little orderly always looked as if he had just jumped out of a brand new band box. His shoes were blacked, uniform fitting like a glove, cap just at the right position, and he would always stop of front of me in the correct attitude, being positive and precise. The same speech would be addressed to me each time.

I went toward General Bradley's headquarters, making up my mind on the way to refuse to talk about whiskey if he approached the subject. In the office the General talked a few minutes about the trip and the Indians. I was afraid he would side track on the whiskey business, so said to him,

"General Smith asked me where your men were, and said that you must be hard up to send a boy out with the mail."

General Bradley laughed right out good and plenty. I don't believe he had laughed that way before for years, even his orderly was surprised.

Then I continued, "I believe General Smith had a favorable opinion of me before leaving on the return trip."

"Yes," the General answered, "General Smith and others speak well of you at Fort Phil Kearny, so the mail states. You must keep straight and not lose your strut."

Then I received a surprise. It was: "Mr. Hart, please be seated." If General Bradley had knocked me on the head with his gold headed cane it would not have surprised me more.

"Now, sir," General Bradley proceeded, "What is this about your horses making a bare foot track with the Crow Indian mark on the right front foot." (He must have received a letter from General Smith.) "I fear you are not letting the old General in on your doings, sir." The buckskin was brought up and the General examined the shoeing and the Crow mark.

"That is a barefoot mark, all right. How did you learn this?"

"By observation, General, by having curiosity, noticing Crow ponies' feet and listening to their lingo about who owned a captured horse. If a party of Sioux trail me up, they are sure to notice the barefoot track and the Crow sign, thereby lessening one half of my danger. They will cease to follow the trail, because they will think a party of Crows passed that way."

"Well, you have succeeded so far quite well. You may go now."

What are we to make of this? These encounters are not reflected where one might expect to find them, in Bradley's own diary. But the diary also leaves some room for

Johnny as mail carrier. Here for the record are all its references to mail carriers, other than large parties, between the lieutenant colonel's first day at the fort, July 27, 1867, and his last, March 31, 1868:

> August 29, 1867: "Raphael [Gallagos] and Jack Stead came in it at daylight with dispatches from Phil Kearny and a bundle of private letters."
>
> September 10: "Started Jack Stead to Phil Kearny at 8 pm with dispatches."
>
> October 1: "Sent mail to Phil Kearny by Crow Indians."
>
> October 5: "Mail carriers returned from PK with mail."
>
> October 10: "Jack Steed came in tonight from PK with dispatches, letters, Indian Commission [news]."
>
> November 8: "Courier arrives today with mail from PK, bringing information that Lieut. Shirly's [Shurly's] train was attacked."
>
> December 3: "Mail came in from below at sundown, bringing letter and papers in abundance."
>
> January 8, 1868: "Richard came in last night with the mail carrier, having ridden from Tongue River, 60 miles."
>
> January 12: "Mail left for Phil Kearny with two Indians and pack horse. Very cold, but the Indians do not seem to mind."
>
> February 7: "Mail came up from Phil Kearny by special messenger."
>
> March 3: "Sent mail down to Phil Kearny."
>
> March 11: "Mail came in about tattoo."
>
> March 21: "Mail from Kearny came in at breakfast time."

If Johnny's tale is true, his first mail trip must have been after November 30, 1867, when Captain Burt arrived at Fort C. F. Smith. Does it speak in his favor that Bradley does not identify the mail carrier or carriers over the winter, with the exception of one mention of Crows—and that, for a couple of dates, he uses the singular?

The case for Johnny—or at least for a solo mail carrier—is reinforced by the diary of George M. Templeton. Templeton mentions mail carriers (plural) several times in 1868. But after his first mention of "Harwood" in January 1868, three more entries, all dated after Bradley's departure, have a man by this name traveling alone with the mail.[9]

8

THE MOUNTAIN CROW WAR DANCE

Most white people who had dealings with Plains Indians, it seems, responded with a mixture of contempt and horror. Private James Lockwood, a much-cited witness to Bozeman Trail events, is typical. Scathing about all Indians and their ways, he regarded all tribes as enemies; at a banquet given by the Crows, he felt compelled to vomit after discovering that he had eaten dog meat.[1]

Observers of another kind, knowing the Indians rather better, often found attractive elements in their societies. The guides and interpreters who facilitated the U.S. conquest of the West, many of them having an Indian parent or an Indian wife, were of this kind. Johnny seems almost to belong to this cadre of go-betweens. He had an ability to enter imaginatively into the life of the peoples who, in a larger view, he was helping dispossess.

Sometime in the winter of 1868, he found himself in a Crow Indian village.

When a war-party returns, the Crow Indians have a war dance. Each one [warrior] must show and act out with life and energy just how he executed each maneuver, and what he accomplished for his safety, and to be victorious, and in capturing and slaying his enemy. They were allowed to exaggerate somewhat, but not so far as to be utterly false.

The war dance was cruel, savage, unmerciful, lively and cunning, wild and terrible. If once witnessed in its original form it is never to be forgotten. It makes you writhe [with] lonesomeness for that which still is ripping through the blood of the human race. No one will be disgusted, but will see what manner of savage age we have just emerged from, in part or in whole. It is all conquering hero, all life and death; in which something had to die [so] that he, the warrior, may flaunt his efforts to the starlit skies.

Charlie Smith (his Crow Indian name Shaspoosa) and I were at the Crow village of Chief Iron Bull and Chief White Mouth one evening a little while before dark in quest of mules. The village was on the Bighorn River about five miles below Fort C. F. Smith. We were talking with Iron Bull. He was quite friendly with us, and [due to his] being at peace with the white man, we did not have to watch our corners very close.

Iron Bull and White Mouth did not have bands separately strong enough to protect themselves, so the "Old Soldiers" made them unite their forces for protection. Iron Bull had been to Washington, D.C., and to other places, so was easier to talk to than any of his people; so we stayed longer than we expected.

All at once this Crow village turned into a hubbub. Indians were hurrying for their ponies, all excited, all shouting, every Indian dog in the village barking; they seemed to have no end of dogs.

Five warriors soon started down the road pell-mell and on up into the higher hills and country. At that time I could not understand much of the Crow language of words, signs and grunts, and was thrown into [a] dilemma to understand what it all meant. Turned to Charlie Smith, who had been raised by the Cheyenne and could understand the Crow language as well as the Cheyenne. Asked him what it all meant.

"The Crows," he said, "have poor Indians amongst them who cannot go on the hunt unless they walk. It is the wish of the 'Old Soldiers' that they be supplied with ponies. A party of experienced warriors were sent out about a month ago to go and steal ponies from the Blackfoot Indians farther to the north, with whom they are at war. The 'Old Soldiers' say who is to go, and they always go: they have to.

"These warriors have communicated to Iron Bull through pickets which they always have placed out from their camp; and they in turn have sent the news here. They use smoke fires from one high point to another and communicate accurately.

"They know one of their warriors will never return. They know how many ponies they [the warriors] have and the direction they are coming from. The warriors who just left the village are going to meet them and escort them into the village. If you and I can receive permission to stay here, you will see one [of] the wildest war dances the imagination can conceive."

We received permission to stay and see the war dance, so prepared to make ourselves at home, though the Crows were not in the habit of allowing outsiders to be present at such times.

Young Crow boys, young maidens, young squaws and older squaws were busy gathering firewood which they piled in order, one large pile of wood in a large circle, then one little pile of wood and then another large pile of wood and so on. The Crows never have a war dance except at night. It was then below freezing, so plenty of firewood was a necessity, and also for light. From the look of preparations going on I thought there would be considerable of a blowout. . . .

In about an hour the warriors of the pelf party came into camp with the ones who had gone to meet them and escort them into camp a short time before. . . . No warrior of a great nation ever strutted with half the pride as these Crow warriors did, nor were they half so important.

Soon after the entire village had enjoyed a supper entirely of meat, the little piles of wood in the edge of the oblong circle were lighted, and now and then a large pile of wood. A large tepa was put up a little west of the north end of [the] oblong circle. All of the warriors were expected to come out of this tepa and enter the circle.

The medicine man of the tribe sat in a little wickiup directly north of the oblong circle. This medicine man had all sorts of things to represent his power of good and evil and the cure of ones when sick. He had bear claws, bear teeth, horse tails, beads, and dozens of other things arranged in weird forms. He was painted in horrible fashion. The Crows could not have this dance without the medicine man.

All members of the tribe soon were sitting on blankets or robes laid on the ground clear around the circle, and all had robes over them for it was below zero; the older ones nearer the center but outside the circle, the younger ones farther out. It depends on how large the tribe is, how large the circle shall be.

The chiefs Iron Bull and White Mouth and their advisers, the "Old Soldiers," were to themselves at the head of the circle near the large tepa. A slight attempt at honoring and crediting the most able members of their tribe. We were given the honor of sitting near Iron Bull this evening, but I think we were placed there in case some of his warriors went wild, as well.

To be respected by the Crows at that time it was well for us to be dressed a little neat. Both of us were even wearing a necktie and rings on each hand; also each wearing very large watch-chains which resembled a miniature log-chain more than anything else. Old Howard advised me to always go among the Crows spruced up a bit. "Then they will take you to be a man of some importance among your people and will show you more courtesy and respect; otherwise they will take you to be nothing but a filler of the race." We were following dear Old Howard's advice.

THE FIRST WARRIOR

Then in a moment one of the warriors of the pony-raiding party came bounding out of the large tepa and stepped into the large circle which had been cleared, and then into another smaller circle of tiny fires burning around him. This was on account of the extreme cold weather; generally this second small circle of fires is not used.

The warrior was finely proportioned, nearly naked except for breechclout over the loins and moccasins on the feet. He was painted on face, legs, arms, and body according to the tradition of the Crows. . . .

He walked around his little circle once, pretending to lead two ponies, trophies of his valor; then acted out the operation of walking miles and miles; for warriors on these expeditions are sent out on foot. After a while he became, Oh, so very tired, but kept at it unfalteringly. I believe he attempted to show he had the faculty of living on the fat of his body after all food had ceased, and afterward experiencing renewed vigor from this body's storehouse.

He hid around in all sorts of places, swam rivers, crossed mountains. So good was this performance [I] could discern the import quite well, and could at times almost see the difficulties he had to overcome.

Then he discovered some Blackfoot ponies and began to stalk up close to them, something like a wolf edging closer and closer to the sharp-eyed antelope. Over fallen trees and rocks he jumped, under other things crawled; and always behind something, and ever had an eye peeping toward his prey, the Blackfoot ponies, and for lookouts that may be placed in hidden places. He was nimble and wonderfully quick. When he became still he maintained a position nearly like a statue, no matter what position his body happened to be in at the time.

Then again, gradually, [he] would stealthily approach his prey, always out from behind so as to be immediately behind another, all the time making no noise. The cracking of the firewood was distinctly heard; otherwise the whole camp still as death. This warrior had to slay the herder of the Blackfoot ponies, so had to use caution while stalking him. The Blackfeet are the despised enemy of the Crows and they consider it no crime to kill their enemy.

At the right time and place up went his right hand to his quiver which hung on his back and at the right of his head, seizing his arrow, and as quickly pulled his bow back and whang, went the arrow (in imitation). Then he jumped like a cat, landing flat on his stomach clear to the other side of his little circle, then jumped almost straight into the air from the ground and ran around in zigzag fashion, jumping this way and that way over things, and in the midst of all this pulling arrows from his quiver and shooting them at the enemy in all sorts of positions; every second his movements changing. After every arrow had been shot from his bow he would jump somewhere; and all the spare time he had [he] was knocking enemy arrows from him with his bow.

Finally after going through a few more Herculean jumps and contortions in which the gait gradually increased, he lifted his bow strung with an arrow and then straightened up, still as a statue, eyes piercing an object in front of him: something had happened. Then he placed his hand to his lips making a high, keen, earsplitting tremolo yell, his hand all the while fluttering rapidly before his lips. It was the Crow war-whoop of death. He had won, but there were too many; a scalp he could not take.

All the tribe immediately afterward gave the same yell, after a signal from Iron Bull; all the Indian dogs barking at the height of their limits. This awful, savage, animal yell scared me a little, so bloodthirsty, so near the Stone Age, and terribly to the point it sounded. It was the worst kind of noise imaginable for the morals and the ear-drums.

That whole tribe under Iron Bull and White Mouth jumped to their feet, casting their robes aside, naked except for the breechclout. All jumped around giving their war-whoop, mixed, like a dozen brass bands playing the same tune out of time and key. Then in unison, all together; and this contrast hit us hard.

They carried the warrior around on their shoulders for a moment, all keeping a half-hop, half-step and jump. Even the little papooses unable to walk did their utmost to imitate the grownups. They had a kind of "tom tom" makeshift of drum for noise which was used at the right time. After this Iron Bull motioned for quiet. He looked over toward the medicine man. The medicine man nodded. It was all right, the medicine hadn't been broken and the Evil Spirit was still absent. Good.

Then this warrior picked out two old conniecotters (old squaws, grandmothers) and handed them each a small stick. One stick was round and notched at one end, the other square and notched at one end, which meant that a stick corresponding to the stick each one held would be found tied to the-pony's mane they were to have, a kind of bill of sale. This made two old conniecotters happy.

The Crows are very kind to their old people. They think a squaw that has borne into the world a brave warrior has accomplished something worthwhile, has not lived in vain. She is cared for, and is prevented from suffering hunger and want of a shelter.

Then a dozen warriors carried this warrior of the pony-raiding party around on their shoulders above their heads for a minute or two, a second time.

Three more warriors, each one in turn, occupied the little ring about twenty feet in diameter which was inside the large oblong ring. After each one had done his part, these Crow Indians edged a little more and more into excited animals. But the three had ponies to give to their poor. . . .

THE LAST WARRIOR

This warrior bounded into the little circle and walked around once, pretending to lead one pony and carrying a buffalo robe which he laid down at the edge of this circle on the ground. He was painted more hideously than those before him, if possible. The Crows thought he was something beautiful: big, high, to be honored beyond the rest.

He went through some of the same maneuvers and contortions in some respects as his predecessors had; but with variations, and the difference [that] he had to battle two Blackfoot warriors, whereas the others only had one at a time and were prevented from getting scalps.

In one of his maneuvers, this warrior had to climb over a rock while fighting a Blackfoot in front of him and one behind him. In short, a kind of a running fight in which his right hand went to his right shoulder to his quiver for arrows about fifty times. He jumped from his rock onto something that must have belonged to the cat family, judging from the splendid imitation of a wildcat's snarling, spitting, growling. . . . He did this while in motion, jumping all over the ring lithe as a panther.

But then he was an extra skillful warrior; having to fight two Blackfoot and an animal of the cat species all at once and at the same time; a warrior indeed. Then on all fours he scuttled around the circle, then in an awkward difficult position, whang: went his bow string and swish: twirled the arrow straight in front of him. Then to fighting the wildcat, and quick he jumped to the other side of the circle, shooting an arrow to his rear. This arrow to the rear went home, for his hand went to his lips, producing that awful Crow war-whoop of death.

Then he jumped to his buffalo robe, pulling from its folds a Blackfoot scalp. He threw this scalp straight up into the air, uttering at the same time an unearthly yell. When it came down, he seized it and commenced to gnawing and biting it like some kind of an animal not of this world.[2]

The whole tribe gave the war-whoop in unison, followed by one in non-unison. After which the warrior threw the Blackfoot scalp to the people of his tribe, uttering that horrible yell with a climax of a dog bark deep down in the throat. All the Crows would bite that Blackfoot scalp. . . . Even the little papooses would touch that scalp and do their utmost to give the war-whoop and execute the scream. . . .

They were at the point where they were hard to control, and that is the reason Iron Bull and White Mouth placed us close to them. If the band turned slightly wilder they would be apt to kill us then and there.

THE MOURNING FAMILY

The member of the expedition that was killed by the Blackfeet was being mourned by his family. Squaw, daughter and son, they set fire to their tepa, and then started out to a little knoll nearby to freeze to death in the severe cold night. They wanted to go to the Happy Hunting Ground so as to be out of their misery on earth. Their warrior, being scalped, could not enter the Happy Hunting Ground. Because he fought and lost, his family felt disgraced. . . .

Some of the braves put the fire out before it gained much headway, thus saving their tepa from destruction. These braves then went out to the little knoll carrying buffalo robes which they wrapped around these mourners. The mourners had slashed and beat their bodies with rocks, their faces were covered with their own blood, a pitiful sight. They chopped their hair off in patches, leaving humps and hollows, splendid for horrible ugliness.

And as the braves carried them to their tepa, they were muttering all the while, a cold wild moan-yell of sorrow deep down in the throat, then louder from the lips. According to tradition of the Crow Indians, the blood must not be washed from the face, out of respect for the missing one. It must be left there to wear off through time.

We went on the fort. Charlie Smith was not bothered at all; he had been through this thing before. I was quite upset, such as savage thing as this being beyond my capacity to understand and enjoy pleasantly.

9

TWO DANGEROUS PRANKS

Johnny's impetuousness, he reports, got him into trouble frequently, often at the expense of the friendly Crow Indians. Neither the admonitions of brother Hugh nor the threats of Lieutenant Colonel Bradley seemed to have any effect; the young man often followed the lead of his half-Indian friend Charlie Smith.

Some of the officers at Fort C. F. Smith wanted blacktail deer meat and offered an extra inducement for supplying the demand on short notice. I knew where a herd of black-tailed deer had been ranging some distance from the fort and were easy to land. So Charlie Smith and I started out for them as a side issue, thinking to be out only a short time.

We were riding along leisurely back to the fort in the evening. We were somewhat disappointed, for the black-tailed deer had entirely vanished, to parts unknown. We were hungry and our horses were beginning to show signs of becoming weary. We had to be content with an empty haul. So I suggested to make camp somewhere in the willows below us where we could not be seen by passers-by from the trail.

We were at the junction of two canyons running down from the Bighorn Mountains, which were dry now, but raging torrents in the spring. The particular place was called Warm Spring Creek. Here I was rather nervous, as [we] were close to a well beaten trail, but the place below and all around was covered with a dense growth of willows and a park now and then. It was a pleasant place to camp. There were numerous beaver dams. The busy beaver had dammed up the spring water that flowed from the rocks below us, making themselves a home.

Down in this place we selected a site where the smoke from our campfire would not likely be seen if caution was used, as it was getting quite dark. A small fire gave us an opportunity to warm our feet and hands, and the horses had a chance to graze their fill of the best grass on earth excepting it was a little dry by the blasts of winter. . . .

We were silent for a while, then up on the hillside, coming down the well-beaten trail above us, we heard the sound of horses' feet. A whack, a pat, and then a thump, for Indians always keep hitting their ponies. They were Indians sure, but what kind? The principal question that concerned us was, were they Sioux or Cheyenne? We were still for a few minutes, which allowed the party, whoever they were, to come directly opposite us. Charlie Smith suggested he go and find out of what tribe they were. Then quickly, like a wolf, away he went on all fours up through the willows clear to the trail before they had time to pass. The Cheyenne had trained him in this sort of running.

Soon afterward he came back to me still on all fours so quietly I had half a notion to be scared. "The Indians passing are Crows," he said, "so have no fear this time." This was quite a relief; the Crows were friendly. We were in the direction from the fort where Sioux where known to be some of the time.

I had been practicing on the Blackfoot war whoop once in a while around the fort some weeks before this, Charlie Smith being the tutor. I never could put the wild sound into the war whoop as an Indian can.

Knowing the Blackfeet were on the war path with the Crows and not giving a second thought on what we were doing, or the consequences, I filled my lungs and gave the Blackfoot war whoop the best I could. Thereupon Charlie Smith brushed me aside, himself giving the true Blackfoot war whoop in its original form.

On ahead up that trail this yell sank in deep in the marrow of that Crow warrior's bones and his two squaws there in the twilight on ahead. And before the sound of Charlie Smith's voice had died away we could hear the whack, whack, of their ponies feet slipping over the rocks and pounding the well worn trail.

Really we were more scared than the Crows, for each of us knew full well that Sioux and Cheyenne were in the vicinity hunting for white man's scalps. Occasionally a small band of Blackfeet would be prowling around as well. Very rarely, more than a dozen of them were ready and prepared to kill all members of other tribes, more especially the Crows. The Blackfeet did not have as good control of their members as the Crows over theirs. Though the Blackfeet never were at war with the white man in the vicinity of Fort C. F. Smith, yet at the same time they would steal everything they could lay their hands on and kill everyone they came across without mercy. These bands were renegades, especially the *five Blackfeet* who always went together and never ambushed an Indian. They were after the white man.[1]

We mounted our horses and started down the well worn trail after the Crows. As soon as we came near enough for the Crows to make us out, instead of stopping, they tore faster down the well worn trail. The more we urged our horses, the more they urged theirs. In a little while this thing degenerated into a kind of race for the welcome protection of the fort.

We soon began to see blankets, trinkets, and all sorts of Indian things along the trail. We, not being very far removed from our teens ourselves, took the cue like a school kid and started to fool these Crows good and plenty. It was plain they were really scared and taking us for the dreaded Blackfeet. Charlie Smith gave the Blackfoot war whoop every little while. The poor Crows whipping their ponies for all they were worth and riding the life out of them as well were expecting a death without quarter.

Not long after this we overtook an old squaw who, on being pressed pretty hard, left the trail. Immediately afterwards her pony fell down. The squaw was not hurt. Never in all my life have I heard such unearthly screams of distress and groans as came from the throat of that old squaw. No living man can make a scream of death like the female. It seemed to me to be like "the breath of an infant and then like the blast of a tornado." Complete opposites. I told her we were not Blackfeet and were going to the fort. Then the pandemonium of screams coming from her throat ceased. She then squatted on the ground in a sitting position and bent her head forward, which signifies, kill me, I cannot stay fate.

She was a frazzled looking old squaw, all torn and scared and at bay. She made a few angry grunts of displeasure and watched us like a lioness in her cage. Her pony still lay at her feet as if dead, so Charlie Smith dismounted and made the pony stand on his feet; then the pony, out of disgust, began to snort, that being the only thing left for him to do. The other Crows on ahead, hearing her screams, supposed that the Blackfeet were dispatching her to the "Happy Hunting Grounds," we judged from the increased whipping of their ponies.

On to the next squaw we rode, on coming close, she immediately commenced the same kind of an unearthly scream; only this squaw seemed to have three throats and worked them all at once under forced draft, so rapidly did she repeat. On coming closer she rode her pony out of the trail and kept pulling her pony's head around so as to keep away from us. This caused her pony to whirl around and around and not make much headway.

Soon she jumped off her pony and ran to his head, all the time keeping up that unearthly scream. She was so scared, she did not know what she was doing. The scream of this squaw was in another key. It was penetrating. It held such a variety of meaning, in its wild thrills and overtones, carrying death, fear, and the last call. All animals know its meaning and import, even the educated man harkens to the call.

Charlie Smith told her we were white men and would not harm her, and were going to the fort. She stopped her screaming and began to moan and see red in turns. Quickly from her pony's head she strode and started in on us in a mixture of Crow and English for our benefit and punishment. In these days it would be called a lecture. She made faces at us, called on her Indian Fathers to give us as feed to the wolves, and raised both her arms pointing them at us, crying:

"White man heap no good! All the time scare squaw, squaw know what to do. No brave man fool squaw, only cowards do that. White man some day scare too much! Kill! You not know much as papoose, year before papoose know anything. You cold! Like moonlight!"

Then after the old Crow warrior we rode. Our horses being grain fed were more able to make time than the Indian grass-fed ponies, so we could crowd him to the limit. But the old Crow warrior had by this time gained considerable of a lead on us; however after some minutes the distance began to shorten. Soon we could see his whip or his arm coming down on his pony in rhythm. The moon then rising gave us a little more light enabling us to see plainer.

Now and then along the road we began to pass more blankets, for we were on the Government road by this time. Then came arrows, ropes, piece of leather, chunks of venison. And then a saddle blanket and finally a white man's saddle which the old Crow warrior had somehow loosened from his pony on the run. How he loosened the saddle from under him on the run is a puzzle.

On and on we urged our horses until the distance became some hundred yards between us and the Crow warrior. Then Charlie gave him a few more of his Blackfoot war whoops and all the time we could see the Crow's whip coming down on his pony regular and timed. It still looked less than a mile to the fort, we dare not chase him too close. Our chances were good to catch him, but his were better to escape to the fort authorities than ours.

We then lessened our speed. By the edge of the road I spied his old Enfield musket. I dismounted and picked up his treasure of a musket. An Indian who will throw away his musket has to be pretty badly scared, he sticks to that to the last. But he, like the squaws, expected to be killed by the Blackfeet, whom he took us to be. Circumstances were against us, we could not catch the old Crow warrior and escape scot free. He, much to our chagrin, rode into the fort and to safety. Then trouble commenced, for the soldiers were ordered out, not many, one company, for General Bradley wanted to keep the Crows friendly. Guns were fired, everybody rushing into the fort from the outside as if twenty thousand Sioux were storming the fort.

When this happened we were very sorry for what we had done, but it was too late to make amends. The moon became pretty well hidden by clouds which lessened our chance of being discovered, so we rode around to our corral which was on the outside of the fort under the welcome cover of dark shadows, hoping to be spared the pain of being caught and punished by General Bradley.

After enjoying a warm supper Hugh prepared for us, our tongues were loosened; from him we never had any secrets, at least myself. So to him we related our adventure, and at the conclusion he said, "I am afraid the two of you will run into trouble. Why do these things John? But where, tell me please, did you get such an old type of an Enfield musket as that leaning against the wall by the door?" I brought Hugh the musket. Then Hugh commenced:

"Boys, these two weasel skins hanging from the breach of this warrior's Enfield musket are to make his musket look pretty, and these pieces of brass hanging from the barrel are for beauty. These rows of beads of different colors on a string and wrapped around the stock are in imitation of a rainbow, because their colors correspond in the order of the rainbow. These brass tacks driven into the wooden stock without any semblance of order denote how many hunks of black-tailed deer he has jerked and laid away for winter. This mark resembling the beak of an eagle is his signature and notifies all people this musket belongs to Crooked Arm. You remember him. These little straight marks near the trigger with the half arrow, three in number, are evidence Crooked Arm has taken three scalps and the scalps are Blackfeet.

"The sight at the end of the musket had been broken off sometime in the past during an awful engagement with the wily Blackfeet, so the old Crow warrior found a chisel or something and pounded up another sight from the end of the barrel. He was at the time a mighty mechanic, even if he did hammer the sight to one side. Therefore this musket is more apt to shoot to one side than straight ahead. It served the old Crow faithfully, but how could he persuade it to shoot straight ahead in a pinch?"

"Stop your description of the musket, Hugh," I interrupted. "You will be apt to make a mistake about some of the fine points of that old musket."

"Yes, John, you will want somebody to show you how to run straight in the morning when General Bradley sends his orderly for you to come to his office."

This next morning we were up bright and early, had enjoyed a good breakfast so were feeling quite happy and contented. Was praising the good points of the old warrior's musket more to tease Hugh than anything else, for he was quiet and peaceable. We were interrupted by a knock at the door.

"Come in!" we shouted.

In came a soldier from the fort. The old Crow warrior, he said, told a fine tale, all about how many Blackfeet he had killed and wounded, and what a running fight he had to make for his life. How they had torn his two squaws to pieces before his eyes, and what a heroic stand he had made for them. That there were hundreds and hundreds of Sioux outside the fort and Blackfeet hunting for Crows.

We had quite a few visitors that morning, were becoming quite popular. It ran along until about ten o'clock when the old Crow warrior we had chased into the fort last night came in. He told us all about how brave he was and dozens of things we knew he never did. Finally he said, "Me go." He walked toward the door, at the same time happened to notice his old Enfield musket leaning against the cabin in the corner. We had forgotten to place it out of sight. The old Crow warrior stopped still as a statue for a moment, his eyes riveted on his pet Enfield musket, then gradually began to edge up closer and closer, actually stalking his own gun for the time being. Finally gazing up and down the length of the Enfield musket with his nose about a foot from it and both legs spread out, so as to brace his body if he should happen to become scared through some unknown witchery.

Then all at once he seized his Enfield musket, turned it over and over, squirmed and wiggled around and stamped his feet, first one then the other. He was so angry he could hardly see. I was afraid the old musket might be loaded and if so it might mean trouble for some of us. An Indian that was as angry as he was then would be apt to do anything under the sun on the spur of the moment.

The old Crow warrior turned around and strode straight to me, mad as a fighting bull that has been goaded beyond endurance. He stepped directly in front of me making a guttural grunt and a kind of growl, which gradually grew louder. Several times he repeated this kind of a grunt before me. He was so angry he couldn't seem to manage his talking apparatus. Soon, however, his tongue loosened, and then he said,

"You white face! You know all, last night! Me catchum pretty soon, pretty soon heap scared! . . . You killum my squaw, One Eye! You killum my run-like-deer squaw, Deer Foot! Takum my buffalo gun! Pretty soon heap big chief come! You tremble like a leaf, go down!"

And off to the fort he strode trying to take five feet at each step and grunting angry grunts to keep his outraged soul company.

"Now," Hugh said, "you are in for it, John. Better behave yourself after this. General Bradley's orderly will be down here in a few minutes. Have you anything that must be arranged before you have to be locked in the guardhouse for a couple of months?"

"No, Hugh, the world is all set for me. I have no rebuttal testimony."

In about twenty minutes, as we expected, down came a dapper little orderly from headquarters. Straight into the cabin he strode and right up in front of me, and said, as he clicked his heels together, "General Bradley orders you, Johnny, to appear before him at once."

Then the dapper little orderly turned on his heel and strode back to the fort. He was like a bantie [*sic*] rooster, only a thousand times more important. But for all that he was pretty much of a man.

So that settled it. To disobey meant that Hugh and I would have to leave the fort. We were making money, the picking was good, we liked the life, and especially the hunting and trapping. Never in all our lives so far did we feel the joy of living so well. We could sleep like a baby, and had an appetite akin to the hungry maw of a threshing machine.

General Bradley at times was a very erratic, nervous sort of a man, sometimes slightly overbearing. When angry he was in the habit of forcing his wishes upon you whether you liked it or not, it made no difference. He always kept tapping the floor with his gold-headed cane, sometimes lightly, at other times viciously, according to how he felt, when talking to you. And you had to watch him and the cane, and not differ with him, lest a rap on the head he would give you, free of charge, with that cane. It was this tapping of the cane on the floor which annoyed all that came before him, more than the man.

The minute I walked into his office the first thing he said was: "How did you get in trouble again?"

"I wasn't exactly in trouble, General."

"How many squaws did you kill last night? Do you know what I am going to do to you? Explain, and be quick about it!" And each question he asked was punctuated by three or four vicious taps of his cane on the floor.

"Never killed any squaws last night, General."

"You never! You mean to tell me that?" the General shouted.

"Yes, sir, I do. We rode up to the two squaws, told them we were not Blackfeet, and it was all right, so far as I know."

"Are you telling me the truth?"

"Yes, sir."

"How did you come into possession of the Crow's gun? Tell me that!" the General commanded, feeling sure he had me fast.

"Picked it up beside the road and brought it in with me. Thought perhaps it may be a Hawkins rifle, but it was an old Enfield musket."

"Are you telling me the truth?"

"Yes, sir."

"Did the Crow shoot at you?"

"No, sir."

"Did he shoot at all?"

"No, sir."

"He tells me that he did."

"He never fired a shot, not one."

"Are you telling me the truth?"

"Yes, sir. I always prefer to tell the truth in trouble and out of trouble."

"You do, eh?"

For a little while the General pounded the floor with his cane. I believed then, and still do, that the General was trying to keep from smiling. Then he twisted his face up, once more becoming fierce and domineering, and ordered me to tell him all about the affair from beginning to end. . . . When I finished, he said:

"You are always stirring up trouble between the Crows and the whites. The Crows boast they have never taken a white man's scalp, and always have been at peace with the white man. Now if they make war on us there will be trouble. Can't you see that! Can't you see if trouble starts all the other tribes will likely join in?

"Now, if I ever hear of any more of your pranks around this fort, [I] will order a file of soldiers behind you, and march you off the reservation. That's all, you may go now."

And he tapped his gold-headed cane until I was out of sight and hearing. I escaped from that scrape better than I expected. General Bradley would give anyone all the leeway he could providing they stuck to the truth. It was the opposite when they tried to hang it over on him. He was more fair than hundreds of people I have met before and since. . . .

That night I went out with the mail. The night was dark and dreary and I did not feel much like traveling. I was somewhat out of tune with my world, so did not care much what happened. Everything I attempted to do went wrong, or slipped my fingers. Something just had to go wrong every so often.

MY WOODPILE, GUNPOWDER, AND THE CROWS

For two weeks I had been bothered by having my wood stolen more than usual. Had the wood chopped in lengths for cook stove and fireplace. A family of Crow Indians were the culprits. They were living close to our cabins in a tepa, and the head of this Crow family was known as Long John.

[John] Tewksbury had three cabins and a corral built along the edge of a hill close up under the fort's protection, but on the outside. By permission from General Bradley I could join my corral with that of Tewksbury and make a comparatively tight enclosure, which then I thought would keep out those troublesome night marauders from my woodpile. General Bradley granted my request and so Hugh and I built a new corral, but the wood still vanished.

One morning the gap in my woodpile was more than I could stand.

"It's no use, Hugh," I said. "We will have to build a new cabin with a heavy door and keep it locked night and day, if we ever expect to have any wood for ourselves."

"I have thought of a scheme," Charlie Smith said, "which will stop Long John and his outfit from stealing your wood, if you boys can furnish a brace and bit."

"And what is that?"

"Suppose, boys," Charlie Smith answered, "we bore a hole in the end of a stick of wood and then fill it with powder, just enough to scare them pretty good, enough to make them afraid of the wood."

Hugh, the cautious, objected to this thing. So we made a compromise whereby I was to build a new cabin, but in the meantime was to go on with this powder and wood business sparingly.

So Charlie Smith and I rustled a brace and bit and bored a hole eight inches deep in the end of a stick of stove wood that was six inches in diameter. Then we opened an Enfield cartridge and poured the powder into the hole in the wood. Hugh said that was enough powder, but I didn't think so, so I opened another cartridge and poured its contents into the hole on top of the other charge.

It didn't seem to be very much power, as the hole was so large. Then we plugged the hole up tight with earth and a piece of cloth. We were afraid the stick would burn up and do no good, so I bored another hole with a gimlet bit nearly into the powder from the side about four inches from the end of the stick. This was somewhat dangerous, but I took the chance. Then we twisted a string and run it into the hole close to the powder. Both holes were then plugged up on the outside neat and clean, so they would not be noticed. Then we laid this fine prepared stick of wood on the woodpile in a conspicuous place, so that anyone prowling around there for wood would be sure to get it.

Then, as it would be dark pretty soon, we went into our cabin and commenced to prepare our evening meal. While busy at this, Charlie Smith found time to go out and examine the woodpile. Soon he came back smiling. "The loaded stick of wood is gone," he said.

Charlie Smith and I ran out of the cabin and around the end of the cabin to where there was a large rock and some poles. We jumped on these and from there on to the top of the cabin, which was roofed with earth and was flat on top. In the meantime Hugh stayed in the cabin keeping the supper cooking for us; we waited on the roof for the commotion sure to come.

We had not been on that roof more than two or three minutes when out from the old Long John tepa next to us about one hundred feet away shot a flame of fire, coals, and wood, as if shot from a cannon, in one grand swish and boom.

The next instant we could see Indians crawling out of that tepa any way they could. Some wiggled and crawled out from under the edge all around in different places next to the ground, others bolted, hitting the sides of the tepa and yelling. Finally two [Crow] soldiers came running out of that tepa and one of them was holding his hand over his eye. The Crows were making considerable noise. The Bad Spirit was working.

Once outside of that tepa and the Crows finding they were still alive [they] began to collect in bunches. The old squaws were grunting and talking, very much excited, for it was beyond their comprehension to understand how wood could blow up.

Three little papooses were groaning as if they would surely die. Not crying, for a papoose is not given to cry. He is taught and partially inherits the tradition that only conniecotters and squaw men cry. He has nerve from his first Indian cradle. The condition of the little papooses excited all the more the old squaws, so they made all the additional noise they could. It was well for they too had received some of the flying splinters and kept rubbing their eyes, both angry and scared at something they did not know.

We could see two little Crow maids who had their hands bruised from the way they favored them, also, one old Crow warrior had his nose bleeding and made a wonderful amount of groans, grunts and spirit noise. He kept repeating, "Long John is killed, Long John is dead!" and limped on a foot that wasn't hurt at all.

The tepa was in danger of burning up, so the two soldiers commenced to put the fire out, and then all the Crows tumbled to themselves and helped. In a short time the fire was under control.

Then around the two soldiers the Crows gathered. And from the action of a squaw pointing to our cabin, we surmised, the soldiers were telling them the cause of the blowout and who the guilty parties were.

Right away over to our cabin the squaws came. They asked for "Shaspoosa," which was the name the Crows gave Charlie Smith, and once in a while we would hear "Masta-cheata," another name for Charlie Smith, but these two last words were Cheyenne, meaning white man.

They were very determined to find Shaspoosa, that was quite evident. Hugh told them Shaspoosa had gone out somewhere, maybe down the Bighorn. The squaws came into the cabin and looked everywhere for him, even in cracks too small for a mouse, their search was very painstaking and thorough. They were telling Hugh all the while, he "lie, white man fool too much, squaw mad. This time catchum Shaspoosa!"

If they had known at the time Shaspoosa and I were on the roof of the cabin, I think very likely Shaspoosa would have had to make a run for the fort, as the Crow squaws were so very angry and wanted him only. Then too we dare not strike back at the Crows so near the fort.

Then as the squaws could not find Shaspoosa they went back to their tepa, but they were not satisfied. They gave the impression that they believed Shaspoosa was hiding somewhere, and that Hugh lie, fool too much.

It was comical seeing so many Crows coming out of that tepa in all sorts of ways, all sizes and ages and all yelling and grunting in turns. We struck a laughing streak when we started to talk it over.

And as each Crow recovered his poise, the first thing [they sought] was something to fight with. They had "blood in their eyes." They wanted to go on the war path; they wanted to kill the Bad Spirit that had made the wood blow up and the White Spirit that coaxed the white men to act so bad.

That stick of fire wood had too much powder in it, for it blew up everything in sight, but at the same time it accomplished a little good, as it removed some dirt along with the skin from the faces of the Crows. And there is no loss without some small gain. So we were getting even with the Crows at the woodpile's expense, together with a little fun and excitement. That stick of firewood was too thick and strong. It's a wonder that some of the Crows were not seriously injured.

In about fifteen minutes all the squaws came back to our cabin, asking as before for Shaspoosa, but we had him safely hidden outside of the cabin. In the cabin the squaws came looking everywhere again for Shaspoosa but without success. They were brave when it was all right to be brave. They told Hugh: "White man lie, forked tongue, no good to fool! Kill Shaspoosa! Make earth shake!"

"Shaspoosa good," Hugh answered the squaws.

Then the whole bunch of squaws gathered around Hugh, all shouting and grunting and making as much of a jumble of mixed noises as a band of excited coyotes. It looked for a minute as though Hugh was going to have to endure a drubbing.

"Lie! Lie!" they kept shouting. "No good white man, fool with papoose, squaw mad, killum!"

Then the angry squaws went away. Hugh was very much relieved. The squaws had upset a bucket of water on the floor and other things were in bad shape, so that Hugh had to clean house.

That evening we had quite a jolly time joking each other. For the Crows blamed everything on Shaspoosa, while General Bradley was sure to blame everything on me. Hugh always came clear. I suppose it was because of his slow going, quiet way. We used to envy Hugh because no one bothered him; he had so many friends.

Always everybody addressed Hugh as Mr. Hart, while the rest of us had to be content with plain Johnny, George, or Jim. We argued that General Bradley's orderly would come down in the morning for Hugh, as it was his time to "walk on the carpet."

The next morning about ten o'clock down came General Bradley's orderly. The same little fellow who sometime when he was a kid forgot to grow. He was very important to a civilian, but on the whole was a splendid fellow. Straight up to me he strode just so and so and so precise. He reminded me of a turkey gobbler in his pride of strut. He said: "The general orders you to appear before him at once!"

Up to the fort I went soon afterwards having for consolation the Godpseed of my companions.

Immediately on entering General Bradley's office, [I] was greeted with a savage scowl and eyes that fairly snapped. A few rapid punches on the floor with his gold-headed cane as a preliminary, and then the storm broke over my head.

"It's been just two weeks since you were here for fooling with the Indians! How long will it be before you are in here again? Are you in partnership with the Devil?"

These remarks were flung at me in an angry jerking fashion, and after each remark an imitation of dance music on the floor with his gold-headed cane, which bothered me in spite of all I could do.

"No, sir, not in partnership with the Devil."

"Well, there is something crooked some place! Why did you blow up the Crow Long John's tepa down there last evening? Out with it!"

"General, the Crows were stealing too much of my wood, which it costs me too much, so concluded to scare them a little, but did not intend to have any of them hurt. Put too much powder into a stick of wood. Some of them were skinned up a little, is all."

"Skinned up! That's what you call it, is it? Suppose they would have only been skinned up, if you had killed some of them. Are you telling me the truth?"

"Yes, sir."

"And by telling the truth will not be sick afterwards, young man!"

"Cannot say as to that, General."

"Be quiet, I'm talking! Now begin at the first of this thing and tell me all about it, and don't you lie to me."

I told him the story straight and when I had finished, General Bradley said, "You make plans to be rid of Shaspoosa, and better plans to improve yourself. The next offense of any nature you commit, I'll order soldiers to march you off the reservation. That's all, you may go now."

I was glad to get out of General Bradley's office, as I had to stand so long it wearied me. General Bradley was like Napoleon in the standing business, because he always made everybody stand in his presence, no matter how long the interview lasted.

10

CAPTURED BY THE CHEYENNE

Shortly after their arrival, Johnny and Hugh had purchased some horses belonging to the notorious Montana Militia, an outfit that began partly as a scam and finished as a minor insurgency.[1] Johnny relates the background rather clearly.

In 1867, the officers of the Territory of Montana asked for a militia. They, or perhaps others, circulated the story that Indians were coming over Bozeman Pass into Gallatin Valley and would kill everybody. So they organized a regiment of militia as a guard to camp on the Yellowstone River. These men bought horses for seven and twelve dollars and sold them to the Territory at fifty dollars, and the same rate of profit in like proportion in everything. The men who served were to receive $5 a day. In the fall, the high authorities discharged these men, refusing to pay them anything except promises. . . .

Captain [Robert] Hughes wanted the men to be paid, so had had all the horses and mules of a whole regiment, some 250 head, tents, wagons, and everything else turned over to him. He then moved the outfit across the Yellowstone and out into the hills, then sent word he would keep the equipment until all men had been paid on the Yellowstone.

Hughes sold the purloined stock wherever he could, including at Fort C. F. Smith. Later, however, the government caught up with him—and the unwary purchasers.

One afternoon about three months after we had bought our horses from Captain Hughes of the Montana Militia, Captain Wishart of Fort C. F. Smith called on me saying during a conversation, a deputy sheriff from Virginia City [in Montana Territory] was at the fort, and in the morning would gather up all the horses branded M.M. and sell them to the highest bidder.

Charlie Smith and I concluded to take our horses, Captain Wishart's one and two of Hugh's, and all of them M.M. horses, nine besides the ones we were riding, away as soon as it was dark to the village of Chief Blackfoot, the Crow chief, on the Little Bighorn, now called Custer River, about twenty miles northeast of Fort C. F. Smith.[2]

As soon [as it was] dark, Charlie and I started for the Crow village, each one of us leading one horse with the others tied each to the tail of the one in front of him, divided into two leads, Charlie and I. Horses can be handled this way to perfection, they cannot get away from you and seldom cause any trouble.

We arrived at the Crow village about two o'clock that night. I was riding in the lead when nearing the tepas. I noticed some of them had fires in them and that they were painted in imitation of war scenes. The Crows never paint their tepas, something was wrong.

My hair commenced to rise all over my head. The fear of something [I] could not understand gripped me by the throat, and there was at least twenty half wolf dogs barking near my feet. I concluded we were in a Cheyenne or Sioux village, so started to turn around, then every Indian in that village gave the Cheyenne war whoop.

At once there were two Cheyenne to every dog all around us. I was pulled from my horse, this way and that way, up and down, around, over and across nearly as fast as lightning strikes. Was nearly naked except underclothes before I touched the ground. It was worse than going through a Dutch mill on short notice, a mighty lively performance while it lasted.

Things for us were happening fast and furious about that time. We could not tell which way we were going among those savage Cheyenne breakers. To be roughly handled, robbed and made nearly destitute of clothing while tumbled about in the air was a new experience [I was] very seldom forced to endure. Once in a lifetime.

These Cheyenne did not want to kill us then and there for some reason. Charlie Smith experienced even more rough treatment than I from the looks of him.

Their chief shoved us into a tepa; no Indian will kill you there. It is not according to Indian justice. The Indian that breaks this law is doomed to death and loses his chance of ever gaining the Happy Hunting Ground, and has no appeal to alter the law, it is set and irrevocable.

Then a Cheyenne chief asked me in broken English what I wanted. I thought instantly of a yarn to tell him.

I told him I came from Fort Phil Kearny and the Great Chief General Smith sent me to him asking for peace. Of course it was a lie, but had to say something, and could not make my mind work out a better answer, I was so excited, scratched and bruised.

The chief slapped me in the face, and said, "Lie! Lie!" Then he placed his fingers over his lips, then pointed them at me, the first and second fingers pointing outward, forked: a sign in Indian language for liar, two stories, different, like the forked tongue of a snake. I had to repeat this statement several times. The chief knew I was not telling the truth, but he wanted us to talk, thinking to find out the truth after a while.

Charlie Smith whispered, "Stick to your story." He had given up at the start and sat down. This band of Cheyenne were not the ones that raised him. He knew that, if there was one Cheyenne among them who would recognize him, these Cheyenne would make his life short in a moment, once outside the tepa.

The Cheyenne raised the sides of the tepa and came in all around us. The old secondary chiefs were kept busy keeping the young warriors from beating us black and blue. One old thin-mouth-and-nose chief would slap the young warriors on the head good and hard when they ventured too close, and for fear of that slap they kept out of his way.

The Cheyenne built three or four fires outside [the] tepa and we were taken out there. Thought it was roasting time and wondered how I would stand it. They had a trial in Indian fashion. The chief first was determined to make me tell the true reason why we were there. It was up to me to stand some torture before death concluded.[3]

And then [I] noticed quite a number of Crow Indians standing around. One of them I knew, we called him Limber Jim. To him I said in a casual way, "I want Blackfoot. Blackfoot!" Blackfoot was the leading war chief of the Crows, and I had known him since my Army days.

Then two half breed squaws came up to take a look at us. I looked at them expecting a little sympathy, as they were dressed up so fine in the heighth of Indian style and fashion.

But no, these squaws laid down on the ground and commenced kicking up their limbs and feet and yelling, "Kill a paleface! Kill a paleface!" This performance worked up the young warriors to white heat, so it was all the old chiefs could do to keep the young warriors from killing us then and there. When an Indian becomes excited his thirst for blood has no bounds.

Just as soon as quiet was restored, the old thin-mouth-and-nose chief gave those two half-breed squaws a good licking and thrashing. He was just as severe on the squaws as on the warriors. Then he made a very able talk for an Indian which lasted about five minutes. This talk further quieted the Cheyenne, so that there was less and less ammunition.

There was an awfully ugly, bony warrior who persisted in kicking and slapping me every time he got a chance. He worried me so, the wish came to me, to be in a position to make him want to run and keep running. Never in my life wanted to straighten anyone out as bad as I did this fellow.

This old bony warrior had a knife in his belt, and knowing the end was near became desperate, so [I] thought I would seize that knife and stab him and a dozen more before they could kill me, as this would be better than burning to death. I was silently watching [for] my chance, pretending to be looking straight ahead, but all the while keeping a shadow of a look to the side of me.

But some of them were watching my eyes. They guessed my plan. Four of them seized my hand and arm and pulled it over my right shoulder, then drew my left arm around my back, tying my two hands together behind my neck. This was painful. The old bony warrior got a whack from one of the old chiefs which made him keep at a distance. This punishment given by one of his own people gave me a small amount of comfort.

RESCUED BY CHIEF BLACKFOOT

In a few minutes after this I noticed there were at least two Crow warriors to every one Cheyenne. The first Crows I had noticed earlier I supposed were visitors, but now that idea was different. A ray of hope, the Crows would save us. In a moment the tall stately form of Chief Blackfoot was before Charlie Smith and me. He looked like a prince then, the best man of blood and flesh I had ever seen, though we were by no means unacquainted.

I quickly told him we had started for his village of tepas, and wanted to stay with him.

Blackfoot and the Cheyenne chief commenced a spirited conversation and argument, in which Blackfoot told the Cheyenne chief in no uncertain terms, white man coming to see him, and he would protect white man. "You no kill white man tonight! We are many, you are few! Me know what to do!"

There both sides stood with drawn bows and arrows and a few old guns.

Every Cheyenne was covered, all up close. The Cheyenne were quick to realize their position, they dared not move. Then the Cheyenne chief lowered his head which was the signal he gave in, he was not the victor. He remained with his head bowed until Blackfoot grunted. . . .

Blackfoot then started forward, untied my hands. By now the sharp pain in my right shoulder was making the sweat run down my face, even if the cold air around almost was freezing, as nearly naked as we still were. As soon as my hands were free, the cowed Cheyenne chief lifted his head away up high and soon was as pert as before, though he was careful not to do anything that would make the Crows angry.

Then I told Blackfoot all about our trip and why we came.

"Humph!," he grunted. "Me right! You right! Come to my tepa."

Then quite a number of the Crows crowded around us, while a goodly number still guarded the Cheyenne. The Cheyenne were singing their war songs. They still disliked to give us up, but the Crows would have killed all of them if they had tried to match their strength in battle. As there was about thirty Cheyenne warriors and about three hundred Crow warriors, the odds were overbalanced.

The Cheyenne had given us up because, according to the Crow method and law, the tribe can always claim the ones coming to see them, be they friend or foe. And, second, we did not know the Cheyenne were there, so were innocent in coming into the Cheyenne village. But I think the point that drove home our release was the greater number of Crows. The Crows claimed us as their guests, but nevertheless the Cheyenne were furious; they had missed a splendid good time and a dandy war dance.

The Cheyenne had camped close above the Crow village that evening before dark to trade with the Crows, as the Crows could buy supplies from the fort over and above their annuities; the Cheyenne, being at war with the white man, could not buy these things except through the Crows. The Crows who told Charlie Smith and I where their village was did not know the Cheyenne were there, as they had left for the fort in the morning, and the Cheyenne had come in afterward. A Crow Indian will not describe to you a location and leave anything out that will cause anyone to suffer disappointment.

Halfway down to the Crow village, Limber Jim, my Crow friend, motioned for me to sit down, which I did. Then he pulled off his moccasins and helped me to get them on. Limber Jim was an excellent friend, one worthwhile, both in trouble and out of trouble.

It was still winter, and walking along in the snow barefooted was not a very pleasant thing to be forced to do. We were lodged in Blackfoot's tepa, which was large and roomy, and served with cold boiled meat. I wasn't very hungry, but the happiest fellow in the world, for I held four jacks and the cuter.[4] . . .

CHIEF BLACKFOOT RECOVERS MY PROPERTY FROM THE CHEYENNE

We went to sleep in a cozy corner Blackfoot selected for us. Late in the morning we were awakened by hearing the noise of Indians going about outside the tepa. We had slept as sound as a log the rest of that night, but my arm pained me now and then where it had been pulled over my shoulder nearly out of joint.

After a breakfast of straight boiled meat, Blackfoot unrolled a blanket. The first thing he pulled out was a boot of mine. He held it up, and at the same time making a grunt, which was equivalent to asking, "Is this boot yours?"

"It is my boot," I answered.

Blackfoot then handed the boot to me in a certain way and position, or it may break the good medicine. This method was rigidly held to throughout until we were dressed once more in what was left of our own clothes. Everything had to be held up by Blackfoot until he grunted before we could claim a single thing. All my things were returned except a pocket knife, so I thought would not say anything about that, as it would stir up more trouble for all concerned. I was very glad to get back what I already had.

Then dear old Blackfoot took us outside to a place where all our horses were tied, and where there was a warrior guarding them. With the horses were all our blankets, bridles, ropes, saddles, and five hundred Enfield cartridges for the old muzzle-loading Enfield rifle that I was taking out to give to the Crow Indians. Blackfoot insisted the cartridges be counted so we would know whether any of them were missing, which was done to please Blackfoot. There was none of them missing. Blackfoot would make the Cheyenne come across even for one cartridge.

I was greatly surprised. If there was anything the Cheyenne wanted just then it was powder and lead. We had thought everything lost that morning, but as guests of the Crows, the Cheyenne must not rob us. We had to look the horses and ponies over to satisfy Blackfoot.

I gave Blackfoot one pony and Charlie Smith did likewise. Blackfoot was not very anxious to accept them as gifts, but after our insisting he accepted them, making his bow of the head and neck accompanied with a grunt, his method of thanking you and at the same time showing you respect.

Blackfoot then untied the ponies and led them to another tree where he tied them again. It wasn't long after this, Blackfoot traded them to other members of his tribe for two old ponies apiece, making four ponies, which he gave to four poor old conniecotters (grandmas) that had no ponies. These old grandmas were very much pleased, they chattered and grunted and made signs to each other like four little girls enjoying their first great treat in life. Blackfoot to them after that was almost as great as the Great Father of the Happy Hunting Ground.

Blackfoot lived by what he thought was right, the thing to do. He had to think in order to decide hundreds of things every month. He was a savage and he was primitive, but he had arrived at a point where the whole of existence for him was to think out the right thing to do as he saw it and understood. So while we slept so peacefully in his tepa he was busy gathering our things from the Cheyenne for us. No one was more faithful than Blackfoot, even if he was an untutored American Indian.

All chiefs of the Indian tribes were the best, ablest, most brave and even-balanced of the Indians. The chiefs were not absolute rulers, as they were accountable to the "Old Soldiers" or "Old Chiefs" for advice and had to pay respect to councils.

These few facts aroused my curiosity, so [I] commenced to learn all I could about the Crows, their methods of handling knotty points and their governing methods.

There follows a lengthy section on tribal customs. Whether or not all of this information was gathered at once, the amateur ethnographer seems to have grown quite familiar with this alien society—and to have been more than a little attracted to it.

The Crows have lawyers in their humble way who settle all disputes by quoting former rulings of great chiefs, and by stating their client's case in the same, and the opponent will claim it is entirely different. With the Crows the Old Soldiers have the final say in everything. It's a good thing, as it keeps an Indian from wanting to run everything and own everything.

I noticed that morning. while [I] was busy learning Indian law, an Indian brave standing on top of a small knoll. I asked Limber Jim what it meant. The thing seemed a little odd as the brave always stood in the same position and never moved.

Limber Jim said, "The young brave was guarding the ponies which were out browsing around among the willows for something to eat, but he tired of his job and came in before [he] was relieved. The punishment was to stand all day in sight of camp from sunup until sundown. He was never to sit down, or turn around, or change position. It was a severe punishment."

About one third of the young braves were detailed to be with the pony herd when they were turned out to grass. Blackfoot's tribe of Crows were rich in ponies, which was due primarily to Blackfoot's shrewd business ability. All ponies are driven to the Crow village at noon and braves detailed to take them out in the afternoon. In the evening all ponies are driven in and are kept in camp, where they can be guarded against thieves from stealing them overnight.

In the evening the Old Soldiers order the young warriors who have ponies to go out at daybreak and ride around the village to learn if an ambush of the enemy has been placed during the night; and also to seek a place to pasture their ponies when they are turned out. The whole country close by must be looked over before any Indian dare turn his pony out.

As a last resort the Old Soldiers are absolute masters over the war chiefs and all other members of the tribe. They say when to move camp and where, when to provide a retreat among timber when a three days' storm is coming, and they always know about these storms in advance. They watch the birds, the animals. . . . They whip with an Indian whip the warrior who does not provide meat for his family, and see to it that the old grandmothers are provided for.

The Mountain Crow Indians have strict rules and laws. All the Old Warriors, or Old Soldiers, as they were then called, and some of the leading young warriors, hold a council on every leading subject and event. Their decision is final and from it there is no appeal. The Old Soldiers say where they are to trade. Select in advance a week or two ahead a camping ground when intending to travel. None but the warriors can leave the village without permission and even they cannot go away very far, or long at a time.

The Old Soldiers order at a certain time, or any time if the supply of meat runs short, for every family to jerk meat against an hour of need. This is to prevent a famine and so they may survive for another year.

They take a buffalo, elk, or blacktail deer hide and fold it like squares before it becomes hard and dry. It is folded about three feet long, two feet wide, and one foot in depth. The hide is folded lengthwise so it will have two covers meeting across the top, and likewise at the ends. It is then packed full of jerked meat, enough, with care, to last five or six Indians for a month. Then they sew this package up tight with thongs, tying it finally in the middle with a peculiar hard knot, which answers for a seal.

Any Crow ordering one of these hides filled with jerked meat without orders from the Old Soldiers will be whipped with an Indian whip by one of the Old Soldiers. It makes no difference who the guilty party may be, man, woman or child. A young sturdy warrior will take his whipping gamely, even though he could tear the Old Soldier to bits. This whipping disgraces an Indian more than any other punishment given him. It hurts his feelings, his standing, his associating with others and brands him as a whipped man for a time.

The Old Soldiers give orders in the evening usually to eight young warriors (depends on size of the tribe) to go to a point two or three miles out, sometimes six miles out, from the village in the morning, east, west, north and south. Always two together to look for the enemy before turning their ponies out to graze. These warriors are supposed to go in advance of the ones spying out near the village. The pony is the Indian's principal wealth, therefore, caution is used to prevent surprise and capture.

If [the] report comes to the village [that] the field is clear, the ponies are turned out excepting a few which are held at camp until noon, when they are replaced by others until evening. Young Crow boys not yet rated as warriors herded the ponies during the day. An old warrior would go with these boys every time. If any danger, several warriors would go with them. But always there would be a few warriors scouting around the outer limits beyond the herd of ponies to be on hand against an attack or surprise during the day.

This Crow village was in a good many respects like a military camp. The ponies were brought in at noon and herders changed and [the] herd returned out to the commons to graze in the afternoon. Nearly every day hunters were sent out to bring in meat.

The Mountain Crows faithfully cared for their old people. The grandmothers were entitled to receive their share of meat from the hunt, and were treated kindly and respected according to Indian customs.

When one of their members became sick with fever, the Old Soldiers would order braves or squaws to drive stakes into the ground about eighteen inches high. Upon these a temporary bed would be lashed. A trench perhaps a foot deep would be excavated in which a small fire would be kindled at one end to burn among rocks. The patient would be stripped naked, placed upon this temporary bed and covered with blankets or robes reaching to the ground.

After a while water would be dashed on the hot rocks in the trench which caused steam to rise under the patient, but there was no fire under the patient. This steam would thoroughly sweat the patient. Then after a time the patient would be taken from his vapor bath and rubbed down, after which a splash of cold water would be thrown on him, and again rubbed down. Usually the patient recovered, providing care was given him of the right sort and he had a good condition. But this treatment killed those suffering with smallpox.

If one of their number suffered with rheumatism and he desired to take the Indian cure, it was given to him. An Old Soldier would detail about six young Indian boys to help cure the patient. The patient was laid on a blanket against the ground, or something solid which would not give. Then the Old Soldier would take hold of the patient and secure his promise to obey him completely during the treatment.

The boys were then ordered to walk and sometimes jump on the patient's aching joints and muscles, arms, hips and limbs. The joint or muscle that hurt the most, the boys jumped on the hardest. The patient would groan and occasionally yell in an agony of pain, but he would hold fast to his promise given to the Old Soldier. This treatment usually cured the patient, at least his joints were loose and pliable afterwards.

The Indians can tell two or three days before a storm, especially one of those three days' storms (blizzards) which Montana and especially Fort Phil Kearny is subject to. Beforehand the Old Soldiers select a place to set up their tepas among trees and willows where shelter can be had to some extent and where the force of the terrible northers' windy blasts will lose some of their fierceness.

The Old Soldiers tell each family where to pitch their tepas, where to herd or keep their ponies, and how much meat and wood they must have. They make preparations with the wisdom of old experienced sages. They have learned this lesson well, they began it, how long in the past no one knows.

When the three days' storm strikes in all his might, the Indians fare quite well, for they have prepared beforehand. When their ponies become hungry, as they are sure to be during these strikes of the northers, they have to eat willows and the bark of trees. The Indians hack down small cottonwood trees for their ponies to browse on in case there is nothing else left, and that is better than letting them starve. But the squaws do most of the hacking of trees for the ponies. The Indian considers that squaw's work.

The Indian knows how to prepare better than the white man for these three days' storms. He has had to learn how for thousands of years.[5] He is schooled in the business. He lives in the open. Will die cooped up in a house.

If one Crow warrior kills another, which is a rare thing, an Old Soldier arrests him, relieves him of his bow and quiver, or rifle, knife, or whatever his killing instruments are. The Old Soldiers would then give him a fair trial according to Indian methods. He could give to the family of the murdered Indian a pony or two. And if they accepted all would be settled, nothing more would be said or done concerning the matter.

Or, if he said he had to kill to prevent being killed and, therefore, was not entitled to pay anything, and if the Old Soldiers thought he was justified in killing in self defense, they told the tribe so. But in that case if peace was not established between families and in the village, he had to go and live with another tribe of Crows if they would allow him to do so.

But, if he absolutely refused to pay anything, was nonchalant and didn't care, the Old Soldiers turned him loose while in the village. He was supposed to leave the village and never return, an exile.

On the other hand, if the murdered warrior's people would not come to the trial, or council, that meant they would not compromise, [they] intended to kill him. If he had to leave the village and home tepa and no compromise reached, he as a last resort could appeal to the Old Soldiers, offering to run the gauntlet stark naked, as pay for the murdered warrior, which if permitted by the Old Soldiers to be administered by the whole village, would clear him of all guilt.

In this case all members of the village who desired to take a hand in the affair lined up in two long rows facing each other. They were placed about four feet apart in the rows, each one having a stick, whip, or something handy to strike with. Down this narrow lane the guilty one must run.

The members of the village were instructed by the Old Soldiers to not draw blood while the Indian ran the gauntlet, and especially to not hit the running Indian over the head or eyes. Nevertheless, the bad Indian came out at the tail end covered with blood, staggering and weak, and it would take him some time to recuperate.

However, if the bad Indian was knocked down while running the gauntlet, he could not be whipped any more. The Old Soldiers would step in and stop things, as to knock him down was not according to rules. This treatment being so severe it usually made a good Indian out of him afterwards, providing the wicked devil part of him did not overlap his good points too far.

As stated before, these Mountain Crow Indians are under strict Indian military rules. They have their chief, the Old Soldiers' council, the advice of experienced warriors, all of which say what shall be done and in what matter. They settle all disputes concerning the welfare of their tribe, but the Old Soldiers have the final say from which there is no appeal. There has to be some semblance of order to curb the stubborn overbearing members. There has to be a kind of military rule to prevent other tribes from annihilating them. . . .

If you had at any time in the past rendered the chief a service, or one of his tribe a favor, he will remember you, and will in your hour of need afterward give his life for your benefit if such had to be. They believed in returning a favor. Once you had fully won their favor in genuine earnest, you possessed that from them until the crack of doom. Not all Indians are good. Some there are that will kill for the pleasure of killing, will steal and rob. But all races of man have the bad breed mixed among them.

It is difficult to shoot a rifle accurately without resting the barrel on something. Nineteenth-century cavalrymen usually dismounted and lay down to fire. Then as now, it was something of an art to shoot without such support, or "off-hand." As part of their exchange of favors, Johnny claims, he taught Chief Blackfoot this skill.

The second day felt fine, though once in a while my right arm pained me when I attempted to raise it too high, and that arm never was what it should have been afterwards. That was one thing the Cheyenne did for me when I wanted to get even with the old bony Cheyenne that kept kicking me.

Blackfoot showed me his rifles and a bunch of trinkets he valued very high; some of them were mere trifles. I looked at everything he showed me with the utmost interest, as to do otherwise would offend him. We were his guests and as such must be as game as he was for us.

The rifle Blackfoot used the most was what we called the Hudson Bay musket, a light flintlock that carried an ounce ball. Blackfoot showed me how he loaded the musket. He poured in a charge of powder, then a ball of wiregrass rolled up hard was rammed down the barrel on top of the powder, then the ball was dropped down in the barrel. This was followed by another ball of wiregrass to hold the ball in the barrel. No one could do accurate shooting with this musket.

The other firearm was a fine rifle that had been given to him in Washington, D.C. He had only two bullets for this rifle left. It was necessary to take this rifle apart and clean it. He had been shooting this rifle the same way as the old Hudson Bay smooth-bore musket and had it badly leaded. I managed to pull the bridge pin out, showing Blackfoot how it operated, how to care for it, its use and how to keep it in order.

Blackfoot did not want me to work with his rifle, but after he understood a leaded rifle wouldn't shoot accurately, and that it was in bad condition otherwise, he gave in. He watched my every move with intense interest, and once in a while he grunted a long grunt, which means "You do right, you no fool." When the rifle was in first class shape, I handed it to him. He was well pleased.

Then I sorted out a bunch of Enfield cartridges. I molded at least one hundred bullets for the rifle. Then I placed a target one hundred steps from me and fired five shots off-hand at the target. The Crows considered the shooting good, as any one of the shots would have killed an Indian standing there. But I was like the fellow that executed something excellent accidentally, I surprised myself, so I said I could do that all day long.

Then I persuaded Blackfoot to load the rifle as I did, and always taking care to patch the ball, and insisted that he shoot off-hand. Blackfoot had a good steady arm and hand, so in three days' practice he matured into a good shot. He was the proudest Indian in camp. Couldn't thank me enough.

I gave Limber Jim twenty cartridges and a good skinning knife, all the other Crow warriors four cartridges apiece, and the balance to Blackfoot.

Seeing a chance to get even with the Cheyenne who bullied him, Johnny once again showed his lack of impulse control—and found himself answering to an authority figure.

While walking around the Crow village I later noticed a few Cheyenne warriors visiting the Crows and trading with them. I spoke to two of them. They shrugged their shoulders, straightened up, would take a step or two away and stare at me like a savage beast, showing their utmost hate for a white man, and make a coarse growl deep down in their throat.

So after that I would not notice them if I could avoid it. I don't believe there is any species of man that can hate like the North American Indian. The fact that the Crows received annuities from the Government and could go to the fort and buy anything they wanted placed them at an advantage over the Sioux and Cheyenne, therefore it became necessary for these Indians to trade with the Crows. This position was gradually making itself felt among the warring tribes of Indians.

The next morning, when we were strolling around Blackfoot's village, [I] noticed two Cheyenne earnestly trying to strike up a bargain for some powder with a wealthy Crow warrior. We were primed with mischief that morning, and I soon noticed [that] the Cheyenne trying to strike up the trade was the old, ugly, bony Cheyenne that had delighted in kicking me so when in their power. That fired me to energy.

"Charlie," I said, "you gather a small rock or something and throw it at that ugly, bony Cheyenne when he stoops over. Be sure to hit him good and hard in the region of the seat. He is the one that wanted to kick me to death. I will keep watch so as not to be seen, and when I grunt throw your rock and be sure to throw it good and hard."

In a moment the chance came. I grunted. Charlie's arm swung around and away went the rock swift and fast like a bullet. Ka-punk it landed square on the ugly, bony Cheyenne's caboose.

That old, ugly, bony Cheyenne jumped straight up into the air and yelled. He turned around and around and kept yelling. He placed his hands on his seat several times, but he never stopped his commotion. Thought was shot. And while he had a little pain then, [he] believed [he] would have more presently. At any rate something had happened to him. "White dog kill me!" he shouted. "Kill a white dog!" He was very much insulted, very much hurt, and he said so.

He bumped into an Old Soldier just as he came out of his tepa and the Old Soldier knocked him down, to stay down for a while. After that there was commotion everywhere. Charlie Smith and I cleared out to Blackfoot's tepa because there is no telling what might happen. We had mixed into something our saner reasoning would have prevented, now it was too late. But we never thought of the consequences afterwards.

The Crows prepared for business if the Cheyenne intended to make trouble. The Cheyenne were not powerful enough to have much say with the

Crows, and that was the thing which stayed action then and there.

Blackfoot questioned us about the affair. We could not fool with Blackfoot. So we told him we did throw the rock in the direction of the Cheyenne, but did not intend to make a commotion and believed he was not much hurt, that we did not knock the Cheyenne down or touch him at all, that the bony Cheyenne was the one that tried to kick me black and blue when they had me captive, that we were willing to pay for what trouble we had caused.

"Cheyenne mad," Blackfoot said. "Bony Cheyenne heap bad. Heap no good. Someday him die to stay dead. You stay away. You pay for trouble, good."

The Cheyenne went to their village and would not come near again as long as we stayed with Blackfoot.

RETURNING TO FORT C. F. SMITH

A while after that I noticed some deer hides folded into squares and tied with a peculiar knot. These hides or hide boxes contained jerked meat which had been packed away against a time of need. The Old Soldiers were going around and opening some of them, taking out a certain amount and then tying the hide box up again with their peculiar knot and seal. I wondered what they were doing that for. The Crows seemed to be making preparations to leave or something. So I asked Limber Jim what it meant.

"The Old Soldiers," he answered, " say there is coming tonight a three-day storm. We move to the cottonwoods and willows. Everything go with us. Ponies live on cottonwood and willows three days. Squaws cut down cottonwoods for ponies when ponies get hungry. If you go home, go now, go fast. Old Soldiers know. If you want to stay, all right, plenty good."

We had visited with Blackfoot four and a half days and this three days' storm so near woke us up. We cut short our visit without much ado and started back to the fort in broad daylight in the afternoon. Blackfoot promised us the Cheyenne would not follow, they would attend to their main business.

On arriving at the fort I learned the fort people knew all about our terrible experience with the Cheyenne. They were as pleased to see us whole and alive. We arrived about twenty minutes before the three days' storm broke in all its fury.[6]

11

LIEUTENANT COLONEL BRADLEY ASKS A FAVOR

The next two days I spent in building another cabin for wood. We had plenty of room in our large cabin of two rooms, but according to [my] agreement with Hugh about the woodpile and the stick of stove wood that blew up the Crows, I had to make my word good with him.

While busy with this new cabin General Bradley's orderly came down to where we were working outside the fort. The orderly walked up to me in his proud fashion, stopping and standing upright as an arrow in front of me. "General Bradley," he said, "orders you to appear before him at once."

A few minutes later when I walked into General Bradley's office I found him in a pleasant mood for once, and this was somewhat of a surprise, his usually severe attitude absent. He commenced with:

"You, sir, will go out to Fort Phil Kearny this evening and take with you General [*sic,* Colonel Johnathan] Smith's nephew. [I] want no objections, the thing must be done."

"I will do it, General, but the risk is great, as I think this nephew cannot stand much of a jaunt."

"Very well, sir. Now here is another item. Here is a wallet Mr. Brown of the freight outfit of Wells Fargo Co. gave me. He said I was to return it to you after a certain length of time providing no one proved ownership together with an accurate description. No one has described it up to date, so I am returning it to you with its gold contents. Its quite a find, something like $800. Mr. Brown told me you found it a few miles below Fort Phil Kearny. Is that true?"

"Yes, sir."

The day was a warm cheerful day, one of the kind that makes us want to live a life eternal. Did not want to spoil it all by going through the night on a mail trip to Fort Phil Kearny, but orders had to be obeyed. And taking this nephew of General Smith's still further clouded the prospect of my trip. This young fellow was a renegade, not much good for himself, a kind of a would-be tough, and at the same time a fellow harboring within his mind the ancient god of fear, especially when the Indian menace stalked too close to all around us. Yet he had been a splendid fellow sometime, but now was the captive of whiskey and gambling and some other things.

He had come down to Fort C. F. Smith from the Gallatin Valley farther to the north. He was a great source of annoyance to the officers at Fort C. F. Smith, so they persuaded General Bradley to nearly force me to take this nephew down to Fort Phil Kearny where his uncle General Smith was in command.

Young [Al] Smith had never ridden in a saddle before to any great extent, at least not lately. He was fleshy and not used to exposure. To have him with me was considerable of a burden and the thought of his safety worried me from the first. I wanted the officers to give him a good horse with an easy gait, but young Smith wouldn't have a horse. He wanted a mule, so a mule he rode to Fort Phil Kearny.

Everything being ready, we started, the sun long since having gone down and the dark night coming in over our heads. Young Smith looked so large and clumsy after he had mounted his mule and rode out to the gate. I begged him to go back and take a horse, because of his stout condition, knowing that a horse can travel better, faster and easier than a mule, but this plea availed me nothing; he would have his way.

We had traveled for perhaps ten miles; and seeing that we were not making time, I commenced to urge my horses a little more, and asked him to do the same. Then for a time after that all seemed to be fine. After I crossed the creek and trotted my horses around a small hill, thinking we were making fine time. On looking around and behind me, young Smith was nowhere to be seen.

Just then from around the little hill I heard young Smith commence yelling for me not to leave him. He couldn't find the crossing. [I] had to go back to him and help him cross the little creek and scold him for yelling. Told him it positively would not do to make a noise of any kind, that an Indian may hear and that would be all up for us.

"I don't care," he answered. "I am not going to be left behind," [reminding me] that I had orders not to leave him.

"Well, Mr. Smith, I am running things here and you are not, so if you do not want to be left behind, keep up close to me and keep the mule coming.

I am not going to run into trouble on your account. I will leave you if necessary."

For another hour we traveled pretty good. Then in going through some timber and crossing another creek, young Smith again fell behind and again began yelling. This time I gave him some pretty straight talk, because one or the other of us had to be captain and give the orders. After this less trouble.

His ankles were paining him quite badly and he could hardly sit in the saddle without being unmercifully chafed. I dismounted and cut the government stirrups or tapaderos so he could slide his ankle partly into the stirrup instead of the toes as before.[1] Then I wrapped cloth around his ankles to prevent them from chafing any more. I arranged his clothes and the saddle in a more convenient position for him.

Then I scared him with a story of the cruelty the Indians were in the habit of dealing out to white men and especially those as stout as he was, and how one time the Indians actually scared a poor fellow so bad he ran away and never stopped running.

"Where is that fellow now, Johnny?" young Smith asked.

"He is away off somewhere a-running yet, Mr. Smith."

"But a person cannot run forever, Johnny!"

"Any man can run forever, sir, especially if he happens to be scared until his eyes pop out of their sockets."

"I will keep up with you, Johnny, but just now I don't know whether I'm sitting in a saddle or a hard rock."

This talk of Indian scare helped, for after that young Smith kept up until daylight.

I was about a couple of miles this side of where [I] usually made a detour into the hills, so I had to hide the horses and the mule among some trees and feed them their rations there. We went down to the creek and washed up for the day. We ate a cold breakfast, as it would not do to make a fire. Then went away a distance from the horses and the mule where I spread a blanket on the ground for young Smith to sleep on and another one for myself and using the mailsack as a pillow, as the mailsack had to be with me always.

The day was nice and warm, for a wonder no wind, plenty of sunshine. We lounged around, slept and rested, but young Smith was so chafed he couldn't sleep to any great extent. I felt rather lenient toward young Smith as I knew he would have the time of his life when we started again at dusk.

There is something peculiar about a man out like this; after a while he became alert and uncommon watchful, like a wild animal, or a dog that seems sleeping, yet half awake. A kind of hidden sense that people in cultured surroundings do not have. So that was the way of my day sleeps. Then a bird flying near roused me, or a squirrel, anything; even a scent entering the nose had an effect. Always wide awake in an instant. For the time [I] was primitive in a measure by force of surroundings.

Never forgot to double up my arm under my head so it would go to sleep. In reality this doubling up of the arm caused the free circulation of blood to be retarded, so that, in about so many minutes, the arm would begin to tingle and cause me to waken. This was to prevent me from sleeping too long at a time.

Along in the afternoon a noisy bird began to twitter among the limbs of a tree over where young Smith was trying to sleep. Smith made more fuss than the bird, but the bird didn't seem to be much afraid of him. The incident aroused me, as young Smith had begun to talk too loud. Young Smith wanted to have wings when he passed over the divide, so he would not have to ever ride a horse again.

Again it was growing dusk, another night coming and soon we would be on our way once more. We were saddling the horses and the mule when young Smith suggested we stay another twenty-four hours. I objected, telling him that [at] any time the Indians may discover our trail, and that a night's ride may mean a world of difference in the next twenty-four hours.

"That's all right," young Smith answered, "these animals are shod and any old Indian can follow a horse that a blacksmith has shod. If they are going to follow our trail, there is nothing we can do to prevent [it]."

"For your own satisfaction, Mr. Smith, lift one of my horse's front feet and examine his shoeing, also notice that the mule is barefooted." I made a short explanation for his benefit.

"Well," he said, "you will do. General Bradley should turn everything over to you, and let you run things, as you are now running me. No one after associating with you a while would have any use for a seat, even in a house of worship. I'll have my uncle put you in the guard house for 90 days when we get to Fort Phil Kearny, if we ever do."

Then we mounted and followed the trail that has no end at night, Smith pretty sore, myself in fine condition as I was used to riding.

SECOND NIGHT WITH YOUNG SMITH

We had on this, the second night, been riding for about three hours, and young Smith kept lagging farther and farther behind in spite of all I could do. He was about two hundred feet behind me when he yelled for me to go on, and that he was going to climb down off the mule and turn him loose, then lay down and die, Indian or no Indian.

I went back to him determined to gag him if he did not stop yelling, as I was a little angry. It was a most foolish thing to do, this yelling. He had thrown away everything he had and given up like a little baby who was denied having his own way.

"Where is your rifle?" I asked.

"I threw it away back there where you had such a time crossing that deep gulch."

"Don't you know you are liable to need that rifle from now on in?"

"I don't want the rifle, Johnny, I couldn't hit anything if I had it. I want to die and go up with the angels and sing the rest of my life."

He was about all in. I was considering whether it would be advisable to leave him and go on to Fort Phil Kearny, then come back later with help and pack him in, but on second thought was afraid he would not stay hidden until I could come back. Then an idea struck me. Why not tie him on the mule like a pack and continue my journey that way?

So I said to him, "Mr. Smith, if you don't want to continue the journey further, I will tie you on the mule like a pack and go with you to the fort that way."

"You can't do it! They will hang you at the fort for that! You are worse than seven hundred kinds of desperadoes, that's what you are!"

"That's what is going to happen to you if you don't keep up from now on, and not another yell out of you. I have worried with you long enough."

"Johnny, the Indians are not half as bad as you. If I ever get out of this awful mule riding punishment, I will never speak to you again, not even acknowledge there ever lived a person of your description. Let me ride the black [horse] from now on!"

"No! I begged you to ride a horse before we left Fort C. F. Smith, but you would not have a horse. Now take your medicine, have a little grit!"

"There is no one that could have any grit around you. You would have them scuttled before the beginning."

"That's enough, Mr. Smith. You keep up, or I will lash you to the mule and gag you besides. The rest of the journey requires quiet and cunning."

This lashing of young Smith to the mule scared him more than Indian stories possibly could at this stage of the trip. "Go on, Johnny," young Smith quietly ordered. "I guess I can ride into Fort Phil Kearny just as well dead as alive."

On we journeyed, and could hear a string of perpetual grunts and groans sounding in the rear. He was suffering from being chafed, and through too much riding in the saddle, but he had better suffer a little than die at the hands of the Sioux in the morning.

After several long, hard hours and numerous spats with my charge, and thoroughly disgusted, I concluded to leave young Smith for a few minutes, as then thought we were about seven miles from Fort Phil Kearny. I rode on ahead to where I had often been before to look down the valley toward the fort. It was good daylight. For a wonder there was no sign of Indians, all looked clear. Then young Smith came trotting up on his mule beside us, a-sitting his saddle limp as a rag.

"Look, Mr. Smith, there is Fort Phil Kearny," I said. "You certainly can make it in from here, it's so near."

"Well, I can, perhaps. I feel like I cannot. I must have died back there on the trail somewhere. I feel so numb, and the flesh on my legs feels like it has all fallen off. I want to get off of this mule and lie down here and die."

"Come on, we're going to make a beeline for that fort."

On we rode down toward Fort Phil Kearny in broad daylight. I had lost so much time with young Smith I threw away prudence in an attempt to be rid of him. We rode into the fort about eight o'clock, whereas we should have arrived there at daylight. Quickly a crowd of people gathered around us including General Smith. It was a little out of the usual thing for the mail carrier to enter the fort so late in the morning, so all were curious.

"Why, Al," General Smith said, as soon as he recognized who was with me, "is that you?"

"Yes," young Smith answered, "this is what is left of me."

"How did you happen to come down here, Al?" General Smith asked.

"Uncle, I came down here with your mail carrier. He ought to be locked up in the guard house for riding me on a mule half to death, and bossing the life out of me. He's too important with other people, that's what he is. I think he must have owl eyes for sight at night."

The next morning some of the officers said, "Why didn't you let the Indians get Smith? We don't want him here. General Smith would have given you something nice if you had left him at Fort C. F. Smith."

"I had to obey orders given by General Bradley to bring young Smith here, Captain. The Indians would surely have scalped him last night if there had been any within hearing distance, for he would yell in spite of all I could do to prevent, sometimes. After this experience I will refuse to take anyone with me again. It's hard enough as it is."

12

RUNNING FIGHT CARRYING THE MAIL

Johnny describes, or at least mentions, eight mail trips. All but one passed without incident. On that one occasion, however, he was forced into an hours-long battle with pursuing Sioux and Cheyenne, ending only at the gates of the Fort C. F. Smith. Johnny provides no date, but the context seems to place this adventure in the late winter of 1868.

This account is problematic. It is hard to believe that so dramatic an arrival would have left no trace in official documents or personal accounts at Fort C. F. Smith, including the diary of Lieutenant Colonel Bradley, who was then nearing the end of his command. At the same time, the unfolding fight is described in such detail that it is difficult to brush it off as pure fiction.

But there is one significant source that provides support to the narrative, albeit at a different fort and a different time of year. In late June Lieutenant George M. Templeton was on his way south from Fort C. F. Smith to Fort Phil Kearny. On the nineteenth he records in his diary a meeting with the mail carrier "Harwood," who accompanied his party until the evening of the twentieth and rode into the night alone. Templeton's entry for the twenty-second reads: "Arrived at Phil Kearney [*sic*] about 10 A.M. Learned that Mr. Harwood had been chased by Indians after leaving us the other night."[1]

Here, in any case, is Johnny's story.

The second night out with the mail was stormy and windy. It sprinkled now and then, and black darkness when I thought it should have been daylight. The change being so slow it was hardly noticeable at the time. I was about twenty miles from Fort C. F. Smith and as I had no trouble with the Indians to speak of so far, or on any of my former trips, I decided to ride on to the fort, by keeping close among the foothills and mesas.

When I came some distance closer to the fort the clouds began to lift, much to my dissatisfaction, as I could be seen more easily if there were any Indians near. The sun began shooting his life-giving rays through the rifts in the clouds. I saw that broad daylight together with a shining sun would witness my ride into the fort.

A few minutes after this I crossed a little creek in the middle of a little valley which lay northeast. Here I stopped and scanned the valley for Indians before continuing my journey, as I would be more in the open for some distance directly ahead. But I could not see a living thing, so resumed my journey. As I rode on ahead it seemed as if Old Howard's voice sounded in my ears. "Don't attempt to ride into the fort in broad daylight!" . . .

When I had ridden about two miles further on, a bunch of buffalo crossed the trail just behind me on the run. Now buffalo do not run unless something is chasing them. This meant I must find out quickly what had startled them, so I rode up behind a point of rock and peeped over using my field glass.

There saw twenty or more Indians coming straight for me and others stringing out back toward the little creek I had crossed two miles back. The leaders were about one half mile behind me. Quickly I put my field glass away and started on the run. I had not gone half a mile when rounding a turn in the trail ran right into three Cheyenne within less than fifty feet of me.

I had my carbine in my hand ready for business. Instantly thought, this is where the advance is, I must fight through them. So I fired point blank at the nearest to me. He was so close I did not take sight, but fired my carbine like a revolver. Then I fired at the second one who was in line. And the last one was a squaw, so fired at her pony, which threw up its tail and hopped out the trail. That settled three Indian ponies.

This rapid shooting and rapid moving completely surprised these three Indians. Then I went faster than ever for about eighty yards, when I busted right into about a dozen Cheyenne who had stopped to learn what the shooting was about, I supposed. Fired four shots into the thickest spots so as to rattle them. They scurried out of the trail as much surprised as I was.

To my left there was a steep bluff thick with cedars, so couldn't think of riding that way with any speed, even if it was the sure way and the trail too narrow for my business just then. There happened to be a draw leading down from this bench, the last one of the mountain, and I followed it.

Through the brush I rode as fast as dare ride for safety. At the mouth of this draw came to a little creek with brush and timber along its course. Down beside this creek I rode at a lively gait. The Indians lost my trail for a few minutes in the draw, which was the thing I desired. . . . It was death both ways if caught, so I had to make a square turn to the left and out in the open plain fifteen miles from Fort C. F. Smith.

I hadn't any plans formed, as I had been running. Now, my only chance for life left was for the fort and the wagon road leading toward the fort, which was within two miles of me and to my right. I must go northwest so as to avoid losing time and distance by making another square turn. The timber on the creek was playing out and would shield me no more on my right, so I would soon be in plain view, a thing I most dreaded.

There was no other way. "Here goes for the fort," I shouted. And the red devils will get the one in front this time if the buckskin and the black play out. So far my horses were behaving well, their breathing regular and their muscles steady as bars of steel. The black kept up beside me whenever space permitted, giving me no trouble at all.

After leaving the creek I soon crossed a small rise. Here I scanned the rear with my field glass to see what I would have to do. The first party in my rear was stealing up on me with good running ponies and were coming straight for me. There was the large party [I] had fired into some distance back, about thirty in all, and others coming behind them. It was no time to fool along, and a slight mistake could not be remedied or lost time be made up. Some Indian ponies, while they look of no account, are in reality as good as blooded horses, can run long distances, and have speed and endurance.

A FIGHT IN THE WAGON ROAD

In about one half mile further on I struck the wagon road, and then let the buckskin and the black out for a good gait, all they could stand in a twelve-mile run. But this was not fast enough, as the Indians were gaining, so I rode a little faster and then my horses began to sweat freely for the first time.

Felt confident I could outrun all Cheyenne and Sioux ponies but two or three, and could fight them off, but soon I discovered much to my surprise there were nine of their ponies as good as the buckskin and the black. There are always surprises coming into your life no matter what you do and how careful things are planned beforehand. These nine pones meant life or death to me before very long.

There were three Indians riding swift ponies a mile and a half to my left, striking for the creek ahead of me about two miles. If they beat me to this creek there would have to be a scrap sure as fate, and from the looks of things they were likely to be there first.

Behind me clear to the foothills could see Indians coming, they were scattered, but all coming as fast as they could. All of them in deadly earnest to capture me. They wanted to have my scalp for some time back in the past.

Rode in the wagon road straight for the crossing, but when I had ridden to within eighty yards of the crossing I turned square to the right, because the three flankers had beaten me to it. And then [I] rode down the creek about one hundred yards, crossed, and struck back for the road.

Hadn't ridden more than thirty-five yards when out came the three Indians from their ambush at the road crossing about one hundred and fifty yards away. Something had to be done on the spur of the moment.

I stopped and dropped to the ground with both feet at the same time so as to be in motion quickly, as seconds counted. I sat down on the ground, elbows on knees, and drawing a quick fine bead. I fired at the first Indian's leg to get an Indian and pony if I could. The pony threw up his tail, both were hit hard. Then I shot the other two ponies, aiming as before at the Indians' legs. They did not fire on me. They couldn't very well, as the Indians and their ponies were out of commission.

I then rode into the road once more, and on looking back saw two Indians standing beside the first one [I] had shot in the leg. Thought I had them buffaloed and like a fool gave the war whoop to let them know I was on the scrap. Was feeling pretty good over my success and guessed now that I could gain the fort.

But this turn down the creek and back to the road and shooting at the three Indians caused me to lose at least three hundred yards, so that the red devils in my rear gained that much on me. Then [I] started on to the fort in real earnest, for thinking thus had roused the possibility of not doing so fine after all. On looking toward the hills I saw three more Indians riding to cut me off from the fort. They were about a mile from me and a little ahead, it was an even break then, thought I.

There were four behind me that were gaining on me, so [I] attempted to whip up, but they still gained, always closer and nearer. Had about eight miles to run yet before the welcome protection of the fort would be mine. It would not do to wind my horses, or the whole bunch would be upon me in no time. Better to fight them three or four at a time and save my horses.

Then on looking back to the rear a few minutes later saw six Indians in the lead. Two more had moved to the front. They had that many; that was their limit of good horses in my rear, besides the three that were trying to cut me off from the fort in front. Nine in all that had splendid speed and staying power. Be they cayuse, mustang, pony or horse, I call that sort all thoroughbreds.

Those behind began to slacken their speed a little, hoping that I would be cut off and that they could all together handle me to their liking. The Indian has some cunning, for if he saved his pony a little and I did not, then he would eventually have the advantage.

THE INDIANS ON FAST HORSES

On looking ahead I saw one of the three flankers was quite a piece behind, so there were only two that could come up in front. I could increase my gait a bit if forced to do so. Then on looking behind I saw seven in the lead. Where did this odd one come from so quickly? That worried me. What if they have more real ponies like that, what if? If I stopped to fight them, the ones flanking me would win. [I] knew they were determined to get me, even at the cost of ruining valuable buffalo ponies. Concluded to urge my horses to their limit, so as to be ahead of the flankers, now two. The seven behind were now managing to just barely keep out of gunshot, a nice piece of strategy.

There was no discounting, these Indians were well mounted and could stay about so close. No scheme of mine could shake them from their purpose. And added to this predicament, there was another bunch of Indians about four hundred yards behind the first seven.

But the thing that began to worry me most was this first fast seven hovering in my rear. They could run in on me whenever they liked. And if so, they would charge me pretty soon, as I was then nearing the fort, and had about four miles yet to run.

On looking back again a moment later I saw there were only five in the lead and one was whipping hard, soon there would be four. They were charging me. I rode on like the wind for a spell and then heard the old familiar army call-to-action. Turned my head sidewise to know whether I was dreaming or hearing things. Never did anything sound more good and welcome.

Sure as my life it was the bugler from the fort sounding double quick plain as printed words while I ran onward for my life. Though the bugle call was somewhat faint, it had a meaning of a whole volume. Instantly the old army life came back to me, floating on the billows of bugle notes, deep seated in its meaning, true and fine: this beautiful music of action, of hustle, of life and power and vitality and "I'm coming." I turned my field glass in front. There I saw several horsemen coming on the run and a company of soldiers out on the road. That was good, if they would only get to me in time. Had outrun the Indians flanking me, so they now joined the ones coming in my rear.

Then on looking behind saw four had gained, but not near enough to shoot with any accuracy and I didn't care to risk a fight so near safety. Then on looking ahead through my field glass I saw the strawberry roan, Hugh's race mare, in the lead and a few more riders coming a hundred yards behind him. On looking back I saw three Indians about as close as I cared to have them, about four hundred yards. Believed three of them could run me down. What noble grand pony horses they were. And they were doing this splendid running on nothing but grass.

I could stop these three, but seven more would be up and others still coming behind them. I must not fight them yet, I reasoned, but must run on a ways and do nothing foolish at the end. If these three wanted a fight, they could force it. On looking ahead I could see Hugh's strawberry roan coming about one thousand yards distant and three more men from the fort behind Hugh and the strawberry roan. Good, I thought. On looking back the Indians had closed up and were going to force me to fight them before I could receive help.

This was plain, as it was their last chance at me, so [I] must fight them then and there. They were coming like the wind so [I] must be ready to hit the ground shooting, be steady, concentrate on what I was doing. One miss would likely be the last of me. Had to plan to shoot at an Indian's leg so would be sure of wounding an Indian or his pony, and if the bead was good, wound both.

The leader in my rear was within eighty yards of me, others were slightly scattered about thirty yards behind him and the next three were strung out just right to shoot one at a time, also there were four more back two hundred yards. Beyond as far as [I] could see were Indians and Indians. They seemed to spring from the grass roots, so fast did they multiply directly in my rear.

But only the three or four near me counted at present, so [I] dismounted and shot offhand, taking care to draw a fine quick bead; a miss and I was gone. The first Indian turned a little to the left, just what I wanted, so fired at his leg and hit the mark. The ball going on wrecking the backbone of his pony as well, the pony fell, never to rise again, on the Cheyenne warrior's shattered leg, so that, for a time, he couldn't do anything. This pony was the best one among the Sioux and Cheyenne that day, perhaps the best in the world, this beautiful dark bay.

On they came, the other three, the second one did not turn, so I fired at forty yards at the breast of his pony and down he went. The Indian riding fell over his pony's head to the ground, regained his feet quick as a cat and charged me with a lance, so I had to drop him. The third Indian's pony fell about thirty yards from me. His rider turned loose on me with a revolver but shot wild, [I] had to drop him, because he might cease to shoot wild. The fourth Indian came on. My first shot did not stop him. He was within twenty feet of me before I again raised my rifle and gave him his quietus. His pony whirled and fled from me before I could capture him. He was a beauty and a mustang at that.

Then I learned the reason these few Indians gave me such a chase. They rode mustangs in whose veins the blood of the Arabian breed flowed. The Indians must have stole them from Mexican travelers coming through from Mexico.

The Indians behind started back, they lost, I won. Then once more I gave the war whoop. The first Indian answered it, the one with a broken leg, and his war whoop was that of the Cheyennes. He was game as any warrior of his race can be. Why he should answer my war whoop was more than I could fathom. It was probably his last call and knew it, as all Indians with a broken leg or a bad wound usually die.

These Indians were as brave as any race of man, but I had an enormous advantage over them in firearms and experience.

THE RESCUE FROM THE FORT

Then Hugh came by my side, dismounting almost before his strawberry roan and finished his last lunge forward.

"John, what is this?" Hugh shouted, all excited. "John, you are covered with blood!"

"I had a running fight with the Sioux and some Cheyenne. I have been working in the lead and refused to play second fiddle for any Indian among these hills. May have skinned my face riding through brush away back there somewhere in a gulch, or it may be an arrow wound, as they shot hundreds of them at me. I can't quite think accurately now that the game is over."

Then Meacham, Brown, and Tewksbury rode up. They wanted to chase the Indians now scurrying away.

"No," I said, "I have all the fight I want today. The Indians have too much the start of us now, and besides there is always the danger of an ambush."

Then Captain Wishart came up and a few minutes later a company of soldiers. Captain Wishart asked, "Johnny, how bad are you wounded?"

"Oh, just a scratch, Captain."

"But you have been bleeding for some time, Johnny! Look at the blood on your face, clothing, and body. 'Just a scratch' is too thin, it won't work with me."

"Oh, yes, now I remember, Captain, was hit by an arrow in the side of the head and one punched my arm a little. The arrow that hit my head glanced [off] and fell out, then [I] noticed it bled a little. I did not know the wound was bleeding still."

"How long have you been running and fighting these Sioux and Cheyenne, Johnny?"

"Ever since a little after daybreak, and back for about twenty miles."

Then the Captain commenced to examine my wounds, and all the men had something to say. The fort doctor then came up and pronounced my wounds that of arrows, so that settled that. [Pierre] Shane the interpreter started toward the first Indian with the broken leg.[2] He asked the Indian how he was hurt and if he could do anything for him.

The Indian said to kill him, as his leg was broken and he would die anyway. He wanted to see me.

I walked up close to him. He looked at me a while, then said, "You heap damn mean, surprise Indian. Run up on rock, jump off on tree, next time down crack in ground, then down valley. All the time go like the wind, all the time shoot, hit! All the time fool Indian. Pooh! Heap big run, scared, then no scare. Some day Indian catch you."

The Captain gathered up all the Indian arms he could find near, then came and offered them to me. I looked at them, then told the Captain he could have them all if he wanted them.

I began to feel a little weak. I went and patted the buckskin and the black. Then I told the buckskin he was a noble horse, and that he had outrun all the red devils in my rear. The buckskin then nosed around my side, it was the only way he could show his affection. Then I placed my arms around the buckskin's neck in a burst of pride and respect for a horse that could run miles and miles.

Then I mounted the buckskin and on looking around at those men saw their faces were a little strained. Men who seem as hard and unfeeling as a piece of flint will at times show a feeling streak for a man that has faced unreasonable odds and won.

Captain Wishart sent a few Indians to tell the Sioux to come and take one of their wounded away.

Then we all went to the fort. I turned the mail over to Captain Wishart and rode to our cabin outside the fort with Hugh. Rolled into bed and went to sleep nearly as soon as my head hit the pillow. I was dead tired, nervous and nearly at the end of my string, think that I may have bled more than I realized.

13

THE CROW ANNUITIES

Major Burt succeeded General Bradley in command of Fort C. F. Smith.[1] Major Burt was more friendly and better liked than General Bradley, more of a good fellow with all men. He possessed a streak of kindness which endured and rendered friends. Citizens as well as soldiers under him were willing to go after results.

Major Burt became firm and decisive when it became necessary, or when unexpected trouble began to brew. It would not do to tamper with him too far, for a surprise would be in store unexpectedly.

Under Major Burt I still carried the mail, but did not receive so many lectures. For some reason I did not get into trouble so frequently; also it was a real nice pleasure to go into Major Burt's office, and not hear that eternal tattoo of a cane on the floor.

By this time the Indians were so bad away from the fort, I gave up trying to furnish meat for the soldiers and citizens; then, too, the elk and buffalo were eating something which tainted the meat. We did now and then make a venture when out of fresh meat but only for mountain sheep as that meat was not tainted. This meat business was a paying proposition while it lasted. The wolf pelts made some money, and the trapping likewise.

As the soldiers carried the mail when General Bradley left for the East, I did not have to make a trip for several days, so had a good rest. My pay of ten dollars a day went on just the same, but then it was all earned in the odds and ends.

Many late pages of the manuscript feature Indian agent Dr. H. M. Matthews. In his prior function as a surgeon, Matthews had spent ten months at Fort C. F. Smith, from its founding until early June 1867. He reappeared three months later in a double role as government representative to the Mountain Crows and as negotiator with all the local tribes, shuttling among the Bozeman forts and to Fort Laramie.[2]

That evening Mr. Matthews the Crow Indian agent came down to our cabin and wanted me to go to the Crow Indian village of Blackfoot and tell him to come to Fort C. F. Smith and bring his band and other bands to receive their $30,000 yearly annuities.

Did not want to go very bad, finally I concluded to go after Mr. Matthews offered me ten dollars a day to make the round trip. I knew Chief Blackfoot's band was on the Clarks Fork of the Yellowstone, about forty miles west.

Started early before daylight the next morning, so as to be at least ten miles from the fort before daylight. Major Burt advised me to take the buckskin and the black, to be well mounted if anything should happen. He said, "The Sioux and the Cheyenne seldom if ever pitch their tepas across the Bighorn River northwest. Your only concern will be wandering tribes of Blackfeet." Packed the black with provisions, blankets, Enfield cartridges, corn for the horses both ways and a few trinkets to give to the old grandmas.

I stopped two hours to rest and feed the horses at noon, then rode to Clarks Fork of the Yellowstone at sundown, then up the river four miles and camped. The next day I came to an old Crow camp about ten o'clock. I followed the trail by dismounting once in a while to learn the direction the Crows had gone.

If a tepa pole drags over a rock or log, the end on the ground will leave the ground some distance ahead of the rock, but as it passes over the rock and past it, the tepa poles fall down close to the rock, therefore the direction traveled was learned. In this case the Crows had traveled up the river. As there were pony tracks pointing in both directions, all quite fresh, I could do nothing accurate with them, so resorted to the tepa poles, which were positive.

I followed this tepa trail all the next day through several camps, coming at last to Chief Blackfoot's village just at sundown. Chief Blackfoot received me kindly and was surprised to see me out so far and alone. After I had fed the buckskin and the black their ration of corn, Blackfoot ordered a young brave to take my horses out on good grass for two hours, then bring them in to make sure nothing happened to them and tie them with his ponies.

I had supper of roast buffalo hump and boiled tongue, a good supper, and breakfast the same. I had mixed lard, salt, and baking powder in thirty pounds of flour before leaving the cabin. At noon I gave his squaw the flour and requested her to give us some of it at every meal, enough for the three of us. That afternoon I gave 250 Enfield cartridges to Blackfoot and the other things I had packed out on the black, with instructions to give them to his people as he saw fit. This made things more pleasant for me during my stay, as I had to stay long enough to rest my horses before going back to the fort. My horses were led out to grass and brought back each time they drove the herd out in the morning and afternoon; two sets of herders serve during the day to make sure a sharp eye is kept on the surrounding country.

THE CROWS GOING TO THE GREAT SPIRIT

There was a deserted soldier in the Crow village whom the Crows called Jim. I learned by talking to him there were two young Crows who were starving themselves to death so as to go to the Great Spirit. They were above the village, so I asked permission to go and see them. We walked to where they were, Jim and I.

They were pretty weak, almost gone. They had their blankets and robes in a good place under a bunch of willows, just across a little spring branch. There was about fifteen Crows there giving them messages to their friends in the Happy Hunting Grounds of their ancestors.

One of them looked at me and said, and faintly in tone: “White man has no Great Spirit, nothing but money. Where will he go when he dies?”

That made me feel cheap, as all the Crows were looking at me scornfully. So I answered, “Show me how to know the Great Spirit!”

“You know if you try,” he faintly answered.

“Tell the Great Spirit I want to be a medicine man so no more Crows be sick,” I answered.

This last speech pleased all the Crows and they were more anxious to accommodate me afterward. It was a good hit.

These young Crows were worshipping as they thought the true god of heaven, the Great Spirit who controls the Happy Hunting Ground for the Crow Indians. And according to their belief, when one of their tribe sacrifices himself to go to the Great Spirit, he went there, nothing could prevent [it]. He passed through the curtain between daylight and dark, to where there was perpetual daylight. It wasn’t necessary for his spirit to return, because once there, it would be sacrilege to stoop to come back. These Crows were just as strong in their belief as any race of people I have ever met.

WITH THE CROWS ON THE TRAIL

Blackfoot sent runners to all the Mountain Crow tribes of villages to be at Fort C. F. Smith at a certain day. This finished my business, so I told Blackfoot I would start back in the morning.

Promptly in the morning started back to the fort with several old warriors. I knew it would be a hard ride going back the way I came in, but the old warriors said, "Me know a shorter way. Me go by trail you do not know, pretty soon come to fort."

We stopped for rest about nine o'clock. We had fresh meat to roast on sticks in a fire and cold boiled meat for the first meal. You see the Indian does not travel steady, and every time he stops expects to eat. After the horses had grazed for an hour and a half, all saddled up to start on toward the fort. An Indian always mounts his pony on the right side, the opposite side of the horse to our way of mounting. And he fills his mouth with water and squirts it on his hands when he desires to wash his hands and face.

Just as we started, about a dozen young Crow braves and squaws rode up to us and said they were going to Fort C. F. Smith with us. An old warrior lined them all up, made a short speech to them, then started them all back to the village of Blackfoot. They made some fuss, but the old warriors made them go quite lively to avoid the lash of his whip which spared no one.

Every hour we stopped to let the ponies rest and passed the pipe around. The tobacco mostly was not the real tobacco, but called by the Crows "ceh-sha," at that it was a variety probably belong to the tobacco family, perhaps far distant removed. I had to travel Indian way when riding with the Indians.

Now, when smoking the pipe with the Crows, it is necessary to take the pipe in your fingers in a certain way and no other, if you do not observe these rules you break the pipe of peace and the Bad Spirit may enter your mouth through the smoke and cause all sorts of trouble. You must take three puffs, the last puff must be breathed down in the lungs, or held in the mouth for a short time, then slowly expelled into the air in a slow steady stream.

When a fellow next to you takes the pipe, you must give him time in which to take the proper position with his fingers. After all have smoked around the circle, anyone can smoke as he pleases, for it then does not disturb the Great Spirit. But with them it was all right to smoke quite often so long as I furnished the real tobacco.

The leader of the Crows traveled at a lope about all the time, and making his hour stops. And they were pretty good judges of time. We arrived on this cut-off trail about dark at the Bighorn River where we crossed the river in a boat, as the river gradually kept rising every hour. This old Crow leader of our day's ride came to see what the agent was going to give them for their $30,000 annuities. Later he seemed to be satisfied with what they were going to receive.

THE MAN WHO GAVE UP BEING A WHITE MAN

A couple of evenings later, Jim came into our cabin and wanted to know if I would help him. He did not have a pony, a rifle, tepa, traps, or anything, and had married in a poor family. His squaw had to do work for the owner of the tepa who gave them shelter, and while they were so poor no Indian would give them anything without double the amount of work for one pay. He had to keep away from the fort, and had given up trying to be anything among the whites.

I concluded he was not worth anything as a soldier and punishment would not improve him. I asked him to come again the next night and then would do something for him.

The next evening when he came to our cabin, I gave him an old Enfield rifle, 50 Enfield cartridges, lead, powder, some cloth for patches, a skinning knife, an old blanket, three beaver traps and a large horse pistol. He was pleased, as even this would lift him more out of the poor class.

He said the Crows would protect him as he had joined Blackfoot's tribe, and anyone doing that was entitled to their consideration, especially after marrying one of their squaws. And that the fort knew where he was, but the Crows refused to give him up, so all he had to do was to keep forever away. He wanted a pair of tweezers to pull out his beard because his squaw did not like a beard.

He walked with me near the sutler's store where I bought the tweezers for him. Going back we passed Matthews' outfit. Jim began to notice things too much to my liking, so I told him to go away, or I would be obliged to report him to Major Burt. Went with me to our cabin where I further gave him some provisions and old cooking utensils. He stepped out of our cabin and I never saw him again.

In the morning there was quite a stir about Matthews' two best horses being stolen. Matthews was very much displeased, but could do nothing then. I always thought Jim was the one who stole Matthews' horses, but I could not then prove it. I made up my mind to leave these deserters alone.[3]

HOW I FORCED MATTHEWS TO PAY ME

Matthews did not offer to pay me for making the trip to Blackfoot's village, so one evening I caught him in the sutler's store and told him I was out six days, at ten dollars a day would be sixty dollars..

"Oh," he answered, "you are getting ten dollars a day from the Government now, and that was a Government job you carried through."

"No," I said, "you promised me ten dollars a day and I want it. I had no order from the Government to do this work for you."

"Well, I do not pay men to do Government work for me, sir."

"I take it then you do not intend to pay me."

"No, because I'm running behind in this Indian agent business and don't know what [I] am going to do," the agent answered quite determinedly.

"You are not running behind much, Mr. Matthews. I can buy for one thousand dollars all you give to the Indians for thirty thousand dollars, and I think you had better pay me without any further bickering. If I tell Blackfoot you are beating them out of nearly all their annuities, there will be trouble. But this is not a threat exactly as it stands, for the moment at least."

"All right, I will pay you the sixty dollars, but do not talk that way around here about me." . . .

There are men in this world who never make their word good to the men they employ, or to anyone else for that matter. It always takes force to make them come through. Matthews knew I could make him trouble by telling Blackfoot, and that Blackfoot was stubborn when someone was cheating him.

BLACKFOOT AND TRIBE CROSSING THE BIGHORN

One day while strolling around resting from one of my mail trips I noticed quite a band of [Crow] Indians coming from the west across the Bighorn River. . . . It was about the time arranged for them to come to Fort C. F. Smith to receive their annuities.

The Bighorn River could not be forded anywhere, it was on a tear. Whoever crossed that river at that time would have to be an extra able swimmer. The water was boiling and swirling and rushing by in surging floods in its hurry northward toward the Yellowstone. Impatient and like a runaway horse.

There was quite a number of these Crows, for I knew them now by the aid of my field glass. And I did not think for a minute they could cross the Bighorn.

No one at the fort would think of crossing except in a ferry boat, as it would be about equivalent to suicide.

But not so with Blackfoot and his tribe. They came to the shore of the Bighorn, unpacked their ponies, and unlashed their tepa poles from their ponies with quickness and dispatch. No one was excited, no on in a hurry, all so and so and very much elated.

These tepa poles were from seven to sixteen feet long. Each pole having a hole burnt in it, back from the top end about half a foot for the purpose of passing thongs through while the tepa is set up and to prevent them from becoming lost while traveling, and also to aid in lashing them securely to the ponies.

The top ends of the tepa poles protruded above the ponies' backs and necks while the bottom ends dragged against the earth behind the ponies as they plodded along over the trails.

The Crows seemed to not be the least worried about the condition of the Bighorn. Quickly they hustled around, shouting, motioning and chattering, in fact having a merry time. I could see them plainly with my strong field glass. General Smith of Fort Phil Kearny gave it to me on my first trip down there with the mail.

They lashed their tepa poles together at the top end, being careful to see that a thong passed through the end of each tepa pole to prevent it from slipping out in the water and floating away. There would be seven or eight tepa poles lashed together on two sides in two sets, which they again lashed together at the upper end where the holes were burnt through the tepa poles. When finished this had the form of a capital A.

Then the Crows laid their tepa robes and skins on the ground, crossing them in every way so as to have them lie on the ground in a round form; then piled their worldly goods on these tepa robes and skins, after which all the sides were folded toward the center forming a large round ball and then was tied with thongs to stay tied.

Several tepa robes and skins are sewed together, wide at the bottom and tapering to a point, because the base of the tepa is wide and round and tapers to a point at the top, each robe made a V. Each one of these Vs varies in length according to the size of the tepa and the tepa poles, but the Vs must be at least a foot shorter than the tepa poles.

Some tepas may require ten or twelve of these V-shaped lengths, while others six or eight. They, by their shapes, made an ideal outer covering for the ball, and varied in size according to how wealthy the Crow was who owned the tepa. Then this ball was rolled in the center of the capital A.

A rope was passed under this ball from the right side of the tepa poles to the other side and around the tepa poles of the left side of the A, then brought over the ball and securely lashed to the tepa poles from which it started. Another rope was passed under the ball from the left side repeating the same operation. This firmly lashing the ball from both sides and holding it securely in the middle of the A. A third rope was tied to the ball reaching across from the right side to the left side just behind the ball, thus forming a capital A.

This A would not upset and would float. Then the A was pushed from behind and pulled to the edge of the water where little papooses were placed on top of this ball. The ones too small to hold on were tied fast to the ball on top. The squaws do most of the work in making ready to cross the river up to a certain time. Then the one in authority orders the conniecotters, old grandmothers, to ride on the ball while crossing the river, the squaws and young maidens have to swim and hold on to the rope behind the ball inside of the A.

Then the most stalwart warriors, four or more according to the size of the ball, tie a long rope to the front end of the A. They then push the A into the water a few feet, when all the old squaws climb on the ball; they always ride because they are old and are the mothers of brave warriors. The young squaws are supposed to hold on and swim for the reason they have strength and their life is all before them.

When all is ready an old soldier, leader of a family, or chief gives the signal. Then the stalwart warriors, each having separate ropes, would mount and ride their ponies out into the swirling, rushing water, holding their ropes in their right hands. When the ponies were far enough out into the water to begin swimming, each stalwart warrior would grip his rope between his teeth and slide off their ponies into the water on the lower side, or the side downstream, which in this case was the left side. His right hand firmly gripping his pony's mane while the left hand steers the pony across the river by means of a rope fastened to the pony's lower jaw and passing through the pony's mouth. The warrior swims beside his pony in the water never once flinching in his purpose.

They came nearly straight across the Bighorn. I could hear the little papooses shouting and playing with one another. Some would splash water on the ones near them. The squaws would scold but it did not quiet the little shavers very much.

The Crows crossed the Bighorn quickly, only a few minutes, and they could cross a river twice the size with as much ease and dispatch. High water or low water, it made no difference to them, and certainly only a passing obstruction causing them no anxiety.

It was astonishing how quickly they made ready on the opposite shore, how quickly they crossed the Bighorn, what confidence they had in themselves, with what speed in a few minutes after crossing the Bighorn they were packed up and going again as if nothing of any consequence had happened. And nothing going amiss, all together working like the tick of a clock.

There must have been three hundred warriors in Blackfoot's band that day, which would mean over five hundred Indians including families. For this many Indians to cross the Bighorn in high flood time without a single mishap, or loss of baggage, or a single life, and in less than thirty minutes, and be packed up and going again, was remarkable. . . . No white man could move a whole tribe across a river with such precise perfection using the things they used and following their simple method. And doubt very much whether the Crow Indian of today can accomplish this thing. Think they have lost the art and the courage. But it was not the crossing in particular, rather the quickness and completeness of it that was valuable. The Indian ponies swam in the rushing water and pulled the big ball in the center of the A, but they pulled it through the teeth of the Crow warriors. Why the warriors swam beside their ponies I do not know, unless it was to give the pony more freedom.

Captain Wishart with others from the fort came down to watch the Crows cross the Bighorn. "If an army," he said, "lightly equipped, could do that very thing, they could move swiftly and quickly across country and no river would be an obstacle. I never heard of a thing like this and never thought such a thing possible. Not a casualty, nothing to mar their perfect performance, and they think it is play."

CROW INDIANS RECEIVING THEIR ANNUITIES

Blackfoot camped south of the Fort. In a short time all their tepas were set up in their usual strategic position. In a few days Iron Bull and White Mouth came to the fort with their bands. They camped close to Blackfoot, all Mountain Crows.

Both Iron Bull's and White Mouth's bands were smaller in numbers separately than Blackfoot's band. They, like Blackfoot, observed the same method in pitching their tepas, the river had to be the base of their formations. Blackfoot was chief of the Mountain Crows.

When the day arrived to divide the annuities among these three bands of Crow Indians, all the annuities was hauled out in front of the fort and unloaded in one place.

Mr. Mathews gave each Crow warrior a cup full of powder, then passed around a half cup full of powder, then last one fourth cup full of powder, making three times. What was left, a goodly amount, went to Blackfoot, Iron Bull, and White Mouth. Then two bars of lead was given to each warrior, then one bar of lead to each one, in all equalling three pounds each warrior received. The balance went to Blackfoot and the other two chiefs. You see, the division had to be made according to the Crow way of dividing, so two or three times around had to be followed.

Caps were divided, so many for each warrior, but the chiefs received the largest portion of anyone of the Crows. Then flour, bacon, sugar, government blankets cut in two so as to go further, butcher knives, beads of several colors and numerous other trinkets.

Each warrior and brave received about three pounds of sugar, the squaws receiving no sugar. The squaws made quite a fuss on being left out on the sugar portion. Their men would not divide with them which made matters worse. About all the squaws received was nearly all the beads, some trinkets and a few kind words.

After everything had been divided among the Crows in Indian fashion, the three chiefs had to sign a receipt, that was the most important thing for the Indian agent.

Blackfoot signed by making a large black foot covering all of the paper. The foot was drawn with ink and was a fairly good human foot, showing the toes, the heel, and the instep quite accurately. He used quite considerable ink in making the foot look black. Iron Bull's signature represented a bull buffalo and good enough not to be mistaken for anything else and did not use quite as much paper or ink as Blackfoot's. White Mouth signed by drawing a large white mouth showing human teeth. The drawing was the best signature of the three chiefs.

All of the signatures were horrible looking things, but there was no mistake in recognizing who they belonged to. We had quite a laugh over them, especially Blackfoot's great big black foot covering the whole page, and destroying the paper to read.

White Mouth was the orator of the Crows. He could talk quite well and his gestures were natural. He is the only chief that out-talked General Bradley, to a standstill. White Mouth was then nearly seventy years old, an unusual age for an Indian to live those days.

14

LAST DAYS AT FORT C. F. SMITH

Johnny paints a rather melancholy picture of the last months of Fort C. F. Smith. Its abandonment, by this point a certainty, could not happen overnight. Outside its little zone of safety, hostile Indian pressure only increased. The monotony of this transitional period was interrupted for the brothers by a visit from Jim Bridger, the most famous of all guides, who briefly had come out of retirement in Missouri to help in shutting down the Bozeman Trail.

I had just returned from a trip carrying the mail and had started down to my cabin for breakfast and a sleep when I met Jim Bridger, the one time Government scout, emigrant train pilot and trapper. Mr. Bridger came to Fort C. F. Smith from somewhere, those old trappers went where and when they pleased. I had met Mr. Bridger on the Sweetwater as a Government scout in 1865 while serving in the Eleventh Kansas Cavalry. Mr. Bridger was quite an

Jim Bridger, the best-known of all the western trappers, guides, and government scouts. Johnny claims to have encountered him twice.
Kansas State Historical Society.

intelligent man, sociable, agreeable, very much alive; but it was hard to persuade him to talk about himself and [the] adventures he had went through. . . .

I invited Mr. Bridger to come and spend the evening with us at our cabin outside the fort.

"I will come, Johnny, but the privilege must be mine to do most of the talking for I am aching to talk to someone who understands American English."

After I had had my sleep out, becoming in a manner refreshed, though not the satisfying sleep of the night time, Mr. Bridger came down to our cabin. We talked for a time and Hugh did himself proud in preparing for Mr. Bridger a splendid evening meal.

"Have you," I asked Mr. Bridger, "that same Missouri double-barreled gun you had when scouting for the Eleventh Kansas Cavalry through the Sweetwater country?"

"Yes, Johnny, I still have that same artillery with me, and more than a thousand times it has been a godsend to me. Sometimes one cap of one barrel refused to go, so I had another cap ready to fall back on by having another barrel.

"And that reminds me of what a time I had while having the two barrels securely riveted together and other things added to suit me by the Hawkins Rifle Company gunsmith in St. Louis, Missouri. It is not much to my credit to tell this one on myself, but I will, because it shows how green a man can become to the ways of a city after living for years out in this wild wilderness, so close to nature.

"Another chap just about as bright as I was put up at a hotel in St. Louis with me. We were having a fine time of it for a while, but for the life of me I could go nowhere without a guide. It didn't seem to fit me at all, for I could guide anyone safely anywhere through the mountains and across the plains of the West and never be lost for a minute. Why did this St. Louis bother me so?

"My partner lost himself in that town and it required three days to find him. When found he was on the war path and wanted to thrash me. He laid his mishaps all on me, as if I was to blame for his actions.

"By this time [I] concluded I could go anywhere and come back to my starting point. One of the streets I named the Canyon of the Yellowstone because it had three and four story building[s] piled up in straight rows on both sides of a wagon road, and a place a few feet wide to walk on both sides of that canyon. Another street was named the Canyon of the Bighorn. It too was honored by the same piles of straight rows of buildings three and four stories high, except now and then there was a little runt of a building the carpenter or brick-mason got tired working on and quit.

"Then there was some other streets that went streaking out toward the prairie or some destination. Some of these streets did not have the straight idea at all, they angled and I called them Bandan [*sic*] streets, or lost streets.

"Well, I wandered around and around somewhere, always seeing strange faces, and not a single one looked anything like anybody [I] had ever seen before. I walked around until I had just about wore my moccasins out and was becoming tired out. I could not find a point where I could get my bearings so as to have a place to figure from, and as it was getting late I picked out a large fine-looking house to roost in for the night.

"I walked up to the house to the front door and knocked and a fine-looking woman with a turned up nose came to the door.

"'Madam,' I said, '[I] wish to stay all night here. This looks like a good enough place.'

"'Oh!' she answered me. 'We do not keep people here overnight. This is a private residence. You should go to a hotel.'

"'I do not want to go to a hotel, madam. It is only a place to sleep and eat tonight. My hotel was lost today and I cannot find it. I have walked about fifty miles already up and down these canyons, and am going [to] quit walking now.'

"Then the lady of the house came to the door, and boys, she was frazzled out better than Farragut's frigates of the Mississippi ever dared to be. There never was a rooster that flew up on the top rail of a fence and crowed with more pride and victory over battle, than this lady of the house acted and talked. She strutted and fumed, was so important and learned. She was like a veneer that will not stand testing, and not near so important as one of these here fool hens in the Bighorn Canyon.

"Where she got so much finery, so many rings on her fingers and others fastened to her ears is a mystery to me. And she wore a hat that looked like a combination between a nest of birds, a whole pack of pelts, and a part of a haystack. She had all her sails set to go on a voyage down one of them there canyons, but I didn't see no captain to manage her. She looked like an angel only she didn't have any wings. And if she would ever have fallen down in one of them there canyons in St. Louis she would have all went up in smoke, because she was top heavy in clothes and common horse sense.

"'There is a hotel,' she says to me, 'down this street four blocks, then five blocks east and one block south and you're there. We don't keep people here. This is not a hotel, kind sir.'

"'I don't know what this is here madam, but where I come from in Montana a man is welcome to stay overnight wherever night overtakes him. The host must take care of me and I must in return take care of him when he needs a roost. It's the law of the land. It's human and kind, like ways I'm used to.'

"'Who are you, may I ask, sir?' this fine lady asked quite important-like.

"'Me? Oh, I'm just a fellow some people call Bridger.'

"'And because you are Bridger, you prefer to wear buckskin and moccasins?'

"'No, madam, I am Bridger because I am Bridger. My dress has nothing to do with my insides, my thoughts, or my life.'

"'Then what do you do for a living? What is your business?'

"'Sometimes I'm a scout, other times a trapper and hunter, and once in a while when I become right real hungry and the snow up north lays on deep, why, I roast a real nice fat squaw for breakfast.'

"'What! Are you a man eater?'

"'No, a fat squaw is a crow. I eat 'em, because they are black, and afterwards want to kill everything in sight. Their black beak gets into my heart, then I have no humanity left in my frame for a time.'

"This lady called a manservant, who was all dolled up in the shadowed livery of the burnished sun, to take me to my hotel and stay with me until the right roost was located. 'Get him there if it costs me a hundred dollars. Do you hear!' then to me she said,

"'We cannot keep you here. My husband would skin me alive. Please go away!'

"'Sure, I'll go away madam, I do not like your looks anyhow, but if you should sometime be so unfortunate as to be in want of my hospitality out in the West somewhere, why, I'll not turn you away. Good afternoon, madam squaw.'

"Then I said to her servant, 'Now, you colored Satan, find out where I belong, or there will be trouble for you before you are ready.'

"'Yes, sir. I hears what you says, and I sure do want to find where you belong. Please, sir, was it a three or four story building?'

"'Three story and a sort of a white front.'

"'Oh, indeed, I directly knows exactly where it is and in no time we will be there.'

"It was not long until we arrived at the hotel where I was staying, and I had walked past the very place several times that afternoon, but being so rattled I could not remember the looks of any building at all. But I think anyone raised out in the free wild country is apt to be green, placed in a place where feet and rods count more than miles and miles.

"But here I do not lose my bearings and never become rattled, even if a hundred Sioux are running all around me and shouting like wild devils. Now I am more all right to visit a large city, as [I] know more about things in large cities. I came to this country when a boy, and never learned any other life other than that of the wild, free, unfettered kind.

"This shows what a fool a man can become when moved into another locality where everything is entirely different. He has to buck the other man's game. In St. Louis I am nothing and cannot command a worthwhile salary. Out here I am something and can command a good salary as a scout and can make three thousand dollars a year trapping. No, the free wild life is mine. Have lived too long now. To try to make the old man over is purest folly.

"But you place the city man out here and see how long they would last. Why, they would be more of a mistake than I was in the city."

Earlier, Lieutenant Colonel Bradley had asked Johnny whether he had come to this remote outpost to escape the consequences of past misdeeds. It was a fair and necessary question, as the following passage reveals.

There was a clerk in Leighton's sutler store at Fort C. F. Smith who never would give a very definite answer to what part of the United States he hailed from. He came to Mr. Leighton in the early fall and said he could do the work demanded of him in the store. Mr. Leighton gave him employment as clerk in the store through the winter. He gave good satisfaction, was peaceable, and did not often leave the store.

One evening this Leighton's clerk quizzed me about the best way to the south. He asked for trails, particularly the ones away from the wagon road. Wanted to know positively if a man on foot could ford creeks and large streams. Wanted directions from one place to another. His question reminded me of what General Bradley once said to me, that some of the citizens at the fort have run away from some mean thing to escape punishment.

In a few days after this my suspicions about this man came true. Leighton's clerk had fled. He helped himself to a new Winchester and plenty of cartridges and what provisions he wanted. His quiet disappearance in the night coupled with his theft was bound to raise real suspicion.

Three soldiers at the fort afterwards said they knew him, but did not know he was a deserter from Fort Kearney, Nebraska, on the Platte, that nearly killed a lieutenant sometime before he came to Fort C. F. Smith.

After checking Leighton s clerk, his habits, oddities of brushing his hair, the scar on his neck and through other means they decided Leighton's clerk was the man Fort Kearney authorities wanted. How this deserter could live all winter under the shadow of Fort C. F. Smith and escape being discovered is a puzzle.

TEWKSBURY APPROPRIATING MY HARNESS REPAIR KIT

[John] Tewksbury was in the habit of going among my harness leathers and taking what he wanted to repair his broken harness once in a while. The quartermaster at the fort always gave me what I wanted to keep my mail outfit up, so I usually kept a small supply on hand. Tewksbury would always tell Hugh what he had taken and offer to lend mules to pack meat to the fort for pay. This was all right, but who wants another rummaging around among your things? We forgave him as it was a habit of his, and also as he would pay us in money if we did not use his mules.

One afternoon while I was in the quartermaster's department I saw a harness repair outfit nearly brand new. It was the very thing necessary to repair harness and saddles. I asked the quartermaster clerk if he would let me have it. The quartermaster clerk as expected made quite a fuss, but after a while gave the harness kit to me. "Take it," he said. "And don't you ever come back here unless I give you a written invitation."

I placed the harness kit under my arm and started home. On my way I passed Tewksbury's door which was open. And of course he had to notice I had something under my arm, so he stepped to the door and asked:

"Johnny, what have you talked them out of this time?"

"Mr. Tewksbury, I have something worthwhile," I answered.

"Well, Johnny, I have a notion to take that dilapidated contraption away from you, old and worn out as I am, and I can do it!"

"No, I don't think you will, Tewksbury," I answered, and passed on to my cabin.

Hugh and I were a minute later examining the contents of the harness kit. There were different kinds of saddler's thread, needles, awls, wax ends, saddler's tools, a roll of leather, a new jerkline and several other articles. We had them all out on the table when Tewksbury came in. He had to see everything. He made quite a talk about how useful this kit would be to me. Then Tewksbury placed all the articles back in the kit and made a run for the door.

I made [a] rush toward him to stop his cute game, for knew he was persistent and domineering. He parleyed and whispered, and all the time kept stepping further away, slipping and sliding like an eel.

"I need these things," he said. "[I] am old and half sick. My years of life can only be spanned by months from now on. I can only talk in a whisper. Go back to the fort and tell the quartermaster you have to be outfitted with a new outfit, as you have met a problem beyond your control." . . . Tewksbury made a clean getaway into his cabin, which was about seventy feet from our cabin.

In about an hour I went back to the quartermaster clerk and asked for a new saddler's kit. The old quartermaster clerk this time nearly fell over backwards. "What!" he yelled. "Back here again? What am I going to do with you, tell me that? You have about used up your welcome for all time to come. What happened? Out with it!"

"Tewksbury has taken my entire outfit and bolted his door. Cannot recover the outfit without force, but don't like to resort to such methods. Tewksbury will give Hugh and I [*sic*] anything he has in a time of distress. [He] has at other times never failed to accommodate us; for that reason it is hard to go after him, and then he isn't long for this world at best."

The quartermasterclerk gave me a new saddler's kit and a small roll of leather extra. [It] was a better kit than the other kit, as it had never been used or opened. This pleased me quite well.

"Now," the quartermaster clerk said, "if your friend Tewksbury takes this kit away from you, [I] will consider your brain has become a wreck. I will stroll down and have a talk with Tewksbury in a day or two, for he is not to have another thing from the department through you. I will make him pay for that kit."

"No! Please, do not bother Tewksbury, this time at least. I have only told you what happened so as to give you the truth, nothing else."

"And that truth business of yours is what has helped you more than anything else around this fort. Now make yourself scarce around here for at least one hour if possible. I am not running a department especially for your convenience. I like to jangle with Tewksbury sometimes, to pass away the time, and will jangle with some more to a nice point."

"Thank you," I answered. "Sometime I will be of service to you. You are a real nice fellow when you give yourself a chance."

"Get out of here!" I heard as [I] went through the door, just as a brand new riding bridle wrapped me across the face and over the head. That too went with my new kit. I could stand a wallop over the head for a new bridle anytime.

MCKENZIE'S MULES STOLEN

About the first of August, 1868,[1] [William] McKenzie came into the fort and complained to Major Burt [that] the Cheyenne and Sioux were worrying his men to such an extent that it was well nigh impossible to finish the wood contract for the fort. He had to guard his men and mules continually. [He said] that he wanted Major Burt to detail about fifteen soldiers to protect men and mules, so he could finish his contract, and that if Major Burt would not do this, then the government would have to stand the loss if the Cheyenne and Sioux stole his mules.

Hugh and I were lucky. We had sold all our mules and horses for a good price except the strawberry roan, Hugh's mare. The Indians at this time were making things very uncertain around the fort, so Major Burt decided to keep all [the] men at the fort against a time of need. And McKenzie had to finish his wood contract for the fort before he could receive the balance of money. The fort was soon to be abandoned, so [Burt] did not need extra wood. McKenzie therefore was caught between two jaws. He did the only thing left for him to do, continued hauling wood.

One evening so many Sioux and Cheyenne stole around them it became impossible to save the mules. All hands could do nothing but save themselves from being annihilated. McKenzie was left without a mule or a horse. So that finished the wood contract for good and McKenzie too, but he was bound by contract to receive pay for his mules from the government.

PREPARATIONS TO ABANDON FORTS RENO, PHIL KEARNY, AND C. F. SMITH

The Indians of all tribes never fancied having forts within what they termed their country. All resented [it], and especially the Cheyenne and Sioux, who would rather have trouble than peace any time when the white man came into the program of the wilderness. But this branch of the Sioux were then in the territory of the Mountain Crow Indians, by and with the consent of the Crows. This branch of Sioux were somewhat nomadic, and had a short time before experienced a real defeat farther to the north.[2] They lost so heavy in warriors and ponies [that they] were afraid to go back to the old grounds. The Cheyenne and Sioux preferred to kill wherever an opportunity came their way, seldom otherwise.

The Cheyenne and Sioux would not disfigure a brave man and usually [would] not take his scalp, because they thought a real brave man was entitled to respect. These two tribes of Indians were a hard lot to get along with those days. It required some pretty severe war medicine by the right parties to make them behave, which they finally received.

While the Mountain Crow disliked the white men coming into their country, they never went on the war path with them, or scalped a white man to my knowledge. This was the proud boast of the Crows. The Crows claimed the pale face were too many, like the hairs on your head, like the trees of the forest, while the Crows were but few; and ahead of the Crow in thousands of ways.

The chiefs of the Cheyenne and Sioux met the government representatives near or at Fort Laramie and signed a peace to last "as long as water ran downhill and grass grew green." The government was to abandon Forts Reno, Phil Kearny and C. F. Smith as the price of peace. Sometime in September these three forts were to be abandoned by the government.

Hugh and I had lived at Fort C. F. Smith so long and knew the surrounding country so well, it was home. We regretted leaving the place and our friends. I resigned the mail carrying business in July 1868, as there would be only one or

Oglala Sioux chief Red Cloud was the leader of the allied Indian tribes in their actions against the Bozeman Trail and its associated forts, a conflict known as Red Cloud's War. *Library of Congress, Prints and Photographs Division, LC-USZ62-91032.*

Ruins of Fort C. F. Smith on the Bighorn River, n.d. (ca. 1920).
Lantern slide, unknown photographer.
National Park Service, Little Bighorn Battlefield National Monument, LIBI_00030_01386.

two more trips and probably not those. We had up to more than two thousand dollars apiece. Hugh was the one who managed it. He saved our money. As long as we were together, the idea of being out of money seemed a thing well nigh impossible. Hugh was all business, all saving, all for the future.

Is this abrupt close intentional? The words "The End," firmly written at the bottom of manuscript page 355, indicate that it is.[3]

The allied tribes' victory on the Bozeman Trail was, of course, transitory. The Fort Laramie Treaty of 1868 held only until 1874, when gold was discovered in the Black Hills in the heart of the newly designated Great Sioux Reservation. There followed new pressures on, and resistance by, the tribes; the Battle of the Little Bighorn, not far from the former site of Fort C. F. Smith; and the restriction of the various Sioux bands to the poorest remnants of their old domains.

A century after the 1868 treaty, American Indian activists would make recognition of Sioux rights under the earlier agreement a key demand. In 1969 they occupied Alcatraz Island in San Francisco Bay, citing, among other things a Fort Laramie treaty provision about abandoned government property.[4] Living some fourteen miles away, I was not yet aware of the irony. It was as if the reverberations of Bozeman Trail history had caught up with some of John Benton Hart's descendants—and with his manuscript, then housed in my parents' home and familiar only to them.

EPILOGUE

THE BOX FROM COLORADO

LAWRENCE HART

Lawrence Hart, the grandson of John Benton Hart, son of Harry Hart, and father of the editor of this book, was an accomplished man of letters and a teacher of the writer's craft. With the aid of his wife, the poet Jeanne McGahey, he made many attempts to edit and market the old frontiersman's memoirs. His introduction to one of these manuscripts adds a poignant postscript to the story.

One day in the autumn of 1946 there arrived on my doorstep in Berkeley, California, a massive carton, sent to me COD by relatives in Colorado.

Lawrence Hart in a children's creative-writing class during the 1950s.
A young John Hart, the editor of this book, is to his right.
Collection of John Hart.

In the carton were the papers of my father, Harry Hart. But the papers were much more than personal. For they contained, with much else, the remarkable story of my grandfather John Benton Hart, a Civil War cavalryman, frontiersman, and pioneer.

I did not remember my father or my grandfather, and a family schism almost caused me to turn the shipment down. My wife and I did not know it then, but in taking the shipment we had just averted what might have been the final loss of a unique historical resource.

And so we began to read, each taking a sheaf from the top of the great mass. There were unskillful novels by my father Harry Hart. There was poetry, mostly bad (but good in spots). There was a great deal of original music. There was an interesting family tree, full of melodramatic incidents. And there was the discovery of an unrecognized frontier character and even frontier hero, who happened to be my grandfather John Benton Hart.

For months we gave our time, all we could spare of it, to reading the manuscripts: amusement, delight, and discovery. There were errors and malapropisms. The captain of the wagon train was "a gentleman from the word go." The Indian brave had "a breech-clout over his lions." But there were other passages, descriptive or emotional, that were simply brilliant. There were original accounts of little-documented historical incidents. There were mysteries too, resulting largely from gaps in the manuscript: notably the mystery of John Hart's connection with the famous mountain man Jim Bridger.

Partly in hope of clearing up such problems, we went to Colorado in the summer of 1947. For me, it was a journey into a past I had lost and disowned. In Harts Basin near Delta, in the attic of my father's house, we found both the typed and long-hand manuscripts of "The Death of Caspar Collins," and, for "The Battle of the Hay Field," a manuscript in longhand.[1] And it was then that we learned something shocking: that a great part of the manuscript, a casualty of family disinterest, had been burned.

Laura Gale, my aunt and Harry's sister, told me that the manuscript sent in 1946 contained only the pages that were typed and bound, and perhaps not all of those. Most of the handwritten material she had destroyed, regarding it as valueless. This included, it seems, an unspecified number of notebooks, something like composition books, identified elsewhere in the manuscript as "Jim Bridger's Journals." Or perhaps these, being more difficult to destroy, were among the papers spared from the first burning. If so, they too were burned, years later, by another aunt in another bonfire.

Aside from Harry Hart, John Hart's oldest son, none of the old man's family seemed to see value in his memories. In his own old age, Harry tried to interest one or another of the family in taking charge of the manuscripts. I was the person who would have recognized their value; but due to our estrangement, now bitterly regretted, Harry did not offer them to me. They came to me—what remained of them—a year after his death. They were in fact my notification of his death. They came, as I found out later, by a fluke or a whim. But they came.

Harry Hart was an unsuccessful writer. Or was he? There is a strange difference between his fiction (atrocious, impossible) and the factual and skillful historical writing in which he collaborated with old John.

An editor, to whom Harry had sent an unsuccessful novel, suggested that he look up one or more of the old frontiersmen, some of whom had finally settled in places like the Colorado mountains. A few were still alive; and it was important indeed, the editor argued, to get on paper what they had to tell.

Old John, of course, was one of these sources. So evening after evening Harry went down to his father's house in Hart's Basin, listened to his recollections, jotted down what he could of his father's exact words. Then he typed what he had been told and brought it back for correction.

Old John himself, who seems to have had an almost eidetic memory, now became interested in this writing process. He began to set down his own accounts. There is no way of knowing how much there originally was of the old man's longhand record. But a little of it, which had been bound, was among the manuscripts sent to me. It was simply written, with surprisingly few errors in grammar or spelling. It must be the source of some, at least, of the charm of the final manuscript.

What occurred here was, in fact, a rather remarkable collaboration. So it was that the funny story of the sweet potato in the Missouri campaign was expanded, in response to Harry's written questions, until it became a day-to-day recollection of the campaign. Harry, in turn, was brought to write more simply, so simply that there was no place for tritenesses or purple passages.

But in 1928, when old John died, the writing team lost its senior member. Harry continued to work with the manuscripts, but the extreme passages became more numerous. I would guess that, while the old man's longhand manuscript was simple and factual, his spoken accounts were much more vivid. Harry would try to recreate this vividness from memory, with results that were sometimes truly bad but often fortunate.

My own part, as a later (and very minor) partner in this collaboration, was nevertheless entirely necessary. Chiefly this was the elision of the sometimes lurid purple passages (Harry's) and the keeping of passages (also Harry's) when they were both vivid and ably written. Sometimes they rose to something almost like poetry.[2]

I sat, one evening that summer of 1947, on the porch of the Finn House on the slopes of Grand Mesa, and looked out over the lights in the river valleys. The air was so clear, I could see so far, that the scattered farmhouse lights were drawn together like the lights of a city. I could not see over the hills, into Hart's Basin, where my grandfather settled at last. But I had seen the cellar of the house where I was born, now open to the sky, full of timbers and the rough webs of the black widow spider. Even the cellar has disappeared now, and the river valleys are filling with smog. And I cannot retrieve what I arrogantly threw away.

But as a great poet may be known first, and best, through his books, so I know Harry and John Benton Hart, in ways in which I think their Colorado family may not have known them, through what I have of the manuscripts.

NOTES

INTRODUCTION

1. William G. Cutler, *History of the State of Kansas* (Chicago: A. T. Andreas, 1883), 520, available online at http://www.kancoll.org/books/cutler/.
2. John B. Hart, in "Roster and Descriptive Roll, Eleventh Regiment, Cavalry, Kansas Civil War Volunteers," microfilm AR116, State Archives Division, Kansas State Historical Society, Topeka, 79, available online at Kansas Memory, http://www.kansasmemory.org/item/227699. Johnny's brother Hugh F. Hart joined the same regiment and company about a year later. Ibid. Hugh's absence from the Civil War portion of the memoir is a mystery.
3. Ruby Roberts Coleman, *Pre-Statehood History of Lincoln County, Nebraska* (Bowie, Md.: Heritage Books, 1992), 81–87.
4. Descendants of Nathaniel Hart, database maintained by David Hart.
5. Principal source is Harry Hart, "Hart's Basin," manuscript in the collection of John Hart, San Rafael, Calif. Legislative service is from Hart's Legislator Record, Joint Legislative Council Library, State Capitol, Denver, Colo. See also Graeme Pente, "Populism in Colorado," last modified Aug. 31, 2017, *Colorado Encyclopedia*, https://coloradoencyclopedia.org/article/populism-colorado.
6. For many chapters of "Over the Oregon Trail," handwritten versions (usually in very faint pencil) exist; I surmise these are the products of dictation. For a few cases there are typed interim versions. I have followed the 1923 typescript. This itself has two layers of edits, one in black ink and a later one, often modifying the first, in red. Except as occasionally noted, I have been guided by the red edits.

CHAPTER 1. UNDER MOONLIGHT IN MISSOURI

1. See, for instance, Douglas C. McChristian and Paul L. Hedren, *Fort Laramie: Military Bastion of the High Plains* (Norman: University of Oklahoma Press, 2009), 236.
2. Michael Tatham, "Because They Were Needed: The History of the Eleventh Kansas Volunteer Regiment, 1862–1865" (MA thesis, Central Missouri State University, 1998), 77.
3. Howard N. Monnett, *Action before Westport, 1864*, rev. ed. (Boulder: University Press of Colorado, 1995); Kyle S. Sinisi, *The Last Hurrah: Sterling Price's Missouri Expedition of 1864* (Lanham, Md.: Rowman and Littlefield, 2015); Mark A. Lause, *The Collapse of Price's Raid: The Beginning of the End in Civil War Missouri* (Columbia: University of Missouri Press, 2016).

4. Samuel R. Curtis, "Return from the Pursuit of Price," in U.S. War Department, *The War of the Rebellion: A Compilation of the Official Records of the Union and Confederate Armies*, ser. 1, vol. 41, pt. 1 (Washington, D.C.: Government Printing Office, 1893), 519, available online at http://ebooks.library.cornell.edu/cgi/t/text/pageviewer-idx?c=moawar&cc=moawar&idno=waro0083&node=waro0083%3A1&view=image&seq=543&size=100.
5. See, for instance, H. E. Palmer, "The Black-Flag Character of War on the Border," *Kansas Historical Collections* 9 (1906): 455.
6. Andrew G. Todd, in "Roster and Descriptive Roll, Eleventh Regiment, Cavalry, Kansas Civil War Volunteers," microfilm AR116, State Archives Division, Kansas State Historical Society, Topeka, 81, available online at Kansas Memory, http://www.kansasmemory.org/item/227699.
7. "The Negro" is not otherwise identified in Hart's account.
8. See Stephen Z. Starr, *Jennison's Jayhawkers: A Civil War Cavalry Regiment and Its Commander* (Baton Rouge: Louisiana State University Press, 1973); and Monnett, *Action before Westport*, 43–44.
9. William Y. Drew, in "Roster and Descriptive Roll," 75.
10. This soldier is not otherwise identified.
11. James G. Blunt, "General Blunt's Account of His Civil War Experiences," *Kansas Historical Quarterly* 1, no. 3 (May 1932): 211–65, available online at www.kancoll.org/khq/1932/32_3_blunt.htm; Monnett, *Action before Westport*, 53, 66; Richard J. Hinton, *Rebel Invasion of Missouri and Kansas and the Campaign of the Army of the Border against General Sterling Price in October and November, 1864* (Chicago: Church & Goodman, 1865; repr., New South Books, n.d.), 88.
12. Greer is not found in the "Roster and Descriptive Roll" but figures significantly in the Battle of the Little Blue and in later actions on the frontier.
13. Colonel Moonlight at this point was not the head of the Eleventh Kansas but of a larger ad-hoc unit called the Second Brigade. The Eleventh provided the bulk of this brigade, but Johnny never mentions the nominal regimental commander at this time, Lt. Col. Preston B. Plumb. See Monnett, *Action before Westport*, 44.
14. Blunt, "General Blunt's Account," 255; Monnett, *Action before Westport*, 53–54; "Report of Col. Thomas Moonlight, Eleventh Kansas Cavalry, Commanding Second Brigade," in U.S. War Department, *War of the Rebellion*, ser. 1, 41(1):591, available online at http://ebooks.library.cornell.edu/cgi/t/text/pageviewer-idx?c=moawar&cc=moawar&idno=waro0083&node=waro0083%3A1&view=image&seq=615&size=100.
15. Howard Monnett writes confusingly: "Captain Greer with Company I was sent south two miles down the [north-flowing] river." Action before Westport, 54. Moonlight confirms that the movement was to the north. Johnny, however, exaggerates the distances. Greer was a mile downstream from the principal crossing, near modern East Blue Mills Road, while Drew was somewhat beyond that.
16. The identity of this fallen cavalryman is unclear. There was no Tom Roderick in Company I per the "Roster and Descriptive Roll"; there is a John F. Roderick, but

he is met again at Platte Bridge Station. No Roderick is listed among the unit's casualties in William G. Cutler, "Eleventh Regiment Kansas Volunteer Cavalry," in *History of the State of Kansas*, vol. 1 (Chicago: A. T. Andreas, 1883), 197, available online at http://www.kancoll.org/books/cutler/sthist/milrec-p12.html.

17. Moonlight reported that Greer "retired without firing a shot, but claims that it was not possible to do otherwise, as the enemy were crossing at all points." "Report of Col. Thomas Moonlight," 592.
18. Sinisi, *Last Hurrah*, 195–96, 199.
19. Blunt, "General Blunt's Account," 256; Monnett, *Action before Westport*, 80–81, 84; Sinisi, *Last Hurrah*, 201.
20. Official records do not support such a high loss. See *Report of the Adjutant General of the State of Kansas, 1861–1865* (Topeka: Kansas State Printing, 1896), 15, available online at https://archive.org/details/reportofadjutantookans.
21. James J. Clancy, in "Roster and Descriptive Roll," 75.
22. Hinton, *Rebel Invasion of Missouri and Kansas*, 173; "Reports of Maj. Gen. Alfred Pleasonton, U.S. Army, Commanding Provisional Cavalry Division," in U.S. War Department, *War of the Rebellion*, ser. 1, 41(1):337, available online at http://ebooks.library.cornell.edu/cgi/t/text/pageviewer-idx?c=moawar&cc=moawar&idno=waro0083&node=waro0083%3A1&view=image&seq=361&size=100; Sinisi, *Last Hurrah*, 245.
23. By most accounts, Moonlight had plenty of "self-esteem." Johnny, however, experienced him as friendly and not at all arrogant, as several episodes omitted here attest.
24. Despite his weakness, Price was expected to strike at Fort Scott, but he decided against it, reentered Missouri north of town, and headed south to Fayetteville, Arkansas. See Edgar Langsdorf, "Price's Raid and the Battle of Mine Creek," *Kansas History* 37 (Summer 2014): 78–99; Sinisi, *Last Hurrah*, 260; and Lause, *Collapse of Price's Raid*, 155.
25. Wiley Britton, *The Civil War on the Border*, vol. 2 (New York: G. P. Putnam's Sons, 1899), 133; *The Union Army: A History of Military Affairs in the Loyal States, 1861–65*, vol. 6, *Cyclopedia of Battles—Helena Road to Z* (Madison, Wis.: Federal Publishing, 1908), 921.
26. The metal was probably bronze, not brass.
27. Johnny's description of the artillerymen's condition suggests that the soldiers, at least, did not experience Pleasonton's pursuit of Price as leisurely.
28. I have not been able to determine the identity of this unit.
29. The same unidentified Union soldier who kidded Johnny about his sweet potato at Lexington.

CHAPTER 2. AT PLATTE BRIDGE WITH CASPAR COLLINS

1. John M. Carroll, ed., *The Sand Creek Massacre: A Documentary History* (New York: Sol Lewis, 1973); Stan Hoig, *The Sand Creek Massacre* (Norman: University of Oklahoma Press, 1961); Arik Kelman, *A Misplaced Massacre: Struggle over the Memory of Sand Creek* (Cambridge, Mass.: Harvard University Press, 2013).

2. Tatham, "Because They Were Needed," 113–15.
3. It may have been Louis Guinard's brother who helped build the bridge, while his nephew, Louis Philip, clerked for him. See John D. McDermott, *Frontier Crossroads: The History of Fort Caspar and the Upper Platte Crossing* (Casper, Wyo.: City of Casper, 1999), 23, and Tom Rea, *Devil's Gate: Owning the Land, Owning the Story* (Norman: University of Oklahoma Press, 2006), 71–72.
4. "Diary of Isaac B. Pennock, First Sergeant Company 'I,' Eleventh Kansas Cavalry," in Pearl T. Ponce, ed., *Kansas's War: The Civil War in Documents*, 197–204 (Athens: Ohio University Press, 2011); Ferdinand Erhardt, "Reminiscences of Ferdinand Erhardt: A Paper Read before the Old Settlers Reunion at Lincoln, 1906," in *Pioneer History of Kansas*, ed. Adolph Roenigk (Lincoln, Kan.: Adolph Roenigk, 1933); George E. Hyde, *Life of George Bent, Written from His Letters*, ed. Savoie Lottinville (Norman: University of Oklahoma Press, 1968), 217–22. Additional accounts by soldiers not of Collins's party include William Y. Drew, "The Platte Bridge Fight by One Who Was There," *Osage County Chronicle* (Burlington, Kan.), Apr. 20, 27, May 11, 18, 25, 1882; Stephen H Fairfield, "The Eleventh Kansas Regiment at Platte Bridge," in *Transactions of the Kansas State Historical Society, 1903–1904*, vol. 8 (Topeka: George A. Clark, State Printer, 1904), 352–62; John C. Friend, "Account of the Platte Bridge Fight Written by John C. Friend," Folder 18, Box 2, William Oliver Collins and Family Papers, WH 73, Western History Collection, Denver Public Library; Henry Lord, "Henry Lord of Dodge City Tells of the Battle of Platte Bridge," *Emporia (Kan.) Gazette*, Aug. 9, 1934; George Morton Walker, "Eleventh Kansas Cavalry, 1865, and Battle of Platte Bridge," in *Kansas Historical Collections, 1915–1918*, vol. 14 (Topeka: Kansas State Historical Society, 1918), 335–38; and Charles Waring, "The Platte Bridge Battle," *Riley County Democrat* (Manhattan, Kan.), Aug. 26, 1909. To these must be added George Bird Grinnell, *The Fighting Cheyennes* (New York: Charles Scribner's Sons, 1915), 216–29. Though not an eyewitness, Grinnell spoke with many unnamed Cheyenne informants and drew on George Bent's reminiscences as well.
5. Grinnell, *Fighting Cheyennes*, 219–20.
6. Pvt. John F. Roderick, in "Roster and Descriptive Roll, Eleventh Regiment, Cavalry, Kansas Civil War Volunteers," microfilm AR116, State Archives Division, Kansas State Historical Society, Topeka, 80, available online at Kansas Memory, http://www.kansasmemory.org/item/227699. See also *Report of the Adjutant General of the State of Kansas*, 410.
7. John W. Holding, in "Roster and Descriptive Roll," 79.
8. Grinnell, *Fighting Cheyennes*, 221–22.
9. Noah Coffman, in "Roster and Descriptive Roll," 78. Pharus E. Hammond, a private from Leavenworth, enlisted in Company I in April 1864. *Report of the Adjutant General of the State of Kansas*, 411.
10. Lord, "Henry Lord of Dodge City Tells of the Battle of Platte Bridge." This account lacks a byline and is written in the third person, perhaps by Lord's son Earl.

11. Charles Bates to R. Ellison, Mar. 16, 1924, copy in John F. Maxon Collection, Fort Caspar State Historic Site, Casper, Wyo.
12. Drew, "Platte Bridge Fight," Apr. 20, 1882. I have not been able to determine the identity of the man killed earlier.
13. Ultimate source for this variant is Sheila Hart, "Mrs. Louisa Lajeunesse Boyd," in *Women of Wyoming*, ed. Mrs. Alfred (Cora) Beach, vol. 1 (Casper, Wyo.: S. E. Boyer, 1927), 139–43 (reprint of Hart, "Oldest Woman Resident of [Fremont] County [Wyoming] Has Passed Away: Was Eye Witness to Fight in which Caspar Collins Was Killed," *Casper (Wyo.) Tribune-Herald*, Dec. 12, 1926). Hart's account overlaps "Seminoe Boy, Son of Lajeunesse, Scalped Cheyenne Indian Caused Battle at Caspar," *Wyoming State Journal* (Lander), Sept. 8, 1938. But this very questionable version is partly based on an otherwise undocumented interview with Mrs. Boyd.
14. Erhardt, "Reminiscences," 120–21.
15. Isaac B. Pennock, in "Roster and Descriptive Roll," 80; *Report of the Adjutant General of the State of Kansas*, 410. Some older sources give his name as "Pennick."
16. After the fighting on the succeeding day, Drew reported finding a note dropped by a captive of the Indians: "You killed one of the principal chiefs of the Cheyennes yesterday, and they swear they will have a fearful revenge on you for it." Drew, "Platte Bridge Fight," May 18, 1882. But it seems unlikely that the fate of High Backed Wolf added much intensity to an attack long planned.
17. Todd Guenther, work in progress, Jan. 2017; Hart, "Mrs. Louisa Lajeunesse Boyd," 141.
18. Lord, "Henry Lord of Dodge City Tells of the Battle of Platte Bridge"; Hart, "Mrs. Louisa Lajeunesse Boyd," 139–43; *In The Court of Claims No. 7806. James R. Whitehead, Administrator of the Estate of Louis Guinard, Deceased vs. The United States, Araphoe, Cheyenne and Sioux Tribes of Indians*, item A22, Fort Caspar Museum, Casper, Wyo.
19. One recent study of Confederate prisoners enlisted to fight Indians on the northern plains is Michelle Tucker Butts, *Galvanized Yankees on the Upper Missouri: The Face of Loyalty* (Boulder: University Press of Colorado, 2003).
20. McDermott, *Frontier Crossroads*, 58; Robert Huhn Jones, *Guarding the Overland Trails: The Eleventh Ohio Cavalry in the Civil War* (Spokane, Wash.: Arthur H. Clark, 2005), 267.
21. McDermott, *Frontier Crossroads*, 55.
22. The Eleventh Kansas was headed at this time by Maj. Preston B. Plumb, but he had been sent farther west with five companies and did not figure in the Platte Bridge story. Former regimental commander Thomas B. Moonlight, whom Johnny had so admired during the Missouri campaign, had been promoted to higher positions in the West before proving so hopeless at Indian warfare that he was dismissed from the army. See *Report of the Adjutant General of the State of Kansas*, 210–11; McChristian and Hedren, *Fort Laramie*, 236.
23. McDermott, *Frontier Crossroads*, 61.

24. Pennock, "Diary," 200.
25. Records show no Bowen connected with the Eleventh Kansas. Johnny here must have meant Major Anderson.
26. J. W. Vaughn, *The Battle of Platte Bridge* (Norman: University of Oklahoma Press, 1963), 33–34; Alfred James Mokler, *Fort Caspar (Platte Bridge Station)* (1939; repr., Casper, Wyo.: Prairie, 1983), 27–29. But Stephen H. Fairfield has Collins, at least, volunteering. "Eleventh Kansas Regiment at Platte Bridge," 357.
27. Hart, "Mrs. Louisa Lajeunesse Boyd," 141; McDermott, *Frontier Crossroads*, 62.
28. Johnny is the only source to say that Collins chose the horse for its appearance.
29. This is the only report of "last words" from Caspar Collins, yet they seem both artificial and ill matched to the situation. Perhaps Johnny, or his amanuensis Harry Hart, embellished a bit. George Bent, watching from the Indian side, did not see an orderly retreat, rather a wild dash for the bridge. Hyde, *Life of George Bent*, 218.
30. The attackers were thronging in from three sides and could and did hit each other. See the *Report of the Adjutant General of the State of Kansas*, 210–11; McChristian and Hedren, *Fort Laramie*, 212, 236; Drew, "Platte Bridge Fight," Apr. 27, 1882; and Hyde, *Life of George Bent*, 218–19.
31. George W. McDonald, in "Roster and Descriptive Roll," 80; James A. Porter in "Additional Enlistments—Co. I," *Report of the Adjutant General of the State of Kansas*, 210–11; McChristian and Hedren, *Fort Laramie*, 411. Both names are listed as fatalities in Cutler, "Eleventh Regiment Kansas Volunteer Cavalry," 195–97. But George Walker reports that Porter, the friend of Henry Lord and (possibly) his accomplice in the scalping on July 25, was killed later on the twenty-sixth. Walker, "Eleventh Kansas Cavalry," 337–38.
32. While there is no Tip Hill, there is a Henry W. Hills in "Roster and Descriptive Roll," 79.
33. Harley L. Stoddard, in "Roster and Descriptive Roll," 81; George D. May, in *Report of the Adjutant General of the State of Kansas, 1861–'65*, 411. The others mentioned here among the wounded are unidentifiable. George Bent also thought that a large number of soldiers must have died. Hyde, *Life of George Bent*, 219. The "yellow boy" is probably a light-skinned African American.
34. Major Anderson sent Johnny and this party out in an attempt to reestablish communications and procure relief. Johnny spends few words on this rather fierce secondary skirmish, described in hyperbolic detail by William Lord and more soberly by George Walker. Lord, "Henry Lord of Dodge City Tells of the Battle of Platte Bridge"; Walker, "Eleventh Kansas Cavalry," 337–38. Apparently only Jim Porter died in this encounter.
35. McDermott, *Frontier Crossroads*, 67–70; Jones, *Guarding the Overland Trail*, 265, 269–70.
36. Louisa Lajeunesse Boyd also tells of the dud artillery shells. Hart, "Mrs. Louisa Lajeunesse Boyd," 142.
37. See Fairfield, "Eleventh Kansas Regiment at Platte Bridge," 357; and Erhardt, "Reminiscences," 120.

38. The "Ohioan" vs. "Kansan" divergence is described in John F. Steinle, "Frontier Artist and Soldier: Caspar Collins," *Ohio Historical Society Timeline* 21, no. 3 (May–June 2004): 3–13. Mokler's *Fort Caspar (Platte Bridge Station)* is an extreme "Ohioan" telling, relying largely on the son of Major Bretney, friend of the living Collins and defender of his memory. Vaughn's *The Battle of Platte Bridge* follows suit.
39. Walker," Eleventh Kansas Cavalry," 336.
40. See Hyde, *Life of George Bent*, 219; Erhardt, "Reminiscences," 119; Drew, "Platte Bridge Fight," May 11, 1882; Grinnell, *Fighting Cheyennes*, 223; Fairfield, "Eleventh Kansas Regiment at Platte Bridge"; and Friend, "Account of the Platte Bridge Fight."
41. The key source for the burning is a lawsuit filed by the Guinard heirs seeking compensation. *Whitehead vs. The United States, Arapahoe, Cheyenne and Sioux*, item A22, Fort Caspar Museum. Compare Bvt. Brig. Gen. W. Myers, "Annual Report for the Fiscal Year Ending June 30, 1868," Omaha, Neb., Aug. 5, 1868, 3, found in Drawer 1, Folder "Inspection and Annual Reports," Barry J. Hagan Collection, Sheridan (Wyo.) Public Library. Archeological investigation has found no trace of the bridge being burned. Richard L. Young, Fort Caspar Museum, email exchange with John Hart, Feb. 24, 2017.

CHAPTER 3. THE WELLS FARGO MULE TRAIN

1. Coleman, *Pre-Statehood History of Lincoln County, Nebraska*, 81–87.
2. I have not found any company documentation of Mr. Brown or Wagon Train No. 4. Unfortunately, the Wells Fargo archives do not extend back to the company's early days. Christy J. Horton, Wells Fargo archivist, email exchange with John Hart, Oct. 14, 2016.
3. How many wagons were in the train? The count is given elsewhere as forty-three, but this may not count "trailer" wagons, which would nearly double the total to be repaired. See Barry J. Hagan, *"Exactly in the Right Place": A History of Fort C. F. Smith, Montana Territory, 1866–1868* (El Segundo, Calif.: Upton & Sons, 1999), 114.
4. On the origins of the name of Crazy Woman Creek, see, for instance, Merrill J. Mattes, *Indians, Infants, and Infantry: Andrew and Elizabeth Burt on the Frontier* (Denver: Old West, 1960), 115; Barry J. Hagan, "An Explanation of the Name 'Crazy Woman's Fork,'" n.d., Elsa Spear Byron Collection, University of Portland Archives, Portland, Ore.
5. The lookout point was not a rock outcropping but a grassy prominence, Pilot Hill.
6. Hagan, *"Exactly in the Right Place,"* 106; Luther P. Bradley, Journal, July 17, 1867, Luther P. Bradley Papers and Journal, U.S. Army Military Research Collection, Carlisle Barracks, Pa.
7. Hagan, *"Exactly in the Right Place,"* 121; Jerome A. Greene, "The Hayfield Fight: A Reappraisal of a Neglected Action," *Montana the Magazine of Western History* 22, no. 4 (Autumn 1972): 8.
8. Hagan, *"Exactly in the Right Place,"* 117.

CHAPTER 4. FORT C. F. SMITH

1. Richard White, "The Winning of the West: The Expansion of the Western Sioux in the Eighteenth and Nineteenth Centuries," *Journal of American History*, 65, no. 2 (Sept. 1978): 336, 339; Francis Haines, *The Plains Indians* (New York: Thomas Y. Crowell, 1976), 147–48.
2. Assessments of the plight of the Crows differ. Susan Badger Doyle writes: "By the 1860s the Crows in the region crossed by the Bozeman Trail had been pushed close to extinction by the Blackfoot alliance to the west and the Sioux alliance to the east. They were saved from certain extermination only by their alliance with the invading whites." "Intercultural Dynamics of the Bozeman Trail Era: Red, White and Army Blue on the Northern Plains, 1863–1868" (PhD diss., University of New Mexico, 1991), 106. James Donovan is more sanguine: "No tribe on the northern plains had resisted the Sioux invasion as the Crows had, even after the Sioux had permanently driven them from the Powder River country." *A Terrible Glory: Custer and the Little Bighorn—the Last Great Battle of the American West* (New York: Little Brown, 2008), 181.
3. John H. Monnett, *Where a Hundred Soldiers Were Killed: The Battle for the Powder River Country in 1866 and the Making of the Fetterman Myth* (Albuquerque: University of New Mexico Press, 2008), xxix.
4. Bvt. Maj. E. B. Grimes, "Report, Fort C. F. Smith, October and November 1867," enclosure to G-172, vol. 2, 1867, RG 393, Letters Received, Department of the Platte, 1866–68, National Archives and Records Administration, Washington, D.C.
5. Bvt. Brig. Gen. W. Myers, "Annual Report for the Fiscal Year Ending June 30, 1868," Aug. 5, 1868, 4–5, RG 92, Annual, Personal, and Special Reports of Quartermaster Officers, 1863–70, 1872–78, entry 1105, National Archives and Records Administration, Washington, D.C.
6. See, for instance, Grace Raymond Hebard and E. A. Brininstool, *The Bozeman Trail: Historical Accounts of the Blazing of the Overland Routes into the Northwest, and the Fights with Red Cloud's Warriors*, 2 vols. (Cleveland: Arthur H. Clark, 1922), 2:140.
7. Hagan, *"Exactly in the Right Place,"* 200.
8. Mattes, *Indians, Infants, and Infantry*, 145–71.
9. Robert A. Murray, "Colonel Johnathan Eugene Smith," in Fort Phil Kearny/ Bozeman Trail Assoc., *Portraits of Fort Phil Kearny* (Banner, Wyo., 1993), 200–202.
10. J. Cecil Alter, *Jim Bridger* (Norman: University of Oklahoma Press, 1962), 335–36; Stanley Vestal, *Jim Bridger: Mountain Man* (Lincoln: University of Nebraska Press, 1946), 294–305.
11. Fort Phil Kearny/Bozeman Trail Assoc., *Portraits of Fort Phil Kearny*, 177–84; John S. Gray, *Custer's Last Campaign: Mitch Boyer and the Little Bighorn Reconstructed* (Lincoln: University of Nebraska Press, 1993), 26, 59, 60, 63, 73; Donovan, *Terrible Glory*, 4, 161, 163.

12. Hagan, *"Exactly in the Right Place,"* 140–42, 203, 225. In Johnny's narrative I have corrected the spelling of the surname to "Colvin."
13. "Diary of Lieutenant George M. Templeton, 18th U.S. Infantry," undated entry under January 1868, Graf 4009, Newberry Library, Chicago, typescript; Hagan, *"Exactly in the Right Place,"* 23.
14. John S. Gray, "The Frontier Fortunes of John W. Smith," *Annals of Wyoming* 51 (1979): 41.
15. McKenzie appears frequently in Bradley, Journal. See also Gray, *Custer's Last Campaign*, 27, 71.
16. Gray, *Custer's Last Campaign*, 27, 68–69.
17. Gray, "Frontier Fortunes of John W. Smith," 39–43; "Diary of Lieutenant George M. Templeton," Dec. 12, 1866.
18. Tewksbury appears many times in "Diary of Lieutenant George M. Templeton."
19. Hagan, *"Exactly in the Right Place,"* 27, 68–69.
20. Bradley, Journal, Bradley Papers, Archives, U.S. Army Military Research Collection.
21. Finn Burnett, "Fort C. F. Smith and the Hayfield Fight," in Hebard and Brininstool, *Bozeman Trail*, 2:159–74; Robert Beebe David, *Finn Burnett, Frontiersman* (Glendale, Calif.: Arthur H. Clark, 1937; repr. Mechanicsburg, Pa.: Stackpole, 2003).
22. James D. Lockwood, *Life and Adventures of a Drummer Boy, or Seven Years a Soldier* (Albany, N.Y.: John Skinner, 1893).
23. "Diary of Lieutenant George M. Templeton," 1867 and 1868 vols.; Hagan, *"Exactly in the Right Place,"* 23.
24. Alexander Wishart, "Diary of Alexander Wishart, 1867," in Elsa Spear, *The Books and Photographs of Elsa Spear*, by Elsa Spear (Family of Elsa Spear Bryan, 1993), 26–38.

CHAPTER 5. THE HAYFIELD FIGHT

1. John D. McDermott, *Red Cloud's War: The Bozeman Trail, 1866–1868* (Norman: University of Oklahoma Press, 2010), 380; Finn Burnett, "Fort C. F. Smith and the Hayfield Fight," in Hebard and Brininstool, *Bozeman Trail*, 2:159–74; David, *Finn Burnett*, 161–95; Greene, "Hayfield," 30–43; Lockwood, *Life and Adventures of a Drummer Boy*, chap. 9.
2. McKenzie's presence at the Hayfield is called into question by other sources; he may have been on his way to Bozeman at this time. See Gray, *Custer's Last Campaign*, 68–69, 71.
3. Navin is described as a discipline problem in Hagan, *"Exactly in the Right Place,"* 120.
4. These numbers are far off. Estimates vary, but it seems there were six to nine workers guarded by perhaps twenty soldiers. David, *Finn Burnett*, 171; Hagan, *"Exactly in the Right Place,"* 120; Gray, *Custer's Last Campaign*, 69.
5. Johnny had not registered the serious wounding of John Hollister, who would survive the day but die on August 2. Hagan, *"Exactly in the Right Place,"* 124–25.

6. Compare Greene, "Hayfield Fight," 12.
7. Soldiers uniformly feared torture if captured, but it is not clear how realistic this was. The propensity to torture varied by tribe; George Bent says that the Cheyenne never tortured. Hyde, *Life of George Bent*, 296. Postmortem mutilation was certainly standard practice and was perpetrated by whites as well.
8. For Bradley's official report, see J. W. Vaughn, *Indian Fights: New Facts on Seven Encounters* (Norman: University of Oklahoma Press, 2009), 237–39.
9. George H. Palmer, "Journal of Lt. George Henry Palmer, 27th Inf." U.S. Army Military History Research Collection, Carlisle Barracks, Pa.

CHAPTER 6. INTO THE MOUNTAINS

1. Probably a species of grouse.
2. David, *Finn Burnett*, 199–206.
3. Bradley, Journal, Oct. 14, 1867. Templeton reports that McKenzie had two others with him. "Diary of Lieutenant George M. Templeton, 18th U.S. Infantry," Oct. 6, 1867, Newberry Library, Chicago, typescript.
4. See Edwin C. Bearss, *Bighorn Canyon National Recreation Area, Montana-Wyoming, History Basic Data* (National Park Service, 1970), 1:68, available online at https://www.nps.gov/parkhistory/online_books/bica/history_data1.pdf; Alter, *Jim Bridger*, 73.

CHAPTER 7. THE MYSTERIOUS MAIL CARRIER

1. Bvt. Maj. E. B. Grimes, "Report, Fort C. F. Smith, October and November 1867," enclosure to G-172, vol. 2, 1867, RG 393, Letters Received, Department of the Platte, 1866–68, National Archives and Records Administration, Washington, D.C. See also Lt. Col. Luther P. Bradley, "Report of Civilian Employees in Q.M. Dept. at Ft. C. F. Smith M. T. October 8, 1867," Department of the Platte, Letters Received, 1866–68, ibid.
2. "Diary of Lieutenant George M. Templeton, 18th U.S. Infantry," undated entry under Jan. 1868, Newberry Library, Chicago, typescript.
3. Unable to corroborate this or to further identify Ben Barkeley.
4. Bradley's rank was actually lieutenant colonel, but Johnny is not alone in promoting him: it is also "General" Bradley in Wishart, "Diary."
5. Johnny does not mention this trophy pelt elsewhere.
6. Not attested.
7. I have not been able to identify this person.
8. Andrew Burt arrived at Fort C. F. Smith at the end of November 1867, so Johnny's first mail trip could not have been before this date. Bradley, Journal, Nov. 25, 1867.
9. "Diary of Lieutenant George M. Templeton," Apr. 17, 22, 27, June 20, 22, 1868.

CHAPTER 8. THE MOUNTAIN CROW WAR DANCE

1. Lockwood, *Life and Adventures of a Drummer Boy*, 172–73.
2. Tribes varied in the importance they attached to scalps as a measure of achievement. The Crows reportedly did not value them highly but did use them in their dances. See Haines, *Plains Indians*, 186.

CHAPTER 9. TWO DANGEROUS PRANKS

1. I have not found other references to "the five Blackfeet."

CHAPTER 10. CAPTURED BY THE CHEYENNE

1. See, for instance, Hagan, *"Exactly in the Right Place,"* 98–99, 144–145. Just when the brothers had the opportunity to purchase militia horses is unclear.
2. This renaming of the Little Bighorn River did not stick.
3. The bicultural witness George Bent denies that the Cheyennes tortured. See Hyde, *Life of George Bent*, 296.
4. I have not been able to locate this piece of slang ("cuter") elsewhere.
5. According to Francis Haines, Indians had only penetrated the inhospitable environment of the plains after about 1200 C.E. *Plains Indians*, 15.
6. Lieutenant Colonel Bradley recorded a storm on March 5–7, remarking, "The Crows said yesterday it would snow today, and for once they told the truth." Bradley, Journal, Mar. 5, 1867.

CHAPTER 11. LIEUTENANT COLONEL BRADLEY ASKS A FAVOR

1. Tapaderos, or hooded stirrups, are closed at the front so that brush cannot poke in and so that the foot cannot be caught in the stirrup if the rider is thrown.

CHAPTER 12. RUNNING FIGHT CARRYING THE MAIL

1. "Diary of Lieutenant George M. Templeton, 18th U.S. Infantry," June 20, 22, 1868, Newberry Library, Chicago, typescript.
2. Pierre Shane, interpreter, was married to a Crow woman. In passages not excerpted here, it is clear that Johnny disliked him. See Hagan, *"Exactly in the Right Place,"* 189–90.

CHAPTER 13. THE CROW ANNUITIES

1. The transfer occurred on April 1, 1868. General Bradley headed south on April 5. "Diary of Lieutenant George M. Templeton, 18th U.S. Infantry," Apr. 6, 1868, Newberry Library, Chicago, typescript.
2. See Hagan, *"Exactly in the Right Place,"* 140–42, 146–47, 191. Matthews was appointed, somewhat after the fact, on November 16, 1867. *Contributions to the Historical Society of Montana* (Helena, Mont.: Rocky Mountain, 1876), 291.

3. Passages that seem critical of individuals, such as this anecdote, are sometimes struck out in the red edit of Johnny's memoirs. In the case of this interesting incident, though, I have elected to retain it.

CHAPTER 14. LAST DAYS AT FORT C. F. SMITH

1. This date is too late. The last of the garrison left Fort C. F. Smith on July 29, 1868. Hagan, *"Exactly in the Right Place,"* 233–34.
2. I have not determined what "defeat" Johnny refers to here.
3. A clue to the brothers' next move may lie in a loose sheet, apparently a planned chapter's title page, found with the other manuscript materials: "Leaving with Story for Montana." Nelson Story was the man who snapped up much of the government property at Fort C. F. Smith and moved it north to Bozeman for highly profitable resale. Hagan, *"Exactly in the Right Place,"* 231–32.
4. Troy R. Johnson, *The Occupation of Alcatraz Island: Indian Self-Determination and the Rise of Indian Activism* (Urbana: University of Illinois Press, 1996).

EPILOGUE. THE BOX FROM COLORADO

1. I have not found a longhand manuscript about Platte Bridge.
2. For this book, I have followed the manuscript closely, minimizing elisions within the selected texts and indicating any that occur.

BIBLIOGRAPHY

ARCHIVES, LIBRARIES, AND MANUSCRIPT COLLECTIONS

Autry Museum, Los Angeles, Calif.
George Grinnell Collection
Denver Public Library, Western History Collection, Denver, Colo.
Ellison Collection
William Oliver Collins and Family Papers, WH 73
Fort Caspar State Historic Site, Casper, Wyo.
John F. Maxon Collection
Kansas State Historical Society, State Archives Division, Topeka, Kans.
Military History of the 11th Kansas, Collection 617
"Roster and Descriptive Roll, Eleventh Regiment, Cavalry, Kansas Civil War Volunteers," microfilm AR116. http://www.kansasmemory.org/item/227699
Library of Congress, Manuscript Division, Washington, D.C.
Edward I. Hartz Papers, MS 66-1415
National Archives and Records Administration, Washington, D.C.
Record Group 393, Letters Received, Department of the Platte, 1866–68
Newberry Library, Chicago
"Diary of Lieutenant George M. Templeton, 18th U.S. Infantry," Graf 4009, typescript
Sheridan Public Library, Sheridan, Wyo.
Barry J. Hagan Collection
University of Indiana, Lilly Library, Manuscript Department, Bloomington
Walter Camp, Camp Manuscript
University of Portland Archives, Portland, Ore.
Elsa Spear Byron Collection
University of Wyoming Library, Laramie, Wyo.
U.S. Army Military Research Collection, Carlisle Barracks, Pa.
Luther P. Bradley Papers and Journal

GOVERNMENT DOCUMENTS

Bearss, Edwin C. *Bighorn Canyon National Recreation Area, Montana-Wyoming: History Basic Data*. 2 vols. National Park Service, 1970. https://www.nps.gov/parkhistory/online_books/bica/history_data1.pdf.

Report of the Adjutant General of the State of Kansas, 1861–'65. Vol. 1. Topeka: Kansas State Printing, 1896. https://archive.org/details/reportofadjutantookans.

U.S. War Department. *The War of the Rebellion: A Compilation of the Official Records of the Union and Confederate Armies*. Ser. 1, vol. 41, pt. 1. Washington, D.C.: Government Printing Office, 1893. http://ebooks.library.cornell.edu/cgi/t/text/text-idx?c=moawar;cc=moawar;view=toc;subview=short;idno=waro0083.

BOOKS, ARTICLES, AND THESES

Alter, J. Cecil. *Jim Bridger*. Norman: University of Oklahoma Press, 1962.

Ambrose, Steven E. *Crazy Horse and Custer: The Parallel Lives of Two American Warriors*. New York: Doubleday, 1975.

"Another Veteran Heard from, John C. Friend, from an Undated Newspaper Clipping." *Annals of Wyoming* 32, no. 2 (October 1960): 236–38.

The Battle of Pilot Knob, Iron County, Missouri. State Historical Society of Missouri, n.d.

Blunt, James G. "General Blunt's Account of His Civil War Experiences." *Kansas Historical Quarterly* 1, no. 3 (May 1932): 211–65. http://www.kancoll.org/khq/1932/32_3_blunt.htm

Britton, Wiley. *The Civil War on the Border*. Vol. 2. New York: G. P. Putnam's Sons, 1899.

Brown, Dee. *Fort Phil Kearny: An American Saga*. Lincoln: University of Nebraska Press, 1962.

———. *The Galvanized Yankees*. 1963. Reprint, Lincoln: University of Nebraska Press, 1985.

Buresh, Lumir F. *October 25th and the Battle of Mine Creek*. Kansas City, Mo.: Lowell, 1977.

Burke, Diane Mutti, and Jonathan Earle, eds. *Bleeding Kansas, Bleeding Missouri: The Long Civil War on the Border*. Lawrence: University Press of Kansas, 2013.

Butts, Michele Tucker. *Galvanized Yankees on the Upper Missouri: The Face of Loyalty*. Boulder: University Press of Colorado, 2003.

———. "Trading Gray for Blue: Ex-Confederates Hold the Upper Missouri for the Union." *Prologue* 37, no. 4 (Winter 2005). https://www.archives.gov/publications/prologue/2005/winter/galvanized.html. Retrieved January 6, 2012.

Carrington, Frances C. *My Army Life and the Fort Phil Kearney Massacre*. Lincoln: University of Nebraska Press, 2004.

Carrington, Margaret Irwin. *Absaroka: Home of the Crows: Being the Experience of an Officer's Wife on the Plains*. Lincoln: University of Nebraska Press, 1983.

Carroll, John M., ed. *The Sand Creek Massacre: A Documentary History*. New York: Sol Lewis, 1973.

Castel, Albert. *Civil War Kansas: Reaping the Whirlwind*. Rev. ed. Lawrence: University Press of Kansas, 1997.

———. *General Sterling Price and the Civil War in the West*. Baton Rouge: Louisiana State University Press, 1968.

———. "War and Politics: The Price Raid of 1864." *Kansas Historical Quarterly* 24 (Summer 1958): 129–43.

———. *William Clarke Quantrill: His Life and Times*. Norman: University of Oklahoma Press, 1999.

Coleman, Ruby Roberts. *Pre-Statehood History of Lincoln County, Nebraska*. Bowie, Md.: Heritage Books, 1992.

Collins, Charles D., Jr. *Battlefield Atlas of Price's Missouri Expedition of 1864*. Fort Leavenworth, Kan.: Combat Studies Institute, 2016.

Connelly, William Elsey. *The Life of Preston B. Plumb*. Chicago: Browne and Howell, 1913.

Contributions to the Historical Society of Montana. Helena, Mont.: Rocky Mountain, 1876.

Coutant, C. G. *The History of Wyoming*. Laramie, Wyo.: Chaplin, Safford and Mathison, 1899.

Cutler, William G. "Eleventh Regiment Kansas Volunteer Cavalry." In *History of the State of Kansas*, vol. 1, 195–97. Chicago: A. T. Andreas, 1883. http://www.kancoll.org/books/cutler/sthist/milrec-p12.html.

David, Robert Beebe, ed. *Finn Burnett, Frontiersman*. Glendale, Calif.: Arthur H. Clark, 1937. Reprint, Mechanicsburg, Pa.: Stackpole, 2003.

Donovan, James. *A Terrible Glory: Custer and the Little Bighorn—the Last Great Battle of the American West*. New York: Little, Brown, 2008.

Doyle, Susan Badger. *Bound for Montana: Diaries from the Bozeman Trail*. Helena: Montana Historical Society, 2004.

———. "Intercultural Dynamics of the Bozeman Trail Era: Red, White and Army Blue on the Northern Plains, 1863–1868." PhD diss., University of New Mexico, 1991. UMI Dissertation Services, 1997.

Ellison, Robert S., and A. B. Ostrander. "The Platte Bridge Fight." *Winners of the West* 3 (March 15, 1926): 6–7.

Erhardt, Ferdinand. "Reminiscences of Ferdinand Erhardt: A Paper Read before the Old Settlers Reunion at Lincoln, 1906." In *Pioneer History of Kansas*, edited by Adolph Roenigk, 119–21. Denver: Adolph Roenigk, 1933.

Fairfield, Stephen H. "The Eleventh Kansas Regiment at Platte Bridge." In *Transactions of the Kansas State Historical Society, 1903–1904*, 8:352–62. Topeka: George A. Clark, State Printer, 1904. Reproduced in *Tales of Kansas in the Civil War*, 29–39. Tucson: A Plus Printing, n.d.

Fellman, Michael. *Inside War: The Guerrilla Conflict in Missouri during the American Civil War*. Oxford: Oxford University Press, 1989.

Fort Phil Kearny/Bozeman Trail Association. *Portraits of Fort Phil Kearny*. Banner, Wyo., 1993.

Gilmore, Donald. *Black Flag: Civil War on the Missouri-Kansas Frontier*. Gretna, La: Pelican, 2006.

Glass, Jefferson. "Crossing the North Platte River: A Brief History of Reshaw's Bridge—1852–1866." *Annals of Wyoming* 74 (2002): 25–40.

———. *Reshaw: The Life and Times of John Baptiste Richard*. Glendo, Wyo.: High Plains, 2014.

Goodrich, Thomas. *Black Flag: Guerilla Warfare on the Western Border, 1861–1865.* Bloomington: Indiana University Press, 1995.

Gray, John S. *Custer's Last Campaign: Mitch Boyer and the Little Bighorn Reconstructed.* Lincoln: University of Nebraska Press, 1993.

———. "The Frontier Fortunes of John W. Smith." *Annals of Wyoming* 51 (1979): 36–53.

Greene, Jerome A. "The Hayfield Fight: A Reappraisal of a Neglected Action." *Montana the Magazine of Western History* 22, no. 4 (Autumn 1972): 30–43.

———, ed. "'We Do Not Know What the Government Intends to Do . . .': Lt. Palmer Writes from the Bozeman Trail, 1867–68." *Montana the Magazine of Western History* 28, no. 3 (Summer 1978): 16–35.

Grinnell, George Bird. *The Fighting Cheyennes.* New York: Charles Scribner's Sons, 1915.

Guenther, Todd. "Pioneers Extraordinaire: A Most Unusual Wagon Train." *Overland Journal* 18, no. 4 (Winter 2000–2001): 3–17.

Hagan, Barry J. *"Exactly in the Right Place": A History of Fort C. F. Smith, Montana Territory, 1866–1868.* El Segundo, Calif.: Upton & Sons, 1999.

Hagen, Olaf T. "Platte Bridge Station and Fort Caspar." *Annals of Wyoming* 27, no. 1 (April 1955): 3–17.

Haines, Francis. *The Plains Indians.* New York: Thomas Y. Crowell, 1976.

Hart, Sheila. "Mrs. Louisa Lajeunesse Boyd." In *Women of Wyoming*, edited by Mrs. Alfred (Cora) Beach, 1:139–43. Casper, Wyo.: S. E. Boyer, 1927.

Hebard, Grace Raymond, and E. A. Brinninstool. *The Bozeman Trail: Historical Accounts of the Blazing of the Overland Routes into the Northwest, and the Fight with Red Cloud's Warriors.* 2 vols. Cleveland: Arthur H. Clark, 1922.

Hedren, Paul L. *Fort Laramie and the Great Sioux War.* Norman: University of Oklahoma Press, 1998.

Heppler, Jason A. "Framing Red Power: The American Indian Movement, the Trail of Broken Treaties, and the Politics of Media." MA thesis, University of Nebraska at Lincoln, 2009. http://digitalcommons.unl.edu.

Hinton, Richard J. *Rebel Invasion of Missouri and Kansas and the Campaign of the Army of the Border against General Sterling Price in October and November, 1864.* Chicago: Church & Goodman, 1865. Reprint, N.p.: New South Books, n.d.

Hoig, Stan. *The Sand Creek Massacre.* Norman: University of Oklahoma Press, 1961.

Hyde, George E. *Life of George Bent, Written from His Letters.* Edited by Savoie Lottinville. Norman: University of Oklahoma Press, 1968.

———. *Red Cloud's Folk: A History of the Oglala Sioux Indians.* Norman: University of Oklahoma Press, 1937.

"Indian Fight at Fort C. F. Smith, M. T." *Army and Navy Journal* (October 5, 1967): 104–5.

Jenkins, Paul B. *The Battle of Westport.* 1906. Reprint, BiblioLife/University of Denver, n.d.

Johnson, Dorothy M. *The Bloody Bozeman: The Perilous Trail to Montana's Gold.* New York: McGraw Hill, 1971. Reprint, Missoula, Mont.: Mountain, 1983.

Johnson, Troy R. *The Occupation of Alcatraz Island: Indian Self-Determination and the Rise of Indian Activism*. Urbana: University of Illinois Press, 1996.

Jones, Robert Huhn. *Guarding the Overland Trails: The Eleventh Ohio Cavalry in the Civil War*. Spokane, Wash.: Arthur H. Clark, 2005.

Kelman, Arik. *A Misplaced Massacre: Struggle over the Memory of Sand Creek*. Cambridge, Mass.: Harvard University Press, 2013.

Kirkman, Paul. *The Battle of Westport: Missouri's Great Confederate Raid*. Charleston, S.C.: History Press, 2011.

Langsdorf, Edgar. "Price's Raid and the Battle of Mine Creek." *Kansas History* 37 (Summer 2014): 78–99.

Lause, Mark A. *The Collapse of Price's Raid: The Beginning of the End in Civil War Missouri*. Columbia: University of Missouri Press, 2016.

———. *Price's Lost Campaign: The 1864 Invasion of Missouri*. Columbia: University of Missouri Press, 2011.

Lee, Fred L. *Gettysburg of the West: The Battle of Westport, October 21–23, 1864*. Rev. ed. Independence, Mo.: Two Trails, 1996.

Levings, Darryl W. *Saddle the Pale Horse: A Novel of the Invasion of Missouri, 1864*. Kansas City, Mo.: Kansas City Star Books, 2011.

Lindberg, Kip. "Chaos Itself: The Battle of Mine Creek." *North & South* 1, no. 6 (1998): 74–85.

Lockwood, James D. *Life and Adventures of a Drummer Boy, or Seven Years a Soldier*. Albany, N.Y.: John Skinner, 1893.

Mattes, Merrill J. *Indians, Infants, and Infantry: Andrew and Elizabeth Burt on the Frontier*. Denver: Old West, 1960.

McChristian, Douglas C., and Paul L. Hedren. *Fort Laramie: Military Bastion of the High Plains*. Norman: University of Oklahoma Press, 2009.

McDermott, John D. *Circle of Fire: The Indian War of 1865*. Mechanicsburg, Pa.: Stackpole, 2003.

———. *Frontier Crossroads: The History of Fort Caspar and the Upper Platte Crossing*. Casper, Wyo.: City of Casper, 1999.

———. *Red Cloud's War: The Bozeman Trail, 1866–1868*. Norman: University of Oklahoma Press, 2010.

Mokler, Alfred James. *Fort Caspar (Platte Bridge Station)*. 1939. Reprint, Casper, Wyo.: Prairie, 1983.

———. *History of Natrona County, Wyoming, 1888–1922*. Chicago: R. R. Donnelly & Sons, 1923.

———. *Transitions of the West: Portrayal of the Indian Problem in the West and the Trials of the Pioneers Who Reclaimed This Country from Savagery to Civilization*. Chicago: R. R. Donnelly & Sons, 1927.

Monaghan, Jay. *Civil War on the Western Border, 1854–1865*. Lincoln: University of Nebraska Press, 1955.

Monnett, Howard N. *Action before Westport, 1864*. Rev. ed. Boulder: University Press of Colorado, 1995.

Monnett, John H. *Where a Hundred Soldiers Were Killed: The Battle for the Powder River Country in 1866 and the Making of the Fetterman Myth*. Albuquerque: University of New Mexico Press, 2008.

Nadeau, Remi. *Fort Laramie and the Sioux*. 2nd rev. ed. Santa Barbara, Calif.: Crest, 1997.

"Obituary of Sigismund Sternberg." *Army and Navy Journal* 5, no. 37 (May 28, 1868), 583.

Palmer, H. E. "The Black-Flag Character of War on the Border." In *Kansas Historical Collections* 9 (1906): 455–66.

Paul, R. Eli, ed. *Autobiography of Red Cloud, War Leader of the Oglalas*. Missoula: Montana Historical Society Press, 1997.

Pennock, Isaac B. "Diary of Isaac B. Pennock, First Sergeant Company 'I,' Eleventh Kansas Cavalry." In *Kansas's War: The Civil War in Documents*, edited by Pearl T. Ponce, 197–204. Athens: Ohio University Press, 2011.

Platt, Steve. "Trails and Aboriginal Land Use in the Northern Bighorn Mountains, Wyoming." MA thesis, University of Montana, 1992. http://scholarworks.umt.edu/cgi/viewcontent.cgi?article=4952&context=etd.

Powell, Peter John. *People of the Sacred Mountain: A History of the Northern Cheyenne Chiefs and Warrior Societies, 1830–1879*. New York: Harper & Row, 1983.

Rafiner, Tom A. *Caught between Three Fires: Cass County, Missouri, Chaos, and Order No. 11, 1860–1865*. Harrisonville, Mo.: Burnt District, 2010.

———. *Cinders and Silence: A Chronicle of Missouri's Burnt District, 1854–1870*. Harrisonville, Mo.: Burnt District, 2015.

Rea, Tom. *Devil's Gate: Owning the Land, Owning the Story*. Norman: University of Oklahoma Press, 2006.

Service, Alex. *The Life and Letters of Caspar W. Collins*. Casper, Wyo.: City of Casper, 2000.

Sinisi, Kyle S. *The Last Hurrah: Sterling Price's Missouri Expedition of 1864*. Lanham, Md.: Rowman and Littlefield, 2015.

Spring, Agnes Wright. *Caspar Collins: The Life and Exploits of an Indian Fighter of the Sixties*. New York: Columbia University Press, 1927. Reprint, New York: AMS, 1967.

Stainaker, Jeffrey D. *The Battle of Mine Creek: The Crushing End of the Missouri Campaign*. Charleston, S.C.: History Press, 2011.

Starr, Stephen Z. *Jennison's Jayhawkers: A Civil War Cavalry Regiment and Its Commander*. Baton Rouge: Louisiana State University Press, 1973.

———. *The Union Cavalry in the Civil War*. Vol. 3, *The War in the West, 1861–1865*. Baton Rouge: Louisiana State University Press, 1985.

Steinle, John F. "Frontier Artist and Soldier: Caspar Collins." *Ohio Historical Society Timeline* 21, no. 3 (May–June 2004): 3–13.

Tatham, Michael. "Because They Were Needed: The History of the Eleventh Kansas Volunteer Regiment, 1862–1865." MA thesis, Central Missouri State University, 1998.

The Union Army: A History of Military Affairs in the Loyal States, 1861–65. Vol. 6, *Cyclopedia of Battles—Helena Road to Z*. Madison, Wis.: Federal Publishing, 1908.

Utley, Robert M. *Frontier Regulars: The United States Army and the Indian, 1866–1891*. New York: Macmillan, 1973. Reprint, Lincoln: University of Nebraska Press, 1984.

———. *Frontiersmen in Blue: The United States Army and the Indian, 1848–1865*. 1967. Lincoln: University of Nebraska Press, 1981.

Vanderzee, Robert. *Encounter with History: The Memoirs, Reminiscences, and Amazing Life of Captain Edmund Richard Pitman Shurly, 1829–1909*. Lincoln, Neb.: iuniverse, 2008.

Vaughn, J. W. *The Battle of Platte Bridge*. Norman: University of Oklahoma Press, 1963.

———. *Indian Fights: New Facts on Seven Encounters*. Norman: University of Oklahoma Press, 2009.

Vestal, Stanley. *Jim Bridger: Mountain Man*. Lincoln: University of Nebraska Press, 1946.

Walker, George Morton. "Eleventh Kansas Cavalry, 1865, and Battle of Platte Bridge." In *Kansas Historical Collections, 1915–1918*, 14:332–40. Topeka: Kansas State Historical Society, 1918.

Webb, Frances Seely. "The Indian Version of the Platte Bridge Fight." *Annals of Wyoming* 32, no. 2 (October 1960): 234–36.

Weeks, Michael. *The Complete Civil War Road Trip Guide*. 2nd ed. New York: Countryman, 2016.

Wellman, Paul I. *The Indian Wars of the West*. Garden City, N.Y.: Country Life, 1954.

Westport 1812–1912. Kansas City, Mo.: Franklin Hudson, 1912. http://archive.org/stream/westport1812191200west/westport1812191200west_djvu.txt.

White, Richard. "The Winning of the West: The Expansion of the Western Sioux in the Eighteenth and Nineteenth Centuries." *Journal of American History* 65, no. 2 (September 1978): 319–43.

Whitehead, Charles. "Old Fort Casper." In *Collections of the Wyoming Historical Society*, ed. R. C. Morris. Cheyenne, Wyo.: Sun-Leader Publishing House, 1897.

Willits, Vie. "The Bozeman Trail." MA thesis, University of Wyoming at Laramie, 1911.

Wishart, Alexander. "Diary of Alexander Wishart, 1867." In *The Books and Photographs of Elsa Spear*, by Elsa Spear, 26–38. Family of Elsa Spear Bryan, 1993.

INDEX

Page numbers in italic typeface indicate illustrations.